Leigh Hunt
and the Poetry
of Fancy

Leigh Hunt
and the Poetry
of Fancy

Rodney Stenning Edgecombe

Madison • Teaneck
Fairleigh Dickinson University Press
London and Toronto: Associated University Presses

Associated University Presses
440 Forsgate Drive
Cranbury, NJ 08512

Associated University Presses
25 Sicilian Avenue
London WC1A 2QH, England

Associated University Presses
P.O. Box 338, Port Credit
Mississauga, Ontario
Canada L5G 4L8

The paper used in this publication meets the requirements
of the American National Standard for Permanence of Paper
for Printed Library Materials Z39.48–1984.

Library of Congress Cataloging-in-Publication Data

Edgecombe, Rodney Stenning.
    Leigh Hunt and the poetry of fancy / Rodney Stenning Edgecombe.
        p.   cm.
    Includes bibliographical references (p.) and index.
    ISBN 0-8386-3571-7 (alk. paper)
    1. Hunt, Leigh, 1784–1859—Criticism and interpretation.
I. Title.
PR4814.E34   1994
821'.7—dc20   94-20741
                                                                      CIP

PRINTED IN THE UNITED STATES OF AMERICA

For Ernest Pereira,
to thank him for his kindness

Contents

Preface and Acknowledgments / 9

1. Fancy and Its Effects / 17
2. Narrative Poems: I / 51
3. Narrative Poems: II / 95
4. Political and Critical Poems / 143
5. Miscellaneous Verse / 182
Epilogue / 237

Notes / 240
Select Bibliography / 259
Index / 271

Preface and Acknowledgments

Once poets, by unanimous critical assent, have been endowed with "minor" status, they are pushed to the margin of literary studies—to be tapped perfunctorily for corroborative data about the period they exemplify or enlisted as foils conveniently pale and derivative for the more robust talents that flourished alongside them. Leigh Hunt has been particularly unfortunate in this regard, not only because the talents he so generously embraced and introduced to the public eclipsed his own in every respect, but also because he has functioned as a convenient whipping boy and a (mildly) evil genius for the failings of some of them.

What I have attempted in this study, therefore, is not so much a revaluation of Hunt—designed to show how grossly underrated the poems have been, and how fine they really are—but rather to find ways of *enjoying* the minority of his decidedly minor poetry. It thus offers itself less as an exercise in reclamation than as one of adjustment. If the talent is slim, need we invoke a magisterial poet like Keats to measure the thinness, or ought we to try to respond to the material on its own terms? Herrick is seldom judged for not being Milton, nor is Collins rebuked for not being Gray, and yet Hunt has seldom escaped the odium of being compared—being compared with poets who outflank him at every turn. One obviously cannot avoid mentioning Dante when discussing *The Story of Rimini*, say, nor Dryden, nor even Crabbe, but perhaps the shrunken plant occasionally needs to be rescued from these overshadowing presences, and brought into the sun to flourish in its own right. Or, to change the metaphor, once I have sieved away the gravel and the sand, I hope at least to acknowledge the presence of some distinctive gold in the pan.

Taking a cue from Hunt himself, and suggesting that fancy is a less strenuous, less aspiring species of the poetic faculty, I have tried in this study to suggest that fancy imposes its own semigeneric constraints. Once we shut out the sublimities of Coleridge's esemplastic imagination from view, and uninvidiously blinker our vision, we are bound to feel a greater contentment with the material in hand. I suggest, furthermore, that fancy has had its own particular vector in artistic history—the playful and lighthearted mode of the rococo.

By stressing the primacy of the rococo mode in Hunt's poetry, I do not mean to belittle the political significance of his career, a career that would in any case be better illustrated by his journalism. In the first place, although I shall be defining the rococo by its "official" manifestation in the history of the arts, I shall try to expunge its taint of frivolity. The mode might have begun as a plaything of the Bourbon elite, but because it crystallized a set of aesthetic universals, its procedures can be detected in the work of anteced-ent artists (whether Longus or Herrick) and later figures such as Wilde and Firbank. In Hunt's case the rococo provided him with a space of recovery, a means to withdrawing from the pain and misery his political courage brought to his life. It can even be viewed as a lighthearted instance of the millenarianism that so often empowers Radical thought. Shelley's meliorism took refuge from a world weary of the past, and hailed the return of the golden age in *Hellas*. Hunt brought those golden years forward, and placed them in a parallel universe into which he could slip at will to refuel an exhausted spirit. Apparent irresponsibility might therefore, as Jerome McGann points out, often turn out to be a displaced species of engage-ment:

> The viewless wings of poetry will carry one to havens of intensity where pleasure and pain, life and even death, all seem to repossess some lost original value. This is the reflexive world of Romantic art, the very nega-tion itself, wherein all events are far removed from the Terror, King Ludd, Peterloo, the Six Acts, and the recurrent financial crises of the Regency, and where humanity escapes the inconsequence of George III, the absurd Prince Regent, the contemptible Wellington.[1]

Such judgments by displacement could be aligned with another potential defense of Huntian rococo, viz., Hazlitt's claim that idealism nurtures the reforming impulse. It is most vividly illustrated by his reservations about Crabbe, whom he called a "Malthus turned metrical romancer."[2] To gloss this criticism, we must recall that Hazlitt attacked Malthus for defending the status quo, and clipping the wings of Godwin and other visionary theorists: "Compared with the lamentable and gross deficiencies of existing institutions, such a view of futurity as barely possible could not fail to allure the gaze and tempt the aspiring thoughts of the philanthropist and the philosopher. . . ."[3]

Crabbe's leaden outlook has (in his view) the same effect of stalling rather than impelling reform:

> The cottage twined round with real myrtles, or with the poet's wreath, will invite the hand of kindly assistance sooner than Mr. Crabbe's naked "ruin'd shed"; for though unusual, unexpected distress excites compassion, that which is uniform and remediless produces nothing but disgust and indifference. Repulsive objects (or those which are painted so) do not conciliate affection, or soften the heart.[4]

The abundant myrtle-bowered cottages and poetic wreaths in Hunt's verse are a function of the rococo mode in which it is often cast, and, as Hazlitt implies, they inoculate against the Malthusian disgust and indifference that would otherwise impede the reader's visionary aspirations.

Since Hunt saw versifying as a sort of therapy, and wrote with a great deal of facility to boot, the body of poems we are dealing with is as large as it is unequal. Moreover, it shows no real progression and development. If, as Hunt's contemporaries suggested, the poet was an "immortal boy"[5] or "a grey-haired boy, whose heart can never grow old,"[6] and if, as Dickens observed, Harold Skimpole resembled a "damaged young man" more than he did a "well-preserved elderly one,"[7] it would be vain to expect from him the progressive, evolutionary art of the great writers. Here there is no *Tempest*, no *Paradise Lost*, no *Hyperion*, but rather the cheerful persistence of a voice found early and found sufficient. Edmund Blunden claims that Hunt had "during his later life become a poet, not remarkably strong and glowing, but clear, various and following his own course,"[8] but I can find little evidence for decisive maturation. And since (as I hope to show) there is little maturation, there seems no point in attempting a chronological history of the poems. I have thus followed the broad generic groupings of the Milford edition (my text throughout this book),[9] and ordered the discussion accordingly. Milford himself based his arrangement on the 1860 edition, largely the work of Hunt himself, though it was Thornton who saw it through the press. There is thus good reason to retain the original taxonomy[10]—Narrative Poems, Political and Critical Poems, and so on—for even if the categories seem a trifle naïve, they are serviceable, and altogether less contentious than those applied, say, by Wordsworth to *his* own poetry.

The volume and inequality of Hunt's achievement has dictated the omission of a good many poems. So, without quite following his own airy procedures as an *arbiter elegantiarum*, sipping here, italicizing there, excerpting, gathering, deleting, glossing over, I have dwelt only on those that to some extent reward the dwelling, and have omitted altogether the obviously immature and derivative ones of the *Juvenilia* (1801), except for purposes of cross-reference and illustration. The same constraints have also forced me to forego treating Hunt's dramatic verse, even *The Descent of Liberty*, which he intended for a "mental" rather than a theatrical staging. Also omitted are his translations, skillful though many of these seem to be. Translations can be assessed only by critics who are thoroughly conversant with the languages involved, for without these comparative poles, one has no means of deciding which of the surface felicities are original and which derivative. Credit for the larger design and structure must obviously go to the original poet. I hope that the general sense of Hunt's achievement will not suffer seriously from such omissions. After all, as he himself observes in his *Autobiography*, "[T]here is no cast of the Venus [de' Medici] which gives a proper idea of the original"[11]—a judgment one could also extend to literary translation.

Hunt's poetry has not yet received any extended critical treatment, the result, perhaps of an *embarras de richesses*. The multiplicity of his talents enabled him to tackle every literary enterprise known to humankind and reach a level of proficiency in all of them. The would-be commentator, still reeling from this abundance, will then turn to a poetic output almost as voluminous and almost as diverse. Further distractions will spring from Hunt's extremely interesting life—his entanglement with Byron, his nurturing of Shelley and Keats, his prescient salute to Tennyson, and his modeling for Skimpole in *Bleak House*—to name only some of many central issues. The bicentenary of his birth came and went in 1984, but none of the papers delivered at the celebratory symposium[12] in Iowa addressed his poetry in a sustained way. James Thompson included a (very important) chapter on the verse in his recent study of Hunt's achievement,[13] but the constraints of space imposed by his subject's range and versatility prevented him from saying all he might otherwise have said; while John Hayden's equally important article on *The Story of Rimini*[14] was likewise forced to limit its scope to the text in hand. This book is the first to address the full range of Hunt's poetry, and even then its quest for completeness has been thwarted by the sheer volume of the output. Most critics, myself included, have probably come to Hunt through Keats, often encountering hostile asides about his influence. Many of us, perhaps, have taken these judgments on trust—as I did before being struck by Hunt's great sonnet on the Nile—and denied due process to a poet who seems to have suffered as a result his own generosity and self-effacement. The following pages will attempt to offer some redress.

I would like to extend my warm thanks to Professor Ernest Pereira of Unisa. He sent me some crucial Huntiana (otherwise unavailable in South Africa), bravely trusting his copy of the *Juvenilia* to the mail. Pene Beamish, Ros Maree, and Evelyn Rosmeisl of the Interlibrary Loans Department at the University of Cape Town, and Celia Walters of the Reference Department in Jagger Library, also deserve my thanks, and so too does the English Department at UCT, which subsidized my interlibrary and postal expenses. Finally, I would like to thank Wyatt Benner, who edited this book.

Part of chapter 1 first appeared in *The Keats-Shelley Journal*, and is incorporated here by permission of the editor.

Leigh Hunt
and the Poetry
of Fancy

1

Fancy and
its Effects

When he differentiated fancy from the imagination, Coleridge stressed its inability to fuse and reconstitute its materials. The esemplastic imagination atomizes and reforms experience in a mysterious alchemy of dissolution, diffusion, and dissipation, while

> FANCY, on the contrary, has no other counters to play with, but fixities and definites. The Fancy is indeed no other than a mode of Memory emancipated from the order of time and space; while it is blended with, and modified by that empirical phenomenon of the will, which we express by the word CHOICE. But equally with the ordinary memory the Fancy must receive all its materials ready made from the law of association.[1]

The fancy, in turn, passes on these materials to the imagination in a complex symbiotic rhythm, much as a water insect breasts the current by alternating "active and passive motion, now resisting the current, now yielding to it in order to gather strength and a momentary *fulcrum* for further propulsion."[2] Catherine Wallace has observed in her exposition of *Biographia Literaria* that although "fancy and imagination are distinct, imagination cannot operate without fancy any more than fancy can operate coherently without the focus or motive that will provides."[3] However, even though the fancy provides an essential base to this noetic structure, Coleridge's description tends to give it a status inferior to that of the imagination. We come away from the *Biographia* with impressions of a faculty less flexible, less resourceful, and altogether more limited by virtue of its indebtedness to the material données of experience. Such impressions clearly influenced Hunt in his hierarchical distinction of fancy and imagination, even though he dispensed with the context of Coleridge's definition in his looser formulation of problem.

Wordsworth's preface to the 1815 edition of his poems, though attended by problems of its own, provided a more pragmatic idea of fancy than that put forward in *Biographia Literaria*:

> The law under which the processes of Fancy are carried on is as capricious as the accidents of things, and the effects are surprising, playful, ludicrous, amusing, tender, or pathetic, as the objects happen to be appositely produced or fortunately combined. Fancy depends on the rapidity and profusion with which she scatters her thoughts and images; trusting that their number, and the felicity with which they are linked together, will make amends for the want of individual value: or she prides herself upon the curious subtilty and the successful elaboration with which she can detect their lurking affinities. If she can win you over to her purpose, and impart to you her feelings, she cares not how unstable or transitory may be her influence, knowing that it will not be out of her power to resume it upon apt occasion.[4]

This definition of fancy takes us closer to Hunt than Coleridge's epistemological speculations, for, by distinguishing the playfulness and lightness of this faculty from the imagination's engagement with "the inherent and internal,"[5] Wordsworth suggests that it operates in a different poetic mode, with its own criteria of judgment. It should therefore come as no surprise that when Hunt put *Imagination and Fancy* together, he should have dispensed with Coleridge's metaphysical complexities and adapted Wordsworth's differentiae, simplifying them still further to enhance their general usefulness. The apparent reductiveness of his procedure has come in for much criticism. M. H. Abrams has written that a "further degeneration of Coleridge's distinction is plainly evident in Leigh Hunt's anthology. . . . In Hunt's introductory essay the difference between these faculties resolves into a difference between levity and gravity in the poet's attitude,"[6] while James Scoggins has observed that poetic "taste in Hunt's criticism is narrowed to an appreciation for the lyric or for the lyrical parts of non-lyric poems, and imagination and fancy are little more than useful badges of relative merit."[7] All this is true, no doubt, but however limited a simple antithesis of levity and gravity might at first seem, it has real critical utility— even while Scoggins deplores the "badges of relative merit," he concedes their usefulness.

Lacking the refinements of Coleridge's definition, Hunt's might indeed seem at first glance to be "degenerate," but we must recall his impatience at the rarefaction of the greater poet's thought and realize that he is trying to salvage a practical tool from abstract discourse. He speaks of fancy

as "the lighter play of the imagination"[8] and attempts to establish a comple-
mentarity between the two, which he sees not as interconnected strands of
an epistemological web, but rather as different preserves of the sensibility.
According to Hunt it is because Shakespeare is capable of fancy *and* imagination (as separate provinces of literary, not epistemological, performance)
that he towers above all other poets. See how effortlessly he is made to
bestride Hunt's categories even as they are being set up: "Imagination belongs to Tragedy, or the serious muse; Fancy to the comic. *Macbeth*, *Lear*,
Paradise Lost, the poem of Dante, are full of imagination: the *Midsummer
Night's Dream* and the *Rape of the Lock*, of fancy: *Romeo and Juliet*, the
Tempest, the *Fairy Queen*, and the *Orlando Furioso*, of both."[9] And look,
incidentally, at the disinterested way in which an avowed romantic admits
Pope to the pantheon along with Milton.

It is because he conceives poetry as a multitudinous (not a monolithic)
thing that Hunt's definition has seemed too multitudinous, and elicited
David Masson's good-natured jibe about being "constructed on the principle of omitting nothing that any one would like to see included."[10] But
that is precisely the virtue of the description. It is *not* a banner statement,
not the sort one-sided, self-privileging utterance you might expect of a
founder or pioneer like Wordsworth or T. E. Hulme, but rather a definition
reflecting a truly catholic position vis-à-vis the subject: "the utterance of a
passion for truth, beauty, and power, embodying and illustrating its conceptions by imagination and fancy."[11] Indeed, there is something inherently
"fanciful" about Hunt's critical procedure in general—it is always spontaneous and untrammeled, and never subordinates individual or local judgments
to doctrinaire a priori assumptions. For this reason, perhaps, Stephen Fogle
has attacked *Imagination and Fancy* for a lack of ideological rigor: "[W]hen
Hunt turns to abstractions, he becomes softly sentimental, taking refuge in
easy personifications that attract attention to their own picturesque quality
rather than to the idea expressed."[12] While a capacity for abstract thought
certainly does not rank among his characteristic gifts, Hunt's thinking only
occasionally tends toward laxness. Indeed the personifications that Fogle
decries often prove "easy" in the sense of being accessible rather than facile,
easeful rather than strenuous. Hunt enjoys the present moment too fully to
bother about conforming to abstract principles, and to that extent anticipates the ad hoc (but powerful) judgments of Dickens as opposed to those
of more systematic thinkers (Coleridge or Arnold or Mill).

Even statements that Fogle derides for rank inconsistency can sometimes be clarified by context: "Again one wonders what the early Victorian

reader, in search of self-improvement, made of such a passage. There seems to be a clear contradiction between the charge that imagination is too material and that one of its highest privileges is freedom from visibility."[13] And so it would seem until we turn to Hunt's text:

> The terms were formerly identical, or used as such; and neither is the best that might be found. The term Imagination is too confined: often too material. It presents too invariably the idea of a solid body;—of "images" in the sense of the plaster cast cry about the streets. Fancy, on the other hand, while it means nothing but a spiritual image or apparition . . . , has rarely that freedom from visibility which is one of the highest privileges of imagination.[14]

There is no inconsistency here at all. With the ease and inconsequentiality that informal essayists can claim as their prerogative, Hunt expresses a personal objection to the fact that "imagination" contains the word "image," which time-honored biblical usage has associated with idolatry. For the prophets, images traduced the ineffable nature of Deity, as for Hunt they traduce the spiritual nature of imagination: his mention of image-pedlars clarifies his *personal* sense of debasement, for what he objects to is not the *visuality* of the word "imagination," but rather its *visibility*—something staid, unaspiring, and tangible in an entirely unglamorous way. It is even possible that for the moment he was thinking of a stricture in Wordsworth's 1815 preface—"I select these writers [of the prophetic and lyrical parts of the Holy Scriptures] in preference to those of ancient Greece and Rome, because the anthropomorphitism of the Pagan religion subjected the minds of the greatest poets in those countries too much to the bondage of definite form; from which the Hebrews were preserved by an abhorrence of idola-try."[15] Hunt's point would thus have presented no problems to the early Victorian reader who, far from feeling puzzlement, would have recognized as it as the jeu d'esprit of an informal essayist. It is not for that essayist to refashion the etymological cast of words to satisfy a personal prejudice, but wryly and half-mockingly to regret them.

Let us return, however, to Hunt's definition of poetry as an utterance "embodying and illustrating its conceptions by imagination and fancy." By this he would imply that variety obtains not only in its subject matter, but also in its form. One might at first be tempted to read "embodying and illustrating" as a hendiadys, but Hunt's further comments make it clear that they ought (in some degree) to be separated and apportioned to imagination and fancy in turn:

It is a passion for beauty, because its office is to exalt and refine by means of pleasure, and because beauty is nothing but the loveliest form of pleasure.

It is a passion for power, because power is impression triumphant, whether over the poet, as desired by himself, or over the reader, as affected by the poet.

It embodies and illustrates its impressions by imagination, or images of the objects of which it treats, and other images brought in to throw light on those objects, in order that it may enjoy and impart the feeling of their truth in its utmost conviction and affluence.

It illustrates them by fancy, which is a lighter play of imagination, or the feeling of analogy coming short of seriousness, in order that it may laugh at what it loves, and show how it can decorate it with fairy ornament.[16]

While the imagination embodies, the fancy illustrates; instead of the integrated emotional fusion of poetic compounds, it offers the loose amalgamation of verse mixtures. Moreover, it plays more lightly than the high-flown imagination; it associates itself less with prophecy than with pleasure, concerns itself not with esemplastic wholes but with whatever discrete items it might bring into focus. The fancy aspires to entertain and ravish, not to transport and ennoble. It deals with ornamental appliqué rather than stylistic integration, with simile rather than metaphor, with analogical rather than symbolic habits of thought. Writing of his own masque, *The Descent of Liberty*, Hunt cheerfully admits that "Fancy, (encouraged by the allegorical nature of the masque) played her part too entirely in it at the expense of imagination."[17] Granting the truth of this—that externality and decoration are the keynotes of fancy, I would further suggest that it is best viewed as something almost congruent, if not identical, with the established tradition of the rococo.

In *The Spirit of the Age*, Hazlitt devoted a single essay to Thomas Moore and Leigh Hunt. Although he does not offer a reason for this collocation, he would seem to imply that their sensibilities converge in significant ways. While his personal loyalty to Hunt prevented him from analyzing his faults in any detail, it is likely that he made the junction as a conscious critical act—judgment, as it were, by contagion. Of Moore he writes:

[M]odern poetry in its retrograde progress comes at last to be constructed on the principles of the modern OPERA, where an attempt is made to gratify every sense at every instant, and where the understanding alone is insulted and the heart mocked. It is in this view only that we can discover that Mr. Moore's poetry is vitiated or immoral,—it seduces the taste and enervates the imagination. It creates a false standard of reference, and inverts or decompounds the natural order of association, in which objects strike the thoughts and feelings. His is the poetry of the bath, of the toilette, of the saloon, of the fashionable world; not the poetry of nature, of the heart, or of human life.[18]

And again:

> Mr. Moore has a little mistaken the art of poetry for the *cosmetic art*. He does not compose an historic group, or work out a single figure; but throws a variety of elementary sensations, of vivid impressions together, and calls it a description. He makes out an inventory of beauty—the smile on the lips, the dimple on the cheeks, *item*, golden locks, *item*, a pair of blue wings, *item*, a silver sound. . . . This dissipated, fulsome, painted patchwork style may succeed in the levity and languor of the *boudoir*, or might have been adapted to the Pavilions of royalty, but it is not the style of Parnassus, nor a passport to Immortality.[19]

If we disregard the animus of Hazlitt's assessment and center instead on its content, we see him presenting Moore as a sort of Boucher or Fragonard, a purveyor of poetic dainties, a rococo artist patronized (as the capitalized "Pavilion" deftly hints) by George IV instead of Louis XV. Furthermore, his stress on the disconnectedness of Moore's poetic apprehension, the itemized blazons he furnishes in place of a continuous plastique—this stress underlines the fact that it is in the fancy that the rococo moves and has its being. Although Hunt had a justified aversion to fat Adonises of fifty and gave their pavilions wide berth, his poetry, like Moore's (though Hazlitt is loath to say so) also reveals a rococo quality, since it is a poetry of pleasure and recreation, not a poetry of prophecy. Taking Hunt's definition of fancy as our measure, and finding fancy's most persuasive embodiment in the rococo, we can begin to assess much of his verse by the right—that is, the most appropriate—generic standard, and so achieve a juster view of his achievement.

Obviously I need to be extremely tactful when I assimilate Huntian fancy to the rococo spirit, not least because of the historical problems involved. Hunt's taste in painting was limited primarily to the *cinque-* and *seicento*, and his sense of the impact of the visual upon the verbal arts takes the form of impressionistic analogues. In "A New Gallery of Pictures" in the *New Monthly Magazine*, he suggested that Spenser's Aurora could best be realized by the brush of Titian, while in *Imagination and Fancy*, having (one presumes) in the meantime discovered a print of the Borghese ceiling, he substituted Guido Reni.[20] Monitoring changes in the way Hunt responded to Spenser, Greg Kucich has pointed out that this invocation of "voluptuous Renaissance paintings . . . introduces Spenser as a painterly poet who lives isolated in 'a beautiful world' absorbed with 'the beauty' and the 'enchantment' of its 'forms'."[21] Which is to imply that substantive iconographic issues will tend to take second place to the personal conflict projected onto Spenser—a conflict engendered by what Kucich calls Hunt's "constantly thwarted wish to shirk intellectual obligations for the indulgence of voluptuous beauty."[22] Subordinated to this and other ideological concerns, Hunt's *ut pictura poesis* procedures can often seem rather loose: Spenser describes Aurora, Guido paints Aurora, *ergo* Spenser is "like" Guido.

If Hunt's methods as a critic of painting and poetry are altogether too cavalier to enable us to posit any clear influences of the one upon the other, we must also recall that for the greater part of his creative life, the rococo had fallen into disfavor. Neoclassicism in France had eclipsed such painters as Watteau, whose rehabilitation took place only after the Goncourt brothers published their famous essay. Because it bore the taint of the ancien régime— Diderot was one of the first to condemn the immorality of Boucher—the rococo can be said to have fallen from grace with the Bourbons. (We know, for example, that David advised a friend against buying a Watteau for his private collection.)[23] Nonetheless, Hunt had at least heard of Watteau, as witness his reference (via Warton) to "a party worthy of the pastoral pencil of Watteau"[24]—and he might even have seen some of the Watteaus discussed by Hazlitt. However misguided an attempt to connect him with specific rococo paintings might prove, I would argue for the existence of a transhistorical conception of the mode—a configuration of values both formal and moral, which need not necessarily occur in conjunction with *rocaille, coquille* and *fêtes galantes*. While "ideology" might be too grand a term to dignify rococo's characteristic postures (though they do have their own intellectual coherence), one could at least speak of a distinctive rococo *sensibility*, embodied as much in the fairy tales of Oscar Wilde as in the poetry of Leigh Hunt. Just as Jerome McGann has argued for a "sharp distinction between *Romanticism* . . . (which is a critical concept with a more or less concealed ideological component), and *The Romantic Period* . . . (which is a critical concept that defines an historic reality),"[25] so I would apply the epithet "rococo" to a synchronic ideological stance, rooted in, but independent of, its historic crystallization in the eighteenth century. The

OED suggests that "rococo" first entered the English language in the late 1830s, and gives it the additional signification of "quaint or antiquated." (*That* meaning, however, can scarcely be said to survive the citations for which it is adduced, since they all conceive rococo as the concretization of an eighteenth-century outlook displaced by its "modern" Victorian alternative, rather as "medieval" might be conceived today.)

Even if they called the rose by another name, however, some romantics still had a definite sense of the values embodied in the style here designated as "rococo." This, for example, is how Hazlitt described the Watteaus in the Dulwich Gallery:

> There is something exceedingly light, agreeable, and characteristic in this artist's productions. He might almost be said to breathe his figures and his flowers on canvas—so fragile is their texture, so evanescent is his touch. His trees have a drawing-room air to them, an appearance of gentility and etiquette, and nod gracefully over-head; while the figures below, thin as air, *vegetably* clad, in the midst of all their affectation and grimace, seem to have sprung out of the ground, or to be the fairy inhabitants of the scene in masquerade. They are the Oreads and Dryads of the Luxembourg! Quaint association, happily effected by the pencil of Watteau![26]

This reads like a detoxified version of the *Blackwood's* attack on Hunt. Even as he acknowledges Watteau's grace, Hazlitt concedes a measure of affectation; even while he salutes his airiness and vitality, he detects the inflections of an urban drawing room. The account is by no means dismissive, but it remains alert to the potential deficiencies of the style, not least its escapism. Taking Watteau as a sort of metonymic counter for the rococo vision, we can also detect Hazlitt's guarded attraction in another dictum—"In turning over the pages of the best comedies, we are almost transported to another world, and escape from this dull age to one that was all life, and whim, and mirth, and humour. The curtain rises, and a gayer scene presents itself, as on the canvass of Watteau."[27] While he remarks of the Dulwich Watteaus that no contemporary artist could match them, he adds: "[N]or do we very devoutly wish it. The Louis the Fourteenths are extinct, and we suspect their revival would hardly be compensated even by the re-appearance of a Watteau."[28] In other words, it is not a style that recommends itself to the politically committed—a paradox to which I shall return later on. First, however, we need to get the actual qualities of rococo art into sharper focus, defining them through the emphases of visual rococo—its lightness, its disconnected interest in surface effect, and its delicacy and concern with entertainment.

A. C. Sewter has observed that the "transition from the Baroque to the Rococo involved no distinct break in continuity, but rather a change of emphasis from the grandiloquent and the splendid to the light and delicate. Generally lacking either the intense religious emotion and drama of the Baroque, or the intellectual rigor of Poussin's classicism, the Rococo aimed above all to please."[29] According to this definition, the rococo takes Horace's compound of *monere* and *delectare*, and reduces it to an almost pure *delectare*. It is an art verging perpetually on the ornamental, ever ready to break out in arabesques, rinceaux, and other sinuous dispositions of line. Even the human figure is reconceived in ornamental terms, as Watteau's slight, tapering forms testify. An art primarily concerned with pleasing will practice selectivity. Whatever threatens the delicate world of the *fête galante* is excluded; whatever is admitted is refined. Donald Posner has pointed out how unlike his immediate sources Watteau often is. While his painting *Le Repas de campagne* might be indebted to compositions by Teniers and van Ostade, his "images differ . . . in important ways from their prototypes. His peasants and their surroundings are relatively neat and clean. Manners seem more country-like than boorish, and people are solicitous of one another when they eat, and gentle and good-natured when a child tries to interrupt a dance."[30] It is above all to this "etherealization" of its matter that the unreality of rococo can be traced, since it is the art of the garden, of nature methodized.

Small wonder, then, that Lockhart's notorious attack on Hunt in *Blackwood's* should take him to task for his "Cockney" (i.e., suburban) vision of nature. While Wordsworth found beauty in crags and snow, Hunt's rose-tinted spectacles made nature over as a magnified rose garden. That this prejudice persisted well into the nineteenth century can be gathered from Masson's suggesting that Hunt mistook texture for form, and reduced global nature to mere vegetation: "Such an affection of the minutiae of vegetation was reserved perhaps for the so-called Cockney poets."[31] Hunt's landscapes, being forged from careful exclusions and selections, are to that extent rococo, close in spirit to the parkland that so benignly embowers Watteau's idylls and *fêtes galantes*. Hence Lockhart's sneer at "fanciful, dreaming tea-drinkers, who . . . presume to talk with contempt of some of the most exquisite spirits the world has ever produced, merely because they did not happen to exert their faculties in laborious affected descriptions of flowers seen in window-pots, or cascades heard at Vauxhall. . . ."[32] Marlon Ross has observed (apropos of this and other onslaughts) that Lockhart represents the "voice of patriarchal culture," a voice that admonishes Keats (and Hunt, his mentor) that such poetry can never be the site of "masculine maturation."[33] Verse that luxuriates in sensuous accumulations will, from this crude perspective, necessarily emasculate itself.

Even commentators less viciously disposed toward Hunt than Lockhart or Croker have regretted his rococo impulse to prettify by suppression. Almost to a person, they view it as a disability rather than an enabling convention. Another Victorian critic, R. B. Johnson, has claimed that Hunt's "limitations were those of a sentimentalist, and resulted chiefly from an inability to enter into certain moods; the tragic and the sublime never appealed to him so completely as the gay and graceful; sustained thought was less congenial than tender fancy."[34] Yet the very essence of rococo is to be located in the license it gives to fancy, to evanescent moods rather than rigorous transcription.

Venice, cradle of the Italian rococo, while it gave birth the Kodachrome exactitudes of Canaletto, also fostered Guardi's distinctive *vedute di fantasia.* Here topographic details evaporate into the subjectivity of the painter, and aesthetic choices are made at the expense of literal truths. These are the painterly equivalents of the literary idyll, as Germain Bazin has pointed out: "[W]ithin landscape painting the essentially Rococo *genre* is that of the *capriccio.* This pastoral or idyllic genre, with its compositions full of fantasy and its decorative aim, was created by Marco Ricci, . . . and continued by Francesco Zucarelli. . . ."[35] The key word here is "decorative," for it is in decoration that rococo finds its raison d'être. Not only are the streaks of the tulip disregarded, but the tulip is itself formalized into a motif, the linear abstraction of itself.

But whereas, say, in the cubism of Cézanne the abstraction functions in a volumetric way—designed to disclose substance and structure—in rococo the abstraction reduces and etherealizes its object. Pattern replaces the fullness of being. Indeed, pattern also substitutes for structure, exfoliating over, and so obscuring, basic form. One has only to look at the Porcelain Room from the Palace of Portici (now in the Capodimonte Museum of Naples) to see the truth of this. As Bazin remarks, the "characteristic of Rococo rhythm in ornamentation is its counterpointing of asymmetrical elements, ordered with an architectural framework where the many curves and counter-curves and re-echoing planes render the whole space vibrant."[36] *Because* the whole space vibrates, the eye is so beguiled by the rococo arabesque that it does not demand the oriented, axial rhythms of classicism that the "line of beauty" has displaced. A. C. Sewter has rightly observed that in "its purest form, the Rococo was a style of interior decoration rather than a language of architectural forms and ideas," and goes on to add that it is typical for its ornament to spread "from wall to ceiling, . . . blurring the structural boundaries."[37]

Ornament, it goes without saying, is essentially generalized. The capital of a Corinthian column resembles a cluster of acanthus leaves in the remotest of ways; only incidentally do the motifs of egg-and-dart call actual eggs and darts to mind. So in rococo one has to do with types—not the lofty platonic types of classicism, but the unassuming types of decorative art. Boucher shocked Reynolds when he confessed to painting without models, and even if he had not made the confession, the essentially decorative stereotypes of his oeuvre would have led us to guess as much. Thuillier and Châtelet make the point succinctly: "Boucher's sense of decoration and his preoccupation with women's finery were so much a part of his artistry, and his psychological insight was so limited, that the few portraits he painted inevitably turn into genre scenes and *tableaux de mode*."[38] What they say applies not only to his portraits but also to his Dianas and Venuses. Whereas Titian produces a history painting from the bath of Diana, Boucher turns it into a festive rococo fashion plate. Even Watteau, an artist infinitely more tender and subtle than Boucher, eschews harsh, intractable specifics for pleasing generalities. What Donald Posner says of his *Mezzetin* applies by and large to all of the artist's works—if we leave the portraits of Pater and Caylus (?) aside: "At its aesthetic core is figural and physiognomic expression rather than feature, and the aching longing expressed by the comedian is meant as a comment on a universal state of soul."[39]

This being so, rococo inevitably centers on activities of recreation, on humankind in tranquil repose. In it we find no effort, no striving. Although its asymmetries and curvatures were nurtured by the baroque, it owes nothing to its grandiloquence and vigor. Bernini designed his baldacchino and *cathedra Petri* with all the resources of visual rhetoric at his disposal; Watteau was content to embellish *boiseries* with patterns of infinite delicacy and attenuation—the rococo is almost calligraphic in the thinness and pliancy of its lines—and Boucher was more than happy to accommodate his designs to the awkward spaces that rocaille decoration bequeathed him: his "mannered grace," according to Bazin, "fitted in well with the Rococo style, and adapted itself perfectly to *trumeaux*—those spaces framed in sinuous forms."[40] Bernini begins with a spatial tabula rasa, and fills it as impressively as he can. The rococo painters accommodate themselves to what they find or what they are given. Theirs is an art of *sprezzatura, en déshabillé* and unshowy.

Finally, the rococo has a distinctly erotic flavor, a factor that might account for its marginality in the minds of critics who, as Jerome McGann observes, deplore "the erotic strain in the verse of Byron, Shelley, and Keats . . . particularly on the grounds that such work lacks the highest sort of artistic seriousness."[41] Such eroticism is no less apparent in Hunt, and, taken in conjunction with his peculiar features of style and structure, renders the rococo classification additionally plausible. Indeed the *absence* of an erotic element deters us from invoking the mode with regard, say, to Cowper, even though he qualifies as a rococo poet in many other respects—in his poetic undress, his domesticity, and his essentially recreational conception of poetry. In Cowper, however, there is not a nude limb in sight, not so much as a nuance of the carnal. It is true that Watteau scarcely ever unclothes his figures, but the reason must be sought in the uncertainties of his anatomical drawing, for almost all the paintings *do* have a strong erotic charge. As Donald Posner has observed of his *fêtes galantes*, "the placid city park is all of nature, and amorous play is the centre of man's universe. It is none of it true, but it is . . . lovely."[42] In Watteau, a peasant playing the musette in a pastoral setting signifies the phallus, and so does a genre scene depicting an enema. Even a *boiserie* design like *L'Enjôleur* enwreathes a sexual innuendo in graceful arabesques. This obliquity yields, in the coarser world of Boucher, to a more blatant sexuality, and Thuillier and Châtelet have noted how the latter's "pastorals, for which he created a vogue, owe very little to the *fêtes galantes* of Watteau: these elegant shepherds sporting with shepherdesses dressed in the height of fashion in a landscape of fantasy are the genuine expression of that libertine spirit of eighteenth-century France which idolized woman as the sole object of desire."[43]

With these broad generic features in mind, I want to turn now to Leigh Hunt. As I have already observed, he does not qualify as a rococo writer by dint of any pictorial translations of Boucher, Watteau, or Guardi, but rather by virtue of his temperament. He inhabits a world of *vedute di fantasia*, a world of tacit and acknowledged omissions, suffused with gentle eroticism. I find it significant that in the preface to *Foliage* he should remark "I need not inform any reader acquainted with real poetry, that a delight in rural luxury has ever been a constituent part of the very business of poets as one of the very best things which they have recommended, as counteractions to the more sordid tendencies of the cities." He goes on to add that, when it comes to the proper view of mercantile enterprise,

> the French in some of these matters are more practical poets than we are; for they refuse to get more than is reasonable, or than leaves fair play for enjoyment; and they spend their afternoons in dancing under the trees or

in-doors, or attending the theaters, where they see imitations of the Golden Age in dances more poetical. The fashionable world among us see a great deal farther into these things, from the mere absence of this yellow atmosphere of money-getting; and it is curious to observe how they come round, in all their refinements, to place their best entertainment in music and dancing, which are two of the most natural and pastoral of pleasures.[44]

The sweeping elisions entailed in these remarks go far toward making the *fête galante* a way of life, and more than that, the only *natural* way of life. Whereas commerce reduces the world to a yellow, jaundiced vision of acquisitiveness, leisure suffuses reality with the golden tincture not only of myth (as the reference to Hesiod makes clear) but also, implicitly, with the golden tones of Claude Lorraine. Assuming we share his primitivist assumption that naturalness is the proper measure for all things, not least poetry, Hunt uses "nature" to urge on us the highly unnatural (because selected and filtered) vision of rococo pastorale. For him, life is a sort of magnified florilegium, a skimmed-off anthology of pleasant sensations and picturesque moments. His very critical procedure of italicizing and so dissociating passages of particular beauty from their context and carrying these with him into imagined pastoral milieux is pure rococo.

Look how Hunt glides over the strenuous and discomfiting elements of *Kubla Khan* to retrieve and recontexualize a single image:

We could repeat such verses as the following down a green glade, a whole summer's morning:

> A damsel with a dulcimer
> In a vision once I saw,
> A lovely Abyssinian maid;
> And on her dulcimer she played,
> Singing of Mount Aborah.[45]

This is the spirit if not the letter of a Watteauvian *fête galante*—infinite leisure, eternal summer, a benign, protective milieu. In much the same way, Hunt's criticism often involves a leisurely culling of poetic blooms. Here, for example, is how he explains a little detour in his account of Milton's Latin poetry: "To wander in the fields of poetry after one set of flowers, and never to pick up another, would be difficult."[46] In the same article, Milton comes close to being conscripted as a rococo pastoralist in the image of Hunt:

He proceeds to say how delighted he is with his books; and that when he is tired with study, he goes to the theatre to enjoy tragedies and comedies. The look of the inside of the house, filled with spectators, is finely painted in the phrase of "*sinuosi pompa theatri*"—the pomp of the *bosomy* theatre. His father, he says, has got a house in the suburbs, near a grove of elm trees; where he is often treated with the sight of companies of young ladies passing along—"*Virgineos choros.*"[47]

One wonders whether, by translating *sinuosus* as "bosomy" and *Virginei chori* as "companies of young ladies," Hunt has not assimilated Milton's sensibility to his own, for it is he, much more than the Puritan poet, who delights in idyllic settings. Kucich has observed how it "was habitual for Hunt to read his aesthetic conflicts onto other writers, particularly when a strong sense of his limitations was involved."[48] Responses like the one above suggest that it was no less habitual for him to claim that greater writers encapsulated his own peculiar strengths and preoccupations. Hunt even reinvents the transactions of commerce as a sort of pastoral excursion. In a memorial essay on the bookseller Ollier, he muffles the clamor of Paternoster Row, offering instead a rococo vignette in the style of Watteau:

This is the way in which Mr. Ollier used to talk of the objects of his own admiration; and to hear him thus talking of them, on a summer's evening over a temperate glass, with open windows before him, looking on trees and flowers, and in a voice as deep as a bee's and talking of as sweet and sequestered things, was a treat which I have missed for the first time these many years in his favourite month of June, and the memory of which has been filling its week of sadness.[49]

From this and many other features besides we can infer that the rococo element in Hunt's thought and in his poetry is not restricted only to visual congruences. Its influence is far more pervasive and ingrained.

The rococo mode also raises some central issues of aesthetic gendering. In his definition of fancy, Wordsworth used feminine pronouns to suggest the subordination of fancy to the "masculine," resourceful imagination: "Fancy depends on the rapidity and profusion with which she scatters her thoughts and images . . . she cares not how unstable or transitory may be her influence, knowing that it will not be out of her power to resume it upon apt occasion."[50] Here the argument makes implicit use of two sexual stereotypes: woman conceived as fecund goddess, on the one hand, and as coquette, on the other. Wordsworth's unstated antitypes are the austerity and abstraction of rational thought (which the patriarchy traditionally conceives as a masculine preserve) and the resoluteness with which it follows its track of premise and conclusion. Furthermore, by thus feminizing fancy, he might also be hinting at its essentially domestic milieu, one set off from the unsheltered sublimity of the "male" imagination. Wordsworth's account of the imagination in book 6 of *The Prelude* tends to confirm these implicit assumptions:

> Imagination—here the Power so called
> Through sad incompetence of human speech,
> That awful Power rose from the mind's abyss
> Like an unfathered vapour that enwraps,
> At once, some lonely traveller. I was lost;
> Halted without an effort to break through;
> But to my conscious soul I now can say—
> "I recognize thy glory": in such strength
> Of usurpation, when the light of sense
> Goes out, but with a flash that has revealed
> The invisible world, doth greatness make abode,[51]

Marlon Ross has shown in this regard how Wordsworth conceives the imagination as an essentially masculine force:

> When Wordsworth compares imagination to an "unfathered vapour," he brings attention to its source of authority, or more precisely to the lack of such authority. He does not use the word "unmothered" . . . because he is not so much referring here to the birth or origin as to the final cause that ordains and justifies existence itself. . . . Wordsworth is saying that imagination . . . ordains itself, is its own justification, is its own source of authority. Wordsworth's allusion to Genesis (the vapour and the abyss) helps establish the idea that desire gives birth to the human (from the male vantage point) world of perception and value in the same way that God gives birth to the universe and its hierarchies, not as a mother who bears her child from an impregnated seed, but as a father who inseminates existence from nothingness.[52]

While Wordsworth might image fancy as a sort of noetic Eve, he conceives the imagination less as a coequal Adam than as the *Deus artifex*, the creative Λογος. Given this gendered fission between the faculties, we should not be surprised to find that fancy has tended to issue in a poetry of "settlement," opposed to the verse predicated on the imagination's prerogative to pioneer new modes and visions. To quote Ross once again, "One reason Romantic poets are so obsessed with climbing mountains is that the activity perfectly emblematizes the poet's charge of self quest and world conquest."[53]

Even as he masculinizes the imagination, however, Wordsworth at the same time annexes "female" prerogatives of sensitivity and responsiveness. Book 13 of *The Prelude* grafts feeling onto the intellect:

> he whose soul hath risen
> Up to the height of feeling intellect
> Shall want no humbler tenderness, his heart
> Be tender as a nursing mother's heart;
> Of female softness shall his life be full,
> Of little loves and delicate desires,
> Mild interests and gentlest sympathies.[54]

Alan Richardson has detected in this and other similar moments a romantic desire to colonize the feminine,[55] though of course they simply extend the heritage of the Age of Sensibility. We need to remember that the *Blackwood's* myrmidons, having taken Wordsworth to their bosom, never mocked the distinctly Huntian tone and emphasis of such passages as that in *Prelude* 13. In the first place it would not have served their political ends to acknowledge Wordsworth's radical extension of "male" sensibility; in the second, they might have assumed that the "effeminacy" of such claims would have been neutralized by the abstract masculine discourse intercalated into the poet's bildungsroman. In addition, Wordsworth's manliness would have been underwritten by his stress on robust activity and on the sublime landscapes viewed during walks and expeditions.

The "colonization of the feminine" also takes another turn. As we move out of the Age of Sensibility, the Burkean antithesis of the sublime and the beautiful tends to be reformulated as an antithesis of the sublime and domestic. Indeed Stuart Curran has isolated "quotidian values" as a hallmark of women poets writing at this time, and has pointed out that "although present and celebrated in the verse of the Enlightenment and Victorian periods, [they] have been largely submerged from our comprehension of Romanticism, with its continual urge for visionary flight, for an investment in symbols."[56] Precisely because Hunt hardly ever assays visionary flights and chooses rather to attend to ordinary, domestic things, he has been marginalized along with many of the women poets whose reintegration into the romantic canon Curran and others are pioneering. Precisely *because* he lived in the "effeminate" (i.e., domestic) suburbs of London and not in the "virile" environment of the Lake District, he was pilloried by Lockhart and Wilson. If there is domesticity in Wordsworth, it is domesticity sublimized, as in these lines from *Home at Grasmere*: "From high to low, from low to high, yet still / Within the bound of this huge Concave, here / Should be my Home, this Valley be my World."[57] In Hunt, by contrast, sublimity is domesticated, trimmed for comfort.

The domestic and the quotidian are near synonyms, as in Keble's famous line about "the daily round, the common task,"[58] and of course there is as much distinctly quotidian material in *The Prelude* as there is in the poetry of Hunt, with one crucial difference. Wordsworth's domestic element is reportorial—it testifies more to the poet's capacity for observation than his engagement with areas he was ready to delegate to Dorothy and later to Mary. In Hunt, on the other hand (and indeed in Moore, whom *Blackwood's* also accused of "effeminizing sensuality"),[59] we have the *projection* of ideal settings and decor—*fantasized* interiors and garden landscapes. Whereas Moore's memoir of Lord Byron rejected Hunt's attack on the poet by suggesting that "domestic life and poetic genius are entirely incompatible,"[60] Hunt's creed of poetic cheerfulness was posited on their congruence. Keats himself endorsed the creed in *Sleep and Poetry* when he claimed that poetry's "great end" is to "be a friend / To soothe the cares, and lift the thoughts of man."[61] In the lead-up to this pronouncement, he (and Hunt with him) rejects "strength" as the sufficient guarantor of excellence, and calls into question the sort of dichotomy that Ross has located at the center of romantic ideology: "When Moore pits domesticity against poetry, when he locates poetic desire within 'Self,' when he views poetry as a grand manly calling, he is simply explicating and extending the logic hidden within the romantic conception of the poet."[62]

What I have called the "rococo" color of Hunt's sensibility is predicated upon an altogether different gendering of the romantic project. Since Sewter contends that rococo is "a style of interior decoration rather than a language of architectural forms and ideas,"[63] poets who share Hunt's affiliation to this mode often create domestic milieux instead of simply relaying them. To that extent they prove "guilty" of appropriating a traditionally feminine function, given the belief that "true men" remain indifferent to their domestic arrangements. Even to this day, interior decoration is regarded as a largely homosexual preserve, whereas "true men," like those of *Blackwood's*, spend their *noctes ambrosianae* quaffing heavy drink. Here, to illustrate the entrenchment of such attitudes, is how the vindictive Croker attacked Tennyson for a similar "vice" in 1833: "[I]n such a dear *little* room a narrow-minded scribbler would have been content with *one* sofa, and that one he would probably have covered with black mohair, red cloth, or a good striped chintz; how infinitely more characteristic is white dimity!— 'tis as it were a type of the purity of the poet's mind."[64] Even Maria Edgeworth is not above sniggering at a decorator, and basing her amusement on the "incongruity" of a man's being interested in texture and color. This is how Mr. Soho advises Lady Conbrony in *The Absentee*:

> I refused, I absolutely refused, the Duchess of Torcaster—but I can't refuse your la'ship. So, see, ma'am—(unrolling them)—scagliola porphyry columns supporting the grand dome—entablature, silvered and decorated with imitative bronze ornaments; under the entablature, a *valance in pelmets*, of puffed scarlet silk, would have an unparalleled grand effect, seen through the arches—with the TREBISOND TRELLICE PAPER, would make a *tout ensemble*, novel beyond example. On that Trebisond trellice paper, I confess, ladies, I do pique myself.[65]

There is no great distance between this and Hunt's account of the decor of his prison cell. Indeed we might even take it as an emblem for the way his poetry often impearls itself about the grit of real suffering and nobility of purpose, and bathes it, even to the point of prettification, with a decorative sheen:

> I papered the walls with a trellis of roses; I had the ceiling coloured with clouds and sky; the barred windows I screened with Venetian blinds; and when my bookcases were set up with their busts, and flowers and a pianoforte made their appearance, perhaps there was not a handsomer room on that side of the water.[66]

Small wonder therefore that, writing divertissement verse about pretty interiors and pleasure gardens, and shunning the sort of strenuous, self-conscious abstraction of Wordsworth's meditative episodes, Hunt should fall foul of the gender codes that had dichotomized domestic and public life, on the one hand, and feeling and reason, on the other. Ross has pointed out that "the potential to have poetic foremothers, as well as forefathers, is much greater for Keats than for Wordsworth, not only because it has become less unacceptable to see women as serious poets and potential mentors for young male poets, but also because the influence of these women has become so palpable and profound that to ignore them wholly would mean ignoring some of the most prominent figures in the contemporary literary scene."[67] Such observations apply as much to Hunt, only fourteen years Wordsworth's junior and ready to valorize the feminine long before Keats put pen to paper. The poetry of Mary Tighe, to which Hunt (like Keats) almost certainly owes a debt, is thickly seeded with bowers, images of a reclusive temperament that in her own words "for cruel battles would not dare / The low-strung chords of her weak lyre prepare."[68] However, in her lines "Written at Rossana," she casts this gendered diffidence aside, implying that the epic materials her femininity "disables" her from tackling have little attraction for her (just as they would later have little attraction for Hunt, the willed effort of *Captain Sword and Captain Pen* aside): "Dear chestnut bower, I hail thy secret shade, / Image of tranquil life!"[69] The narrow scope of the bower might limit the range of the refugee's experience, but it also exempts her from the masculine brusqueries of public life. Ever since Chaucer applied the epithet to Diomede in *Troilus and Criseyde*, the word "sudden" has in some circumstances, not least these, acquired a harsh "manly" color: "And though no lively pleasures here are found, / Yet shall no sudden storms my calm retreat affright." Thus while it might be true, as Nancy Armstrong has claimed, that the eighteenth century produced "a culture divided into the respective domains of domestic woman and economic man,"[70] Tighe and "feminizing" poets such as Hunt, far from kicking against the pricks, quietly foregrounded that domestic domain as offering the moral high ground and used the pastoralism of the bower to validate their choice.

Even though Hunt had the benefit of hindsight in 1837, we can nonetheless see how in *Blue-Stocking Revels* he detects certain proto-Huntian elements in the women poets of the Regency—the domestic *enclosure* implicit in the "nooks and old houses" he attributes to Charlotte Smith, and the sense of informality and relaxation he ascribes to Felicia Hemans, qualities perfectly compatible with the grandeur she can produce from her keyboard ("Thrale, Brunton, Trefusis, her heart pit-a-patting, / And Hemans, behind her grand organ-loft chatting").[71] (And how contemporary, by the way, the feel of that surnominal catalog, anticipating the recent parity rule that refers to women writers by their surnames.) It is impossible to determine now whether in *Blue-Stocking Revels* Hunt was advancing judgments that had been revised during the decades that followed his debut as a poet, or whether they testify to his sense of having from the start absorbed the "feminine" options of tone and materials they made available to him. Whether consciously embraced or not, the influence seems real and points to the poet's flexibility, his unanxious openness to alternatives that poets such as Byron were eager to scorn.

Mary Poovey has pointed out how the idea of the "proper lady" evolved in the course of the eighteenth century into a restrictive behavioral paradigm,

repressing or deflecting the aspirations it failed to accommodate. The definition of the "proper gentleman" likewise issued in an exigent gender stereotype. When Hunt chose to diverge from established norms, he opened
himself to charges of effeminacy from the *Blackwood's* bullies, who judged
his poetry "unnatural" in more ways than one. Not only was Hunt mocked
for mistaking the artificial approximations of a pleasure garden for nature
itself, but he was also mocked for his "deviancy," his failure to render the
"natural" avocations of the male. Poovey suggests that, in the eighteenth
century, social constructs had been insidiously "naturalized" into the dis-
pensations of providence:

> Throughout this period, then, the dual function the ideal of feminine
> propriety served was, implicitly if not explicitly, to harness the appetites
> men feared and associated with women to their own more reliable mascu-
> line wills and then, by extension, to protect the property upon which the
> destiny of both individuals and an entire society depended. . . . The fact
> that references to the dual function I have identified reappear throughout
> this period but are increasingly subordinated to other, more idealizing
> descriptions of women's nature and role attests to the success with which
> compensations for these anxieties and interests were simply assimilated to
> definitions of "nature." By the end of the eighteenth century, in fact,
> "female" and "feminine" were understood by virtually all men and women
> to be synonymous. Before I turn to an examination of the image of pro-
> priety itself, it is important to trace some of the factors that helped to
> naturalize femininity and, in doing so, helped to formulate the stereotype
> with which most woman compared or identified themselves.[72]

She goes on to identify these factors as religion, middle-class morality, and
property arrangements, some of the issues to which Hunt addressed himself
as a Radical journalist on *The Examiner*. A generous and tolerant man who
was ready to examine alternatives to the status quo, he offered a target for
various reactionary shafts, not least the accusation of effeminacy. When the
romantic poets "colonized the feminine," they did more than develop a
capacity for pathos: the gender stereotype encompassed other traits as well.
    One ideological template for cutting women down to size equated
femininity with the absence of emotional restraint. Adam Smith claimed
that

> Humanity consists merely in the exquisite fellow-feeling which the spec-
> tator entertains with the sentiments of the persons principally concerned,
> so as to grieve for their sufferings, to resent their injuries, and to rejoice at

their good fortune. The most humane actions require no self-denial, no self-command, no great exertion of the sense of propriety. They consist only in doing what this exquisite sympathy would of its own accord prompt us to do.[73]

This is to suggest that masculinity inheres in the conscious control and expunction of humane impulses, and that negative capability turns less on the suspension of self than on the suspension of manhood.

Hunt challenged such absurd categorizations in poem after poem, inviting the charge of "epicureanism." Even though his politics occupied a comparatively small place in his poetry, his adversaries found a Radical taint in everything he said and did, not least in his trespassing on preserves that the patriarchy had marked as essentially feminine. If Mary Wollstonecraft wrote her disquisition on the rights of humankind to invade a traditionally male field and signal "her determination to transcend the limitations she felt her sex had already imposed on her,"[74] then, in an analogous way, Hunt chose *not* to write with the sort of *gravitas* and rigorous abstraction ordinarily conceived as being "manly." In this way, he registered his determination to transcend the sexual limitations that had been demarcated for men in turn. When Wollstonecroft characterized the socially imposed feminine gestalt in *A Vindication of the Rights of Woman*, she might have been offering an account of Hunt's peculiar temperament: "Women, commonly called Ladies, are not to be contradicted in company, are not allowed to exert any manual strength; and from them the negative virtues only are expected, when any virtues are expected, patience, docility, good-humour, and flexibility; virtues incompatible with any vigorous exertion of intellect."[75] Such, indeed, are the leading features of Hunt's oeuvre—its leisured absence of striving, its surrender to pleasure, its cheerfulness, its pliancy.

Several other aspects of the gender division are also worth remarking. For instance, there is the issue of Hunt's sensitivity, a faculty inherited from Cowper, Gray, and Smart, and manifest above all in his revulsion against cruelty. The "huntin', shootin', fishin'" ethos of *Blackwood's* manifested itself, by contrast, in the brutality of its attacks, a brutality no doubt reinforced by the sort of ideological cleft that assigned "susceptibility" and "humanity" to the female sex. Fecklessness and dependency also figure among the charges brought against Hunt's character, as indeed they figured in traditional formulations of the feminine. The avowed escapism of his verse might at first glance seem to explain these negative judgments, but we ought never to lose sight of his heroism in *choosing* to be a martyr for the freedom of the press, however much some would wish to claim that he neutralized the martyrdom (by a stroke of interior decoration and landscape gardening) to a rococo idyll. To judge Hunt for this sort of strategy is, perhaps, to misconstrue the half-conscious thinking that informs it. Jerome McGann has pointed out how the "grand illusion of Romantic *ideology* is that one may escape such a world [i.e., a world of suffering] through imagination and poetry. The great truth of Romantic *work* is that there is no escape, that there is only revelation (in a wholly secular sense)."[76] And again, "What is true of Byron's work is true of Romantic poetry in general. It is a poetry of ideas, of Ideals, and—ultimately—of Ideology, which is why displacements and illusions are its central preoccupations and resorts. Consequently, its greatest moments of artistic success are almost always those associated with loss, failure, and defeat—in particular losses which strike most closely to the Ideals (and Ideologies) cherished by the poets in their work."[77] Elsewhere, McGann remarks that "one can (and should) assent to this view [that romanticism is a reactionary and 'escapist' movement], but only after one also sees that the 'reaction' of Romanticism is also an intense expression of critique."[78]

Since it is Keats more than any other romantic who has been blamed for secularizing the *contemptus mundi* topos, and thus reinventing poetry as a refuge from the fever and the fret of living, we need to remind ourselves once again that in this regard he owed something to the example of Hunt. *Politics and Poetics* explicitly addresses the issue, and the *Autobiography* likewise confesses an experiential fissure between public life and the imagination:

> I was in the habit, though a public man, of living in a world of abstractions of my own; and I regarded him [Keats] as of a nature still more abstracted, and sure of renown. Though I was a politician (so to speak), I had scarcely a political work in my library. Spensers and Arabian Tales filled up the shelves; and Spenser himself was not remoter, in my eyes, than my new friend. Our whole talk was made up of idealisms. In the streets we were in the thick of the old woods.[79]

If, as McGann has suggested, "in Keats we begin to hear whispers of the motto of his great inheritor, D. G. Rossetti: *Fiat ars, pereat mundus*,"[80] it would be tempting to think that they began sotto voce in Hunt's own verse. But the poet's claim to remoteness notwithstanding, the motto does not really fit him. A truer sense of Huntian values would be found in its amendment to *Fiat ars, floreat mundus*.

However much Hunt might deprecate his political stature with a "so to speak," he remains the most *actively* political of all the romantics, Shelley included. This practical engagement in the cause of reform might be said to have earned him the right to the recreational verse he habitually preferred to write, along the lines of that philistine (yet plausible) argument that grants Schönberg the right to atonality because *Verklärte Nacht* had confirmed his mastery of the precedent tradition, and that sees Picasso's cubism as somehow being validated by his mastery of academic drawing. *The Story of Rimini*, like Oscar Wilde's famous ballad, was written in jail, but whereas this circumstance led Wilde for once to shed his preciosity, Hunt found aesthetic refuge in a medieval narrative. We need to remember, however, that escape does not necessarily entail escapism and, with that, the dissolution of social and moral responsibilities. Although McGann has described Heinrich Heine's essay "The Romantic School" as an "attack upon the Neo-Catholic ideology of German Romanticism and the movement's generally escapist and reactionary character,"[81] he observes that Heine could still claim a part for Ludwig Uhland (one of his targets) in the "War of Liberation": "Heine's proof of this position is twofold. First, he points out that Uhland forsook his poetry in the latter part of his career in order to become 'an ardent representative of the rights of the people in the Württemberg Diet' and 'a bold speaker for civic equality and thought.'"[82]

If this can much be conceded to Uhland, the argument will apply still more justly to Hunt. We can follow Heine and claim that practical politics rehabilitate (or at least inoculate) the disengaged *Träumerei* of Hunt's romanticism. While medieval nostalgia might bear poisonous fruit in the mind of an arch-Tory like Scott, it can remain perfectly venial in the dreams of a Radical. His sensibility will rejoice in the externalities of archaic costume and architecture, not in the repressiveness of an archaic ideology. Being in some sense a dramatic work, *The Descent of Liberty* falls outside the purview of this study, and yet we can observe similar displacements in that particular poem. Lisa Vargo claims that Hunt here "attempts to ironize aspects of the court masque, and thus to transcend the limits of the genre," taking "what must be one of the most elite forms of literature, a pageant in praise of a monarch, to write a paean to democracy."[83] This is so, and yet much of the masque, written during the poet's prison sentence, is eager to wreathe decorative garlands about its topic. Hunt has taken Puck's tetrameter monologues and Shakespearian flower catalogs and an image from Marvell's "Bermudas," and, filtering them through his own inimitable sensibility, produced a charming pastiche:

> . Lilacs then, and daffadillies;
> And the nice-leaved lesser lilies,

Shading, like detected light,
Their little green-tipt lamps of white;
Blissful poppy, odorous pea,
With its wings up lightsomely;
Balsam with his shaft of amber,
Mignonette for lady's chamber,
And genteel geranium,
With a leaf for all that come;[84]

The political significance of such verse is negligible, especially when it is set alongside the plangent indictments of Shelley's *Mask of Anarchy*, a poem that Hunt's masque partly inspired. Yet we need to bear in mind that Hunt wrote *The Descent of Liberty* in prison, while Shelley composed his poem in the comparative comfort of his Italian exile. As Timothy Webb observes, Shelley's "poem is 'of the exoteric species' and was specifically intended for *The Examiner;* Leigh Hunt, who had suffered enough for his frankness, preferred not to publish it till after the Reform Bill had been passed."[85]

Having thus glanced at the ideological weight placed on the frail shoulders of Hunt's fanciful poetry, let us now turn to aesthetic issues of structure and style. Hunt has long been condemned for formal slackness. His editor, H. S. Milford, has claimed that he wrote nothing perfect from the point of view of form. This I find unnecessarily harsh. Just as we would never judge Watteau by the compositional gravity of Poussin, so we should give up demanding that Hunt conform to the standards of Dryden or Pope. The rococo, like the baroque, involves a shift from classical frontality and balance to rhythmical asymmetry, and centers on deflected rather than anticipated resolutions of stress. Hunt perceived himself as the pioneer of alternatives to classical decorum. In his view, a native English tradition (beginning with Chaucer and ending with Milton) had been betrayed at the time of Charles II when poets turned to French neoclassicism, and although he was readier than Wordsworth or Keats to acknowledge Pope's greatness, he felt that it reduced poetry to "bead-rolling" couplets.[86]

This metaphor, rejecting a notion of the poetic line reduced to something hard, discrete, and globular, also rejects a poetry of calculated grading and stringing. While bead necklaces might begin and end in predictable ways, it is clear that Hunt has little patience with the principles of composition they embody. In *The Story of Rimini* he accordingly deformed some (but not all) of the individual beads—and it is perhaps worth remembering in this connection that the term "baroque" derives from the Portuguese for an irregular pearl, and that its strenuous irregularities were the precursor of the rococo's more graceful deviancies. Whereas the neoclassical couplet demanded closure and succinctness, Hunt enjambed and loosened his, and so supplanted a finite, squared-off structural procedure with the liquidity of the rococo arabesque. William Keach has suggested that an expressly political purpose underpinned this innovation, a coupling of Reform and reform: "Keats was caught up, then, in a squabble between Tory traditionalists, for whom the balanced and closed Augustan couplets had become something of a cultural fetish, and the liberal reformers who set out to establish 'a freer spirit of versification,' as Hunt says in the Preface to *The Story of Rimini*, along with a freer society."[87] Be that as it may (though it fails to account for Jeffrey's love of Crabbe), Hunt reformed the couplet to make it accord with one of his critical dicta—viz., that the "spirit of enjoyment is a spirit of continuousness."[88] Insofar as this prioritizes momentum above terminal finish, it provides a key to the greater part of his verse.

In the following passage from *The Nymphs* we see the rococo arabesque gather up the two-line units in the unfolding linearity of its curve, incising a larger verse paragraph onto the couplet bricks:

> They screen the cuckoo when he sings; and teach
> The mother blackbird how to lead astray
> The unformed spirit of the foolish boy
> From thick to thick, from hedge to layery beech,
> When he would steal the huddled nest away
> Of yellow bills, upgaping for their food,
> And spoil the song of the free solitude.[89]

An image of errancy requires an errant rhythm, and so the relaxation and slippage of the opened, "arabesque" couplets doubles up as a mimetic resource in this and many other instances. Related to such effects of effortlessness is Hunt's idea of poems as free improvisations, as ad libitum driftings from item to item within the confines of an adaptable topic. His idea of the essay as an easeful exercise also applies to his mode of poetic composition: "[W]e hereby commence a series of articles, in which we propose to be as easy and *ad libitum* on the subject, as if we were poking about the shelves of a curious library with our friend the reader, and talking of any book, part of a book, or anything about our book, that came pleasantly our way."[90] And again, "[W]ithin this pale we shall allow ourselves great liberties, and take up book or subject, or piece of either, just as it suits our humour."[91] The most orthodoxly structured poems by Hunt are his translations, where the compositional spadework has already been done for him and he simply has to tinker with surface effects. In Coleridge's book, and to some extent in Hunt's, the fancy cannot fuse its materials, and the elements of a Hunt poem are seldom melded "esemplastically" but rather juxtaposed, their transitions smoothed and oiled by the grace of the versification and casual insouciance of his modus operandi.

Hunt's effort to aerate and desolidify the texture of his poetry can further be observed in his readiness to write in trisyllabic meters. No poet before him seems to have written anapestic verse in such quantity, nor to have exploited its spirited prance to the full. Skelton and Brome had used the anapest as a hammer, and Cowper (with dubious success) had used it as a sobbing rhythm, but in Hunt's hands it turned into a *valse de salon*. Most trisyllabic meters draw attention to themselves, because they more obviously stylize the movement of the speaking voice than disyllabic measures. Their tendency to emphasize a fleet, mobile pattern of stress has distinct rococo possibilities. Hunt's versification, however, is only one facet of his efforts at lightening and loosening his utterance. Not content with the counterpoint of syntax against lineation as he unspools his couplets, he also relaxes the tension of his sentences within the linear unit. Again and again he sidesteps expected patterns and emphases, as when, in the extract above, the parisonic symmetry of "thick to thick" gives way to the lopsided slew of "hedge to layery beech," or when he inserts a preposition after the object in "steal the huddled nest away / Of yellow bills," disorienting the expected line of the sentence by reshuffling its units. Once again the adapted form helps reinforce the mimesis of the line. Not only does the preposition sever the nest from the fledglings; it also acts out the forced removal by creating a distance between the verb and the object it governs. At another point in *The Nymphs*, Hunt's syntactic experiments become even more daring. By collocating adverb and adjective in a single act of attention, he achieves a dreamy languor, a sense of energies suspended in a pleasant incoherence. Of course it is the *circles* the pigeons describe that are "large"; their *progress* is slow. In that drowsy, suspended vision that Keats was later to make his own, we are allowed only the vaguest sense of the distinction:

> A troop of clouds, rich, separate, three parts white,
> As beautiful, as pigeons that one sees
> Round a glad homestead reeling at their ease,
> But *large and slowly*, . . . [Italics mine][92]

Rococo decoration blurs structural boundaries in a way almost identical with Hunt's erasures in the end-stopped heroic couplet.

There are also other rococo impulses at work in *The Nymphs*. That the mode favors relaxation above formality can be gathered from its recreational *fêtes galantes* and from the domestic quiet of its genre pictures. Even so, it remains highly conventional, governed by a decorum just as insistent (if less obviously rigorous) than that which shapes a Poussin history painting. For Hunt, classicism fetishized the Roman spirit, a spirit he perceived as being "inexpressibly cold and critical; and the people themselves . . . a nation of gladiators,"[93] and he blamed the neoclassicists for "their gross mistake about what they called the classical, which was Horace and the Latin breeding, instead of the elementary inspiration of Greece."[94] Even so, "elementary inspiration" brings with it its own conventions, for, unlike Wordsworth, who tried in theory to denature the artifice of poetry, Hunt acknowledged the fissure between reality and art, and even, by the determined selectivity of his vision, privileged art above the real. The sort of feminine influence I posit above might have some relevance in this regard, if we bear in mind that in *Blue-Stocking Revels*, Hunt calls Mary Tighe "her own Psyche,"[95] suggesting that she generates her own palatial fancies or fancied palaces, the sort of enclosed, privileged space that Marlon Ross has accorded to her diction: "Unlike either Wordsworth or Keats [but, one might subjoin, like Hunt], . . . Tighe accepts the naturally 'artificial' status of poetic language, accepts it both because it provides her a bower of protection in which to write her own poetry as a woman and because it can help protect her readers from the ravenous reality of envy, fierce wrath, and cruel hate."[96] Much the same, mutatis mutandis, could be said of Hunt's solution to the issue of poetic diction. His response to Augustan decorum was to create a decorum of his own—habitual violations of Augustan taboos—and that is why his mannerisms remained with him throughout his career. Displacing poetic diction as a framing device, they signal his decision to write poetically.

Classicism has its inflexible rules, but it is not so much a state of rulelessness that Hunt envisages, as a free adaptation and adjustment of conventions—a "natural artificiality" à la Tighe. We can observe this in *The Nymphs*. The poet does not wholly dispense with neoclassical tropes and procedures; he simply treats them with insouciance. Look, for example, at his invocation. Whereas in Milton's *Paradise Lost* we find a cletic hymn to Urania, in *The Nymphs* Hunt treats the same convention with an unawed familiarity, as though a song from a Regency parlor had somehow been pressed onto a solemn epic occasion:

O Spirit, O Muse of mine,
Frank, and quick-dimpled to all social glee,
And yet most sylvan of the earnest Nine,
Who on the fountain-shedding hill,
Leaning about among the clumpy bays
Look at the clear Apollo while he plays;—
Take me now, now, and let me stand
On some such lovely land,
Where I may feel me, as I please,
In dells among the trees,
Or on some outward slope, with ruffling hair,
Be level with the air;
For a new smiling sense has shot down through me,
And from the clouds, like stars, bright eyes are
     beckoning to me.[97]

Where Poussin's nymphs and deities are friezed and choreographed, Hunt dissolves that formal arrangement and disperses them casually, even inelegantly, through his landscape. They "lean about"—not a usual posture in history painting! Yet, by retaining the form of the invocation, Hunt has allowed us to sense and measure his departures from the norm, as in the excitable, boyish impatience of "now, now." When Keats rejected poetry that seemed to have a palpable design upon him, he might have been remembering one of Hunt's obiter dicta, for again and again the older poet's criticism takes issue with studied, deliberate effects. The frigidities of Ciceronian rhetoric leave Hunt cold, and even while he acknowledges the cumulative weightiness of Burke, he laughs at it: "a certain architectural style in eloquence, proceeding step by step, one point built upon another, till you come to an apex that will not bear another pin."[98] In much the same way, he attacks Thomas Campbell for "eternally balancing his sentences, rounding his periods, epigrammatizing his paragraphs"—in a word, for allowing rhetoric keep "a perverse pace with the poetry."[99]

How then can poetry best be unbuttoned and destarched? In an essay written towards the end of his life, and whimsically entitled "An Effusion upon Cream and a Desideratum in English Poetry," Hunt set forth a sort of retrospective poetic credo. While ostensibly pointing to a dearth of purely fanciful poems in the heritage of English poetry, he seems all the while, whether consciously or not, to be characterizing and defining his own work. He says he has recently lighted on a little jeu d'esprit he believes might be by Thomas Peacock,[100] and feels impelled to share the lyric with the readers of the *Musical Times*:

[T]here suddenly presented itself to our eyes, in the *Manchester Examiner*, the following charming effusion of animal spirits, which adds all that we could have desired to add on the subject, and which is of a class of writing which it is much easier to think easy than to find so. Let any one who supposes otherwise, and who is not accustomed to consider this species of composition, try, with a running pen, or with any pen that does not feel itself charged with its subject, to snatch the swift and happy flow of its manner and matter, the fancies never wanting, the rhymes never forced, the words never out of their places, and their whole felicity of a thing which the author himself perhaps may consider a trifle (for such conclusions are not unnatural to powers so genial), but which nobody else has a right so to regard, in any sense of the word that implies commonness or want of value.[101]

Here are set forth some of the characteristic strivings of almost all Hunt's poetry—effortlessness, the sense of free improvisation *currente calamo*, the sense of fanciful plenitude, of inexhaustible invention at the ordinary (as opposed to the sublime) levels of existence, the adaptation of rhyme to circumstance (often a recipe for "Cockneyism") rather than the procrustean reshaping of thought to fit tyrannical pattern, and a sense of rightness achieved through *sprezzatura*. He goes on to point out that poetry of this ilk has seldom been accommodated by the English national character, though it flourishes in the carnivalesque atmosphere of the Mediterranean: "[V]erses of less merit than these, but of the same class of uncontrolled and joyous utterance, are great favourites to this day in the south of Europe, and this not only with the humblest but the highest people; indeed in proportion to the height of their perceptions, and their superiority to the dull mistake of confounding animal spirits with silliness."[102]

These "animal spirits" provide a key to the nature of fancy as the foster parent of good-natured, whimsical ebullitions, and they provide a touchstone in countless of Hunt's critical judgments. Again, he finds the English character deficient in this regard:

In English poetry, as in English prose, there is plenty of wit, plenty of humour, plenty to make you laugh, after a fashion; but the fashion is rarely of a sort to make you happy—that is to say, not thoroughly so, not thoroughly contented either with yourself or with the writer. English animal spirits, for the most part, are too apt to turn sour, and run to satire. They are not wholly of the right sort; not good-natured or happy enough themselves, to wish to make others happy.[103]

Now of all the poets of the nineteenth century, none more than Hunt has the right to claim felicity as the goal of his or her poetic enterprise, and none comes so close to fulfilling the desiderata he sets forth above. What he admires in Peacock's "Can of Cream from Devon" he would certainly admire in his own verse—its neologisms, for example, which testify to improvisatory suppleness, dishabille, and spiritedness all at the same time. Hence we find him applauding on-the-spot coinages in the poem:

> Skinner (a good clergyman, by the way), in the gaiety of his animal spirits, writing in praise of the reel of Tullochgorum (and to the tune of it), ventures such rhymes as "Philosophorum," and "Whigmegorum"; and O'Keefe's songs in his farces take advantage of farcical licence to indulge in the right native intoxication of merriment. The very jargon of the burdens of them is replete with significance. We have no such things in English. The mere innocent compound-adjective, "melt-in-the-mouthy," in this "Can of Cream from Devon," is an audacity so rare that it will startle the ordinary critic; though nothing could possibly be more warrantable, or to the purpose.[104]

But not, we are no doubt expected to murmur, the ordinary critic acquainted with the poetry of Leigh Hunt.

Many of Hunt's characteristic effects are designed to sidestep all premeditated ponderousness, to lighten the traditionally solemn. And simply because he eschews it at all costs—"Mr. Burke . . . was too elaborate, and studious of effect"[105]—he has sometimes veered too far in the opposite direction, and so irritated his detractors. Graham Hough's ferocious attack on *The Story of Rimini* is a case in point. Notice how his judgment relies for its validation on the presence of Dante: "It is a handling of the Paolo and Francesca episode from Dante, debased to utter vulgarity by an affectation of colloquial ease and a sort of chatty pertness. He combines this with a cocky sniggering appreciation of female charms."[106] And yet the distinctiveness of Hunt's poem lies precisely in its refusal to be awed by Dante, to build upon him as the temple-haunting martlet built in the eaves of Inverness. He was shrewd enough to know his limitations, and to realize that since the sublime was not his province, there was little point in competing with Dante on home ground. In *The Story of Rimini* tragic discourse is replaced by rococo discourse, rather as Gounod, hugging the coast most congenial to his talent, disengaged the lyricism of his *Faust* from the sublimities of Goethe's.

Returning to *The Nymphs*, we see how unselfconsciously Hunt takes up the idling tenor of his muse ("as I please"). He dispenses with any strenuous resolves (such as that of justifying the ways of God to humankind) and seems to be encouraged in this by her intimate, unclassical mien. Of course "quick-dimpled" faces would never be found in Poussin, but they abounded in nineteenth-century drawing rooms, and they fairly describe the countenances depicted in Watteau's *fêtes galantes*. We are not obliged to stigmatize this familiar tone as something vulgar or even prurient. If we leave aside the case of Boucher, we can say that rococo generally offers a disembodied kind of sexuality—the idea of carnal pleasure rather than its realization. While Michael Levey has attempted to show that Watteau's famous Cythera painting in the Louvre is a departure from, rather than an embarkation for, the isle of love, his reading has been challenged by Donald Posner, among others. The poignancy of Watteau must not be confused with *tristitia post coitum*. His pathos centers rather on a sense of the frailty and vulnerability of his world to the lowering realities he has banished from the confines of his parks. So, too, in Hunt I find no "cocky sniggering appreciation of female charms." He was undoubtedly possessed of strong sexual emotions, confessing in his *Autobiography* that the monastic flavor of Oxford and Cambridge made them unattractive to him, and construing even the austere (masculinist) abstractions of philosophy as a sort of courtship that astonishingly supplants *philia* with *eros*: "A Philosopher in fact, or in other words a Lover of Wisdom, claims no more merit to himself for his title than is claimed by the lover of any other lady; all his praise consists in having discovered her beauty and good sense. He is, like any other submissive swain, a mere machine in her hands. It is his business to echo and to praise every word she says, to doat upon her charms, and to insist to everybody he meets that the world would want its sunshine without her."[107]

Behind this little parable we can detect Hunt's discomfort with abstract thought, and his preference for more imaginative and emotional forms of discourse. But the erotic impulse that dictates the maxim is chaste, even Petrarchan. Hunt's poetry does offer an "appreciation of female charms," and (with that) an erotic potentiality, but throughout his life he recoiled from a sensual appetite bent on its own gratification. As soon as the mentally erotic became the actual, the subject's humanity was likely to be compromised. Look, for example, at his judgment on Sheridan, made in 1840: "a strong, a sensual, and therefore essentially coarse nature, none the less so for a veil of refined language, which was his highest notion of the dress of the heart."[108] Yet again we find him differentiating between erotic and profligate art with regard to his translation of Atys: "I think that voluptuousness, in the proper sense, is rather an ill-used personage; but grossness

I abominate; there is neither in this poem; and he would be guilty of real grossness, the essence of which is inapplicability and degradation, who would not see that all other associations in it are overcome by its gravity and awefulness."[109] Hunt's pervasive eroticism is often diagrammatized and so kept chaste by synecdoche. In *The Nymphs*, for example, the muse's "quick-dimpled" face is too fleetingly touched in to bear comparison with the glistening pout of Boucher nudes, while the "bright eyes" that beckon the poet at the end of the invocation seem as impersonal as the stars. In the description of the naiads, moreover, Hunt tessellates fleeting impressions of limb and form not in the spirit of a striptease but rather in empathy with their dolphinlike dartings and disportings:

> Some with an inward back; some upward-eyed,
> Feeling the sky; and some with sidelong hips,
> O'er which the surface of the water slips.[110]

(It is possible that Hunt knew Raphael's *Galatea* and Poussin's *Triumph of Amphitrite*, so we need not invoke Boucher's *Triumph of Venus* as a possible source for this section.)

The "inward back" of the passage alerts us to that concern with graceful linearity so typical of the rococo, and shows how Hunt, even without con- sciously embracing the arabesque (or line of beauty), nonetheless repeatedly dwells on notions of curvature. A single page of *The Nymphs* yields a "pil- lowy place," "rounded banks," a "curving jut," a "down-arching thigh / Tapering with tremulous mass internally" and an "eye-retorting dolphin's back."[111] Taken together, they help confirm the notion of a rococo sensibil- ity capable of recrudescing at any point in history.

That brief catalog of arabesque elements also points to another typical feature of Hunt's style: its spirited neologisms. Once again, critics have, almost from the start, rejected this playful approach to language as a kind of disfigurement. A nineteenth-century writer, Cosmo Monkhouse, regrets the "habit constant through [Hunt's] life of using words in an unusual if not mistaken sense, which spoils so much of his best work, especially in po- etry."[112] We can avoid his censoriousness, however, if we relate the habit to rococo principles, to its conscious departures from neoclassical norms and fixtures. Just as the couplet "beads" of *The Nymphs* often display a purposeful irregularity in the rolling, so Hunt takes care to avoid words and phrases conforming to Augustan dictates. Appraising an anecdote about Roubiliac in Hazlitt's *Plain Speaker*, for example, he notes that the "familiarity of this termination does not put one out. It is part of the humanity of which Mr. Hazlitt never loses sight, in his highest flights."[113]

Pindar's divergence from the narrow prescriptions of neoclassical decorum also meets with approval: "[L]ike a truly great poet, he has not hesitated to mix the homeliest natural truth with the loftiest idealism (for Nature, who makes every thing, disrespects nothing)."[114] Familiarity, domestic relaxation (especially in the sphere of diction), Hunt therefore views as the guarantor of humanity. In some respects his program resembled Wordsworth's, but his solution took a very different form. Indeed his attitude to Wordsworth remained ambivalent throughout his life, focused on what he perceived to be "stubborn affectations" and "magazine commonplaces."[115] He found his paradigm for the diction of poetry not in the language of ordinary people, but rather in the variety and splendor of Spenser's. Adjectives with *y* suffixes were especially attractive, hence the "clumpy bays" and "pillowy place" in *The Nymphs*. These (and such devices as the improvised hypallage of "curving *jut*") Hunt used to emphasize his liberation from neoclassical decorum, and his own freedom to coin and adapt as the impulse dictated. The language of neoclassicism, like the austere pictorial tenets propounded by Poussin, could, in hands of epigones, turn into a procrustean bed. Hunt not only refused to conform, but also claimed license to make his own rules and to break those if need be. It ought to be remembered that the Académie created the genre of the *fête galante* in order to admit Watteau; and Hunt similarly forged a new vision of language to match his new vision of poetic form and his ad libitum sense of poetic structure. For *The Nymphs* and its congeners are not shapely poems in any conventional sense. Caught up in a sequence of present moments, the poet cheerfully puts the larger pattern in abeyance and finally forgets it. The division of *The Nymphs* into parts 1 and 2 is arbitrary, and the variety of creatures in the one is balanced only loosely by the exclusive emphasis on nepheliads in the other. Their own song (in tetrameter couplets) has no counterbalance in the other wing of the "diptych" (if such a term does not in itself confer a formal balance where there is little balance to be found).

Hunt conceived of neoclassicism as "a school of wit and ethics in verse,"[116] and, reacting to its cult of aphorisms and detachable proverbs, quite often produced "holiday" verse, poetry in which very little is done though much is enjoyed. His best poems (such as *The "Choice"*) manage to combine the *fête galante* with a fairly strong ethical component, but there are a number in which the action dwindles to a trickle, and masquelike ecphrases eke it out. This emphasis on descriptive tableaux is typical of the rococo, and it manifests itself also in the many self-identifications we find in the poetry of Leigh Hunt. And not only there, but in any form of literature where fantasy needs to tag itself and create a mode distinct from reportage and realism. For example, it is not unusual for the characters in Gilbert and Sullivan to say "We are dainty little fairies" (*Iolanthe*) or "We are gentlemen of Japan" (*The Mikado*) or "Twenty love-sick maidens we" (*Patience*). The level of action in *The Nymphs* is as slight as that of a Watteau painting, its characters touching up nature here and there (in the manner of Milton's Adam and Eve). For this reason, the emphasis falls on being rather than doing, as in the nepheliads' straightforward, existential announcement:

> Ho! We are the Nepheliads, we,
> Who bring the clouds from the great sea,
> And have within our happy care
> All the love 'twixt earth and air.[117]

We find the same emphasis on being and self-identification in *Songs and Chorus of the Flowers*, itself a title that belongs to the fantastic world of the romantic ballet and the Victorian pantomime: "We are blushing Roses," "We are lilies fair," etc.[118]

A corollary of this decorative indolence, this dreamlike suspension, is a certain indifference to psychology. Just as Watteau shows little interest in characterizing his actors, picnickers, and country folk, so Hunt hardly makes an effort to individuate his nymphs. Some might ride the clouds and some the waves, but, in keeping with the decorative and atmospheric nature of rococo art, he simply situates them as fantastic guardians of his landscapes, landscapes that in turn are decorative and generalized in the manner of *vedute di fantasia*. Even in *The Story of Rimini*, a poem more fully committed to realistic psychology, he invests most of his energy in lavish pageants and pictorial detail. Far from viewing this as an evil, we should acknowledge its importance to the mode in which he has chosen to recast his material. The result is not Dantesque—far from it—but it often proves as light and airy and decorative as a Tiepolo fresco. Lacking a sense of how the rococo functions, and of the emphases it customarily makes and the routes it avoids taking, we are all too likely to reach the harsh conclusions of Graham Hough and others before him. Who would want to break a butterfly upon a wheel when "butterflies are free"?

2

Narrative Poems: I

THE STORY OF RIMINI (1816)

Of all poetic kinds, the verse tale would at first sight seem the least suited to Leigh Hunt's sensibility. How, one might ask, could a critical anthologist who isolates and recovers luminous moments from his reading, and assembles these for the reader's pleasure, prove equal to the epic long view, the planning and sustension required by narrative poetry? Did not Dryden, one of the great narrative poets, stress the primacy of design above texture in this field: "Now, the Words are the Coloring of the Work, which in the Order of Nature is last to be consider'd. The Design, the Disposition, the Manners, and the Thoughts, are all before it. . . ."[1] Design, strenuously conceived as the disposition of neoclassical topoi, was never a feature of rococo art (essentially atmospheric and relaxed in its mode of arrangement) and it is seldom evident in Hunt's poetry; yet he has managed to write some successful verse tales.

Hunt chose to place *The Story of Rimini* at the portal of the 1860 edition of his poems, and indeed his poetic reputation rests to a greater extent on this than on the spirited rococo jeux d'esprit that are more obviously the products of the fancy. Indeed, it can be said to have both made and broken his reputation, so completely does it typify the strengths and weaknesses of his craft. Yet, at the very time he gave it apparent pride of place, Hunt had begun to doubt its value, even to the point of uttering what might at first seem like a palinode. To quote Blunden, "He felt now that *Rimini*, apart from a fine line here and there, was 'conventional, not rich and aromatic, and tending to prose.' He was 'not unwilling to be judged, as to final amount of capacity, by the *Mahmoud*, the *Ben Adhem*, *Inevitable*, *Wallace and Fawdon*, and one or two others of the smallest pieces.'"[2] Some of Poe's microphilia seems to have crept into Hunt's autumnal judgment on himself, and we need not take this apparently harsh valuation at face value. If the lyric alone becomes the yardstick, almost all narrative poetry will de facto "tend to prose." And if *The Story of Rimini* does indeed reveal structural and linguistic flaws, these can more plausibly be traced to an overzealous pursuit of "richness and aroma," to his submission to present impulse, to recurrent exaltations of decoration over form.

Hunt conceived the possibility of a narrative poem about Francesca da Rimini as far back as 1811, but it was completed and published only in 1815, and then suffered an altogether typical spate of "tinkerings" at least until 1844. Discussion of these changes, both narrative and textural, can be postponed to a later point of the chapter. What concerns us for the time being is its narrative procedure, and the way in which the poet has turned this to his advantage. For, examining *Rimini* closely, we find that Hunt has evaded demands that would otherwise have fallen beyond the compass of his gift, and has in the process forged his own kind of rococo narrative. Epic has always had its breathing spaces, its moments for decorative elaboration, whether they be the forging of Achilles' shield in the *Iliad* or the analogous description of Aeneas's in the *Aeneid*. But in the first canto of *The Story of Rimini*, Hunt allows these static elaborations (called ecphrases) to colonize virtually the whole of his narrative. Indeed the entire first canto resolves itself into an atmospheric cavalcade, its pageant formation a convenient means for blocking out the spaces of his canvas. An obvious precedent for such a procedure is supplied by the progress poem so favored by the eighteenth-century poets (and deployed by Hunt himself in *The Progress of Painting*).[3] John Hayden has also observed that the "procession itself seems to be patterned after Sir Walter Scott, especially the entry of the hero in the first Canto of *Marmion*, although there is not the same turn for medieval jargon. . . ."[4]

While these derivatives unquestionably inspired Hunt to some degree, it is almost certain that he also went back to more "authentic" sources to fashion his pastiche—sources such as the prologue to *The Canterbury Tales*, with its sequential progression through the line of pilgrims, and, more germane still, part 3 of *The Knight's Tale*. Here is a sample by way of foil to Hunt's modus operandi in *Rimini:*

> With Arcita, in stories as men fynde,
> The grete Emetreus, the kyng of Inde,
> Upon a steede bay trapped in steel,
> Covered in clooth of gold, dyapred weel,
> Cam ridynge lyk the god of armes, Mars.
> His cote-armure was of clooth of Tars

Couched with perles white and rounde and grete;
His sadel was of brend golde new ybete;
A mantelet upon his shulder hangynge,
Bret-ful of rubyes rede as fyr sparklynge;
His crispe heer lyke ringes was yronne,
And that was yelow, and glytered as the sonne.
His nose was heigh, his eyen bright citryn,
His lippes rounde, his colour was sangwyn;
A fewe frakenes in his face yspreynd,
Bitwixen yelow and somdel blak ymeynd;[5]

And here, to contrast, is Hunt's pastiche, written with clear memories of Chaucer in mind, and supplemented no doubt by recollections of Benozzo Gozzoli and other quattrocento painters, of the many decorative cortèges of Spenser, and of the imposing progress structures find in *The Bard* and *The Progress of Poesy*. Nor must we forget the more immediate instances of medieval *pasticcio* in the novels of Walter Scott—Blunden has noted that in 1814 Hunt attacked the "mediaeval costumery" of that writer[6]—an influence that no doubt also contributed its imaginative grist to Hunt's mill:

A suitable attire the horses shew;
Their golden bits keep wrangling as they go;
The bridles glance about with gold and gems;
And the rich housing-cloths, above the hems
Which comb along the ground with golden pegs,
Are half of net, to shew the hinder legs.
Some of the cloths themselves are golden thread
With silk enwoven, azure, green, or red;
Some spotted on a ground of different hue,
As burning stars upon a cloth of blue,—
Or purple smearings with a velvet light
Rich from the glary yellow thickening bright,—
Or a spring green, powdered with April posies,—
Or flush vermilion, set with silver roses:
But all are wide and large, and with the wind,
When it comes fresh, go sweeping out behind.
With various earnestness the crowd admire
Horsemen and horse, the motion and the attire.
Some watch, as they go by, the riders' faces
Looking composure, and their knightly graces;
The life, the carelessness, the sudden heed,
The body curving to the rearing steed,

> The patting hand, that best persuades the check,
> And makes the quarrel up with a proud neck,
> The thigh broad pressed, the spanning palm upon it,
> And the jerked feather swaling in the bonnet.[7]

Karl Kroeber has written that this "gorgeous pageantry of medieval Italy carries the mind far from the damp and sooty England of the Industrial Revolution,"[8] and he certainly seems right in suggesting that the poem emerges in part from Hunt's nostalgia for an age more ceremonious and decorative in its externals. The poet's desire to find imaginative escape from his imprisonment also played its part, no doubt, though we must bear in mind the fact that the composition of canto 1 predated Hunt's sojourn in Surrey Gaol, and indeed was first conceived as a "melancholy theme of verse . . . to steady [his] felicity" at a euphoric point of his life.[9] Now because *Rimini* was written with at least some escapist motives in mind, its sensuous detail tends to overgrow the plot, and texture is dwelt on for its own sake rather than for any thematic or psychological illumination it might provide. The descriptions thus seem in the last resort to be a touch bodiless, as though Hunt were thumbing his way through bolts of rich fabric in a warehouse, each swatch cataloged but somehow never given a larger scenic coherence. Louis Landré has traced this rampant descriptiveness to a lack of self-control: "Hunt could discipline himself far less than Keats and Shelley; hence the over-abundance of descriptions and overrefined terms."[10] This might be so, but we must remember that someone writing a poem in part for therapeutic reasons will not voluntarily put brakes on the imaginative flight to which he owes his escape in the first instance.

In pastiche it is always the unfamiliar or the remote that fascinates the imitator and prompts the imitation. Unlike that of *Rimini*, the ceremonious pageantry in *The Knight's Tale* is incorporated because Chaucer found it in life, not because he sought it out. Moreover, it is there both for its own sake *and* because it centers on the *characters* at the heart of the story. Where Hunt is deflected from his narrative by the charm of beautiful surfaces, Chaucer digs beneath them to find an additional layer of emblem or symbol. Unspecified plurals indicate a certain generality in Hunt's procedure—"Some watch, as they go by, the riders' faces / Looking composure, and their knightly graces"—and so too does his protocinematic use of synecdoche. John Hayden says some illuminating things in this regard: "It would not be inappropriate to use such movie jargon as 'pan' and 'zoom' to describe Hunt's techniques. The focus does tend to shift, taking the reader's attention from wide scenes to small details and back."[11] It is just possible that this piecemeal annotation of the scenes is also due to a failure of historical nerve—if one registers effects with glances rather than with stares, factual solecisms are less likely to surface. But of course the synecdoche serves primarily to facet and fragment the scene with the dizzying swirl of a kaleidoscope. Even its busy-ness is achieved at the cost of clarity and placement: "The patting hand, that best persuades the check, / And makes the quarrel up with a proud neck, / The thigh broad pressed, the spanning palm upon it, / And the jerked feather swaling in the bonnet." (Attempting a historical pastiche in *The Eve of St Agnes*, Keats opted for a similar strategy of metonymic zooms, and might even have been influenced by *The Story of Rimini* in this respect. Could that "jerked feather swaling in the bonnet" be a possible source for Keats's isolating "shot" of Porphyro's plume as it brushes past the cobwebs?)

While Chaucer moves from surface detail to the psychology it indexes, Hunt is content to linger and itemize without making sustained narrative connections. We are none the wiser about Francesca and Paulo as people by the end of canto 1, but our senses have been indulged to the full. Here is abundant evidence of an impulse to relax and prettify its subject matter, and also of the rococo tendency to give decorative impulse free rein and to allow the surface detail to spread over structural elements and colonize whole spaces at a time.

While Hunt might conscientiously try to reproduce the surface detail of a medieval cavalcade in the manner of Spenser, Gray, and Scott (the last two antiquarians with a strong sense of period detail), he is more than ready to sacrifice that detail to the idyllic impulses so characteristic of his sensibility. Look, for example, at the proem of *Rimini*:

> The sun is up, and 'tis a morn of May
> Round old Ravenna's clear-shewn towers and bay,
> A morn, the loveliest which the year has seen,
> Last of the spring, yet fresh with all its green;
> For a warm eve, and gentle rains at night,
> Have left a sparkling welcome for the light,
> And there's a crystal clearness all about;
> The leaves are sharp, the distant hills look out;
> A balmy briskness comes upon the breeze;
> The smoke goes dancing from the cottage trees;
> And when you listen, you may hear a coil
> Of bubbling springs about the grassy soil;
> And all the scene, in short—sky, earth, and sea,
> Breathes like a bright-eyed face, that laughs out openly.[12]

Hunt knew from quattrocento art that medieval city-centers had no trees and springs to speak of, and yet it was essential for him that some sort of *fête galante* be set in place: a coulisse of leaves, a plot of grass, intimate cottages (the hearth smoke familiar from Collins and Cowper) and bubbling springs. These are the realities recalled and stylized in the constructed bowers and fountains he will later implant in the city-center. Furthermore, he wants to recreate the *reverdies*, the spring songs, of the troubadours, but he knows that love and spring can be connected only outside the walls of Ravenna, which is where he begins his description. As Blunden notes, the "first canto of *Rimini* opens, true to Hunt's philosophy, with a May morning."[13]

As true to his philosophy is the need for human presence to animate his landscape. That is why he feminizes the topography itself, domesticating its details to produce a landscape of reassurance, not of grandeur. Such "anti-sublime" impulses run counter to the general trend of romantic verse—though Keats would at first be inspired by his example—and they remained with Hunt throughout his career. They can be detected also in the way he buttonholes his readers and takes them into the scene with him; there is nothing of the prophet or the *vates*, no ritual or hushed solemnity—"And when you listen, you may hear a coil / Of bubbling springs about the grassy soil." The buildup is achieved rather by the poet's confidentiality, which gathers the details and focuses them on the festive occasion.

The fact that the birds "to the delicious time are singing" could be construed as a "naturalistic" reference to the spring, or—in keeping with the poet's medieval pastiche—as a romance improbability. For example, it is not unusual for romance to posit a supernatural connection between the human and the natural, an effect we see again in the way the Ravennese ships are eager to greet the festal day. Hunt gives their random movements purpose and direction by using *epanorthosis*—"come up" / "Come gleaming up"—a design that recalls (and reverses) the recessive formulation of "She follow'd with her Sight the flying Sails: / When e'en the flying Sails were seen no more" in Dryden's *Ceyx and Alcyone*.[14]

> And the far ships, lifting their sails of white
> Like joyful hands, come up with scattery light,
> Come gleaming up, true to the wished-for day,
> And chase the whistling brine, and swirl into the bay.[15]

It is also worth noting that Hunt uses a romance superlative on the one hand ("A morn, the loveliest which the year has seen"), and on the other naturalizes it with an aside about weather conditions. This bifocal blending of ancient and modern typifies the whole enterprise.

While *The Story of Rimini* is to some extent a pastiche of medieval narratives, it does differ significantly from Scott's. The latter's pastiche might be termed "archaeological," for he supports it with footnotes (either inserted into the narrative as glosses or placed at the foot of the page). Such pastiche tries to reproduce the full cultural ethos of the story, even to the point of introducing archaic words and sentence patterns. Although Georg Lukács quotes Scott as saying that "it is necessary for exciting interest of any kind that the subject assumed should be, as it were, translated into the manners, as well as the language, of the age we live in," he claims at the same time that the author of *Ivanhoe* "*never modernizes* the psychology of his characters."[16] A partial guarantee against modernization inheres in Scott's "Ha-ings" and "Thou-ings" and inverted sentences, whereas Hunt avoids archaic fustian. It might be the case, as John Hayden suggests, that Francesca sounds like a shop girl when she admits Paulo to her pavilion, but it is also the case that Scott's Rebecca sounds like a ham actress. Both writers might be said to have failed in these particular instances, but it is Hunt who arguably comes closer to the Lukácsian desideratum that "the more remote an historical period and the conditions of life of its actors, the more the action must concern itself with bringing these conditions plastically before us, so that we should not regard them as an historical curiosity, but should re-experience them as a phase of mankind's development which concerns and moves us."[17] The question is simply whether that plastic immediacy should be reconstructive, or should seek contemporary analogues for the irrecoverable past.

In the context of the fine arts the word "pastiche" does imply a sort of Scottian reproduction, as witness the following definition in the Murray *Dictionary of Art and Artists*: "An imitation or forgery which consists of a number of motives taken from several genuine works by any one artist recombined in such a way as to give the impression of being an independent original creation by that artist."[18] The literary analogues of that enterprise must obviously be sought in the work of Macpherson and Chatterton, and Hunt's own (honest) archaeology in *The Tapiser's Tale*[19] and *The Shewe of Faire Seeming*.[20] Here the syntax and spelling strive (far more diligently than Scott's) to reproduce the accents and colors of their models. In poetry less ventriloquial, license has to be granted, and space made, for the poet's own peculiarities and nuances of vision. Hence when Hunt constructs his looser, more adaptable pastiche, he always allows a contemporary view to supervene upon the historical.

As Kroeber has noted, there "is nothing genuinely historical about *The Story of Rimini*."[21] The proper parallel to adduce here would not be visual but musical pastiche, pastiche like that in Tchaikovsky's *Pique Dame* and *The Sleeping Beauty*, for example. The purveyor of visual pastiche attempts to conceal his or her fingerprint, whereas composers working in the same genre make only some compromises with their characteristic contours of melody and harmonic color.

Hunt is attracted to the outward show of the Middle Ages, but finds many medieval values repellent. He therefore secretes a contemporary outlook into the antiquarian husk of his story, and also gives the diction a contemporary color. The first reviews of *Rimini* were almost unanimous in finding this strange, and their resistance attests to the fact that Hunt was breaking new *generic* ground as much as new metrical ground. For instance, Hazlitt and Jeffrey, writing in the *Edinburgh Review*, lodge their objection to "cant phrases,"[22] while the *Eclectic Review* speaks of "the easy graceful style of familiar narrative."[23] Like musical pastiche, Hunt's is not a mimeographic reproduction, but rather a loose, colorful, allusive reworking. At the same time, it differs from the "imitations" of the seventeeth and eighteenth centuries because the updating is only partial, and there is no thoroughgoing transposition of mode and manner of the sort that we find, say, in Dr. Johnson's imitations of Juvenal. A related matter is that of decorum, the adjustment of language to genre so central to any appreciation of eighteenth-century verse, and by no means in abeyance at the start of the nineteenth or even the twentieth. There is no *generic* sanction for the sort of lexical experiment that Hunt is making. Here is Barnette Miller, for example, voicing the reservations of an Edwardian reader: "His poetical epistles suffer without injury such departures from dignified diction, but in other cases, of which the *Story of Rimini* is a notable example, a grave subject in the garb of everyday language is degraded into the incongruous and prosaic."[24]

Finally, between the pastiche of Hunt and of Scott there is the *via media* of *The Cenci*. Shelley agreed with the Huntian principle, if not the Huntian practice, of a historical poem cast "in the familiar language of men,"[25] but, disingenuously perhaps, diverged from Hunt's "error" of modernizing ideology: "I have endeavored as nearly as possible to represent the characters as they probably were, and have sought to avoid the error of making them actuated by my own conceptions of right or wrong, false or true."[26] That the reading public eventually acclimatized to Hunt's innovativeness can be gauged from an article in the *Retrospective Review* (1820), which, in the summary of Lulofs and Ostrom, praises "Hunt's *Indicator* . . . as a fine collection of

stories from antiquity, rendered into 'the spirit of modern times' with 'luxu-
riance of fancy' and a 'hearty feeling for the humane and beautiful.'"27

Since the historical shell of *Rimini* is there primarily for its charm and
color, it naturally follows that Hunt would want to elaborate it to the fullest
possible extent. What Chaucer would supply without need to justify, a happy
concourse on a wedding day, the Regency poet feels compelled to explain:

> And well may all who can, come crowding there,
> If peace returning, and processions rare,
> And to crown all, a marriage in May weather,
> Have aught to bring enjoying hearts together;28

Those "enjoying hearts" derive from Hunt's philosophy of cheer; they do
not strike an authentic medieval note. Indeed, the opening canto, far from
looking back to earlier narrative forms, anticipates rather the effects of
Scribian grand opéra, which would burst upon Europe in the 1830s. The
opening of *Rimini* has the feel of *La Juive* or *Guillaume Tell* or *La Muette de
Portici*, and it seems to cry out for the hand of an Auber or a Meyerbeer to
supply it with dominant pedals and melodic snatches before a grand processional march.

Of course, there are no dominant pedals and half-stated melodies for
Hunt to conjure with, but he generates his excitement by other, equally
telling means. The obvious poetic analogue to fragmentary tunes is metonymy, close cousin of the synecdoche discussed above. Hunt uses metonymy as Meyerbeer would use his chorus, to zoom in on details that
measure and suggest the larger movement of the crowd. This he registers at
first in vocal terms, foregrounding individual sounds in the collective buzz:

> Already in the streets the stir grows loud
> Of expectation and a bustling crowd.
> With feet and voice the gathering hum contends,
> The deep talk heaves, the ready laugh ascends:
> Callings, and clapping doors, and curs unite,
> And shouts from mere exuberance of delight,29

Note how, as if by adjustment of a volume control, that laugh is stranded out
of the deeper, collective sound, which Hunt registers as a "heave." "Heave"
is a curiously oceanic term that recurs throughout the passage to strike a
note of effortful power—hence the "heaved-out tapestry," "then heave the
crowd" and "after a rude heave from side to side." The compactness and

density it summons up are relieved in turn by images of release, the most pleasing of which is the ornamental fountain in the midst of the arbors:

> A lightsome fountain starts from out the green.
> Clear and compact, till, at its height o'er-run.
> It shakes its loosening silver in the sun.[30]

The intransitive loosening of the water droplets as they recurve upon the earth at the same time loosens and lightens the mood of the onlooker packed close among the spectators. Hunt sustains this sense of spectatorial engagement with the scene by employing such directives as the crowd itself might have used to focus attention on special features. Look, for example, at the way in which Guido Cavalcanti is brought to our notice: not only by the characteristics of his costume, but by a nonce adverbial indicator that assures us our gaze has been properly directed—"He with the pheasant's plume—there—bending now." And later, a false alarm about Paulo's appearance is rendered in an identical way, with all the immediacy and self-contradictions of speech uttered currente calamo: "Ah—yes—no—'tis not he—but 'tis the squires / Who go before him when his pomp requires."[31] These improvisatory touches in a narrative so brocaded and formal are entirely typical of the poet's sensibility. Just as the fountain supplied a grace note of liberty to the massed densities of the crowd, so by a parallel effect of contraction and release, Guido's concentrating audience relaxes once his witticism has been received and acknowledged:

> Something he speaks around him with a bow,
> And all the listening looks, with nods and flushes,
> Breaks round him into smiles and sparkling blushes.

While the "sparkling blushes" might at first seem like a solecism, a compression made too loosely and unobservantly, reflection shows that the distant spectator's view would in fact fuse and compound the red cheeks with the glittering eyes above them. Still keeping Guido in focus, Hunt has Paulo give him a jewel at the end of the canto, subtly recapitulating the same rhythm of contraction and release in his description of its passage from hand to hand. Just as the fountain had suggested an unraveling chain of silver, so the slippery gold has the effect of liquefying as it passes from donor to recipient: "And loosening, as he speaks, from its light hold / A dropping jewel with its chain of gold, / Sends it, in token he had loved him long, / To the young father of Italian song."[32]

The buildup having thus worked its effect, it is time for the heroine to make her entrance. But here again we find Hunt deflecting our expectations of the obvious; she is given no grand *aria di sortita*, but a pensiveness that Keats must surely have had in mind when he came to introduce Madeline in *The Eve of St Agnes*. Look at the way the monolithic attention of the crowd slews off the abstractedness of Francesca. Whereas the reader was earlier placed within the throng, and like his or her neighbor unable to hear what Cavalcanti was saying to those about him, the authorial focus now takes us into the center of Francesca's meditations, obliterating the outer noise in the silence of her thought:

> But every look is fixed upon the bride,
> Who pensive comes at first, and hardly hears
> The enormous shout that springs as she appears,
> Till, as she views the countless gaze below,
> And faces that with grateful homage glow,
> A home to leave, and husband yet to see,
> Fade in the warmth of that great charity;
> And hard it is, she thinks, to have no will;
> But not to bless these thousands, harder still:[33]

An apparent catachresis—the application of a separative epithet to an inseparable noun in "countless gaze"—proves to have been thought through, for it registers the way in which Francesca senses, at the same time, an innumerable number of eyes and an easily measured attentiveness. Again at this point the modernity of Hunt's pastiche declares itself, for, set in opposition to the superficial festivity, is the passiveness of a woman socially disallowed from making her own life choices. The rights of women, which Dante does not begin to consider in his account of the Rimini saga, enter tangentially through this brief interior monologue.

But once that qualifying monologue has its course, Hunt falls back on the pastiche formula of the blazon. Proceeding to catalog Francesca's beauty by means of the approved Petrarchan checklist, he nonetheless introduces touches of his own:

> What need I tell of lovely lips and eyes
> A clipsome waist, and bosom's balmy rise,
> The dress of bridal white, and the dark curls,
> Bedding an airy coronet of pearls?
> There's not in all that crowd one gallant being,
> Whom if his heart were whole, and rank agreeing,

> It would not fire to twice of what he is,
> To clasp her to his heart, and call her his.[34]

The rhetorical device of *occupatio*, of pretending to omit that which you intend to include, gives the blazon a casual tone at odds with the thoroughness it ordinarily evokes. That is part of Hunt's *sprezzatura*. But he also tries to aerate and Huntify the description with a characteristic neologism— "clipsome" renders the Petrarchan beauty *accessible*, not only to the embrace of the describing poet, but also to that of almost any voyeur in the crowd "to clasp to his heart." One imagines, moreover, that the undemocratic rider about rank is there only to provide a perfunctory nod towards the social values of the period. So fully does "clipsome" embody the values and stylistic procedures of the poet that the parodists Martin and Aytoun could use it without modification in a takeoff of Hunt's diction ("Didst thou not praise me, Gaultier, at the ball, / Ripe lips, trim boddice, and a waist so small, / With clipsome lightness, dwindling ever less, / Beneath the robe of pea-y greeniness?"[35]).

Before rehearsing the usual argument against this sort of sexual objectification, we need perhaps to bear in mind that Paulo himself becomes the subject of a blazon later in the canto. Indeed, this inset, which structurally balances the description of Francesca, is altogether surprising. A Marlowe, bent on being outrageous, might be expected to insert a detailed description of male beauty into his *Hero and Leander*, but Hunt, though he is writing a pastiche *epyllion*, is under no generic constraint to include one. He has, moreover, no Marlovian ax to grind on the topic of homosexuality—or is it possible he does? We know, for example, that he held unusually tolerant views on the subject. Donald Reiman says he "had enough confidence in his whole humanity . . . to defend the sonnets of Shakespeare that his contemporaries felt nervous about,"[36] and cites the following recollection of an acquaintance: "[T]owards the end of the evening, there was an admirable talk between B__, Hunt and Blanchard on the Shakespeare Sonnets— those at least addressed to Lord Southampton. It was chiefly carried on by Hunt, who gave an admirable (but somewhat *alarming*) account of them, with reference to the equivocal expressions in which they abound, under the supposition of their being addressed to a man."[37] Hunt moreover seems to have felt a peculiarly intense (though unconsummated) affection for Shelley, as witness his initial sense of being more worthy than Mary to keep the poet's (physical) heart.

Even given these progressive views, one should perhaps be cautious about connecting them to the accounts of masculine beauty in *Rimini*.

What we have here is probably an instance of negative capability. This is all the more striking if we remember that no comparable accounts of the male form exist in the poetry of Keats, except for an obviously Huntian moment in his *Specimen of an Induction to a Poem*—"Wherefore more proudly does the gentle knight / Rein in the swelling of his ample might"[38]—which could apply as much to the knight's horse as to his physique:

> So fine are his bare throat, and curls of black,—
> So lightsomely dropt in, his lordly back—
> His thigh so fitted for the tilt or dance,
> So heaped with strength, and turned with elegance,[39]

Once again we observe that characteristically Huntian stress on lightness; the Wardour street antiquity of "lightsomely" is designed to buoy up something otherwise massive, and so to keep notions of the Farnese Hercules at bay.

Earlier in the cavalcade Hunt had shifted from riders to steeds, balancing the passages with the same anaphoric format, and suggesting (by a some /others division) two equivalent centers of interest for the crowd:

> Some watch, as they go by, the riders' faces
> Looking composure, and their knightly graces;
> The life, the carelessness, the sudden heed,
> The body curving to the rearing steed,
> The patting hand, that best persuades the check,
> And makes the quarrel up with the proud neck,
> The thigh broad pressed, the spanning palm upon it.
> And the jerked feather swaling in the bonnet.
> Others the horses and their pride explore,
> Their jauntiness behind and strength before;
> The flowing back, firm chest, and fetlocks clean,
> The branching veins ridging the glossy lean,
> The mane hung sleekly, the projecting eye
> That to the stander near looks awfully,[40]

Proof of the "innocence" of Hunt's homoerotic focus can be found in the fact that an identical sensuousness pervades the descriptions *both* of the riders *and* of their horses, with the same sort of lingering, atomizing emphasis, and the same obsession with graceful strength. He repeats the effect in his description of Paulo and his horse in turn, helping incidentally to shore up the canto's structure with isomeric elements in the design, and at the

same time blending human and horsey energy to create the icon of a cen-
taur:

> His haughty steed, who seems by turns to be
> Vexed and made proud by that cool mastery,
> Shakes at his bit, and rolls his eyes with care,
> Reaching with stately step at the fine air;
> And now and then, sideling his restless pace,
> Drops with his hinder legs, and shifts his place,
> And feels through all his frame a fiery thrill:
> The princely rider on his back sits still,
> And looks where'er he likes, and sways him still.[41]

The continuity of will and muscular mass has the effect of assimilating one
to the other.

Canto 2 is subtitled "The Bride's Journey to Rimini," a subtitle that
effectively characterizes this section as a *hodoiporikon* or journey poem. Like
many journey poems, it turns out to be the record of psychological change.
Before he can get Francesca underway, however, Hunt has to fill in some
narrative gaps. It is at moments such as these that his weaknesses become
most evident, since he is forced to put his decorative, exfoliating ecphrases
aside. Strip away the ornament, and the building seems woefully plain. The
narrative flatness and lameness bring Crabbe to mind, but at the same time
Hunt lacks Crabbe's compensating strengths of penetration and compassion. I find it interesting that he should choose to forego the omniscience of
romance narrative at the start of the canto, and register the bafflement and
irritation of the crowd as it senses a non-event. This goes some way toward
justifying the flatness, but there can be no mistaking the fact that the poet
himself has lost interest at this point, and wants to get through the longueurs
with all possible despatch. The anthologist in Hunt is anxious to reach the
next stretch of purple, with the result that his "dead" passages (an almost
inevitable feature of epic, as E. M. Tillyard has pointed out),[42] seem all the
deader for the way in which they are managed in *Rimini*. "The truth was
this:—The bridegroom had not come, / But sent his brother, proxy in his
room."[43] After all the climactic processional of canto 1, we are confronted
with an anticlimax, and the *occupatio* turns out for once to be no rhetorical
sleight of hand, but rather the sign of real perfunctoriness—"We'll pass the
followers, and their closing state."

I have stressed the pastiche elements of *Rimini*—the fact that Hunt is
using his medievalism as the vector for contemporary thoughts about mar-

riage and parental choice. That is one of the reasons for the self-consciousness slanginess of such utterances as "She had stout notions on the marrying
score," so long the butt of anti-"Cockney" attacks. Far from attempting to
traduce period grandeur, however, Hunt is using his diction to signal a
transition in focus from antiquarian shell to contemporary kernel. But while
the stylistic signal functions quite clearly, the passage misfires because of its
intellectual poverty. The contemporary relevance Hunt injects has no depth
or resonance. We have only to set the flat, enfeebled disquisition on Francesca
and Guido against a poem like *The Frank Courtship* to see that, while Crabbe's
verse is comparably flat at moments like these, the thinking behind it is
altogether more profound. The theme of this 1812 tale resembles that of
Rimini—tension between father and daughter on the issue of marriage—
but there the resemblance ends. Such telescopic paradoxes as "an arch look
of gravity" would seem to fall outside the compass of Leigh Hunt's observation, limited as this often is to the decorative and superficial:

> Till a tall maiden by her Sire was seen,
> In all the bloom and beauty of sixteen;
> He gaz'd admiring;—she, with visage prim,
> Glanc'd an arch look of gravity on him;
> For she was gay at heart, but wore disguise,
> And stood a Vestal in her Father's eyes.[44]

Lacking this order of insight, Hunt's verse seems to lose quality when it can
offer no rich detail to deflect our attention:

> Guido knew
> The prince's character; and he knew too,
> That sweet as was his daughter, and prepared
> To do her duty, where appeal was barred,
> She had stout notions on the marrying score,
> And where the match unequal prospect bore,
> Might pause with firmness, and refuse to strike
> A chord her own sweet music so unlike.[45]

The poverty of characterization betrays itself here in a poverty of language,
where an album-verse epithet ("sweet") is repeated in the space of seven
lines, and the conceit of music-making and dissonant chords proves on
examination to have no intellectual substance. (A chord, whether it be
dissonant or harmonious, cannot function as an *alternative* to "sweet music"

as Hunt makes it function here; nor has he taken the trouble to develop the duet image that alone would give the marriage tenor room to work.)

The complaints against *Rimini* have perennially targeted the "frills" of Hunt's language, but in my opinion it is far more vulnerable to attack at such moments as these, where it has no rococo embellishment to conceal the banality of its ideas. How superficial Francesca becomes, for example, when Hunt has her succumb to Paulo's address, since this is simply a transposition of his own creed of cheer, buttonholing and familiar, and set in contrast to Giovanni's Kemble-esque solemnity. Compare "a sore of cloud / Hanging forever on his cold address, / Which he mistook for proper manliness"[46] with "an air so frank and bright, / As to a friend appreciated at sight, / That air, in short, which sets you at your ease, / Without implying your perplexities."[47] In a review of Hunt's novel *Sir Ralph Esher*, G. H. Lewes complained of "a want of intellectual ventriloquialism—all the characters speak Leigh Hunt more or less and they are all subtle and refining."[48] The charge is a just one, for while Hunt might be able to describe masculine beauty without embarrassment, or might try to inhabit the muscular being of a horse, he often fails at the level of intellectual disinterestedness. His pastiche procedures have exempted him from trying to inhabit attitudes and values foreign to his own. Francesca, conforming too patly to his own creed, becomes the proxy for his own complacent self-commendation.

This and other failings account for the thinness of the narrative as opposed to the descriptive segments of the poem. For all its gossipy bustle, it fails to achieve very much: "By telling him, that if, as he had heard, / Busy he was just then, 'twas but a word, / And he might send and wed her by another,—." While some critics would condemn a want of period dignity, it could be argued that the self-generated rules of Hunt's pastiche exempt him from the charge. However, more damaging and unanswerable criticisms might be directed instead at the thinness of the verse. Hunt's impatience to get on, to gloss over, tends both here and elsewhere to fudge his effects. For example, a prolepsis that might otherwise have carried dramatic irony (the sexual implication of "know") is so casually handled as to become a slightly tasteless joke: " [']For when you see the one, you know the other.'"[49]

Once Francesca's journey is underway, though, the poem picks up again. Hunt is much better at analysis through description than he is at analysis *in vacuo*, because he is little drawn to abstract thought, an incapacity as much evident in his criticism as in his poetry. Texts like *Imagination and Fancy* lack the broad intellectual sweep of a Coleridge or even a Hazlitt. Its interest resides rather in the critic's alert, sensitive response to individual poems and moments in poems. And much the same could be said of *The Story of Rimini*. Hunt tells us more about Francesca through his landscape painting than he is able to say *in propria persona*. He implicitly invites us to compare and contrast the return journey with the festivity and color of Paulo's cortège in canto 1, using it to forge objective correlatives for the heroine's state of mind. These are far from obvious, and testify to Hunt's subtle mind. He could have staged a romantic thunderstorm, and curtained the scenery in rain, but he chooses to paint instead an Italian idyll, expressly evoking the opening fete in order to balance it:

> It was a lovely evening, fit to close
> A lovely day, and brilliant in repose.
> Warm, but not dim, a glow was in the air;
> The softened breeze came smoothing here and there;
> And every tree, in passing, one by one,
> Gleamed out with twinkles of the golden sun:
> For leafy was the road, with tall array,
> On either side, of mulberry and bay,
> And distant snatches of blue hills between;[50]

Let us compare this with Ann Radcliffe's account of a journey in *The Mysteries of Udolpho* also undertaken by a stricken heroine, but cobbled together from all the statutory clichés of the sublime. The "sublimity" fails here because its calculated imprecisions are manufactured. Look, for example, at the automatic recourse to superlatives and open-ended description:

> Mountains, whose shaggy steeps appeared to be inaccessible, almost surrounded it. To the east, a vista opened, that exhibited the Apennines in their darkest horrors; and the long perspective of retiring summits, rising over each other, their ridges clothed with pines, exhibited a stronger image of grandeur, than any that Emily had yet seen.[51]

Radcliffe's writing is deliberately intemperate: even the adverbs of degree and the comparatives that pretend to modify the absolutes have been used only as flavor-enhancing condiments. Hunt is too subtle for this sort of posturing. Instead he relies on the poignant ordinariness of the landscape to intensify Francesca's grief. In *Dejection: An Ode* Coleridge had established the pathos of emotional disconnection from a lovely setting, an issue almost as important to romanticism as reciprocity between subject and object.

In the opening canto of *Rimini*, Hunt had half enlisted nature in the festivities, as though bowing to romance convention. Now that the participation is perceived to have been unreal, vestigial memories of the celebration lurk only in the imagery. The "poplar's shoot," for example, because it "like feather waves from head to foot," recalls the "swaling feather" in Paulo's cap, and the vines bring to mind the loops of bunting: "And still from tree to tree the early vines / Hung garlanding the way with amber lines."[52] We saw how distrait Francesca was when she made her entry in canto 1, and how the excitement of the occasion served to detach her, like Keats's Madeline, from her physical circumstances. The same dislocation occurs in canto 2, but for different reasons. Now it is a numbed, sorrowful retrospection, not anticipatory excitement, that displaces the heroine's thoughts:

> With dreaming eye fixed down, and half-shut ears,
> Hearing, yet hearing not, the fervent sound
> Of hoofs thick reckoning and the wheel's moist round,[53]

What a curious description of a muddy road this is: it intentionally confuses fervency with mud as though to suggest the enmirement of hope in the slough of despond. And how programmatically loose and vague the syntax becomes later in the same passage, where two successive appositional phrases fail to lock on to the syntax: "And looking up, half sigh, half stare, / She lifts her veil and feels the freshening air." While this sort of syntactic tricksiness might not be to every reader's taste, nobody would scorn the imaginative coup that converts a bridal to a mourning veil.

At first Hunt makes his point by having Francesca fail to apprehend the scenery. The moment she *does* focus her attention on the landscape, however, outer and inner landscapes converge. Pine forests had already imported their monotonous sterility into Pope's *Eloisa to Abelard*—"The darksome pines that o'er yon' rocks reclin'd / Wave high, and murmur to the hollow wind"[54]—and had also been used atmospherically in Crabbe's tale *The Patron* ("All green was vanish'd, save of pine and yew / That still display'd their melancholy hue").[55] What makes them remarkable here is the fact that by describing these gloomy conifers, Hunt has foregone the typically indulgent luxury of his idylls. They constitute a disinterested effort at the sort of sublimity for which he otherwise felt no attraction. While Pope and Crabbe may well have supplied the inspiration for his choice, it is much more probable that Boccaccio lies behind the description of the pine grove. For in Dryden's translation, *Theodore and Honoria, From Boccace*, Theodore has his infernal vision in just such a setting: "'Twas in a Grove of spreading Pines he stray'd; / The Winds, within the quiv'ring Branches plaid, / And Dancing Trees a mournful Musick made."[56] He sees a specter pursuing a woman who had spurned him in life, and whose heart and bowels he feeds to his hounds in retribution for her coldness towards him in life. In his 1844 edition of the poem, Hunt strengthened the allusion, and then in 1855 spelled it out in detail: "And have her heart, through pitiless wide wounds, / Torn from her shrieking side to feed his hounds."[57] Perhaps he intended some irony by contrasting a legend that punishes a failure of love against his own, which centers rather on its misdirection. It is better in Hunt's book to have loved and sinned than never to have loved at all.

Returning to the pine grove, we can note that there are further interesting touches. How odd, yet true to the psychology of grief (with its strange, impertinent fixations), is Hunt's repeated focus on the sound of the wheels and the different textures they traverse:

> And now with thicker shades the pines appear;
> The noise of hoofs grows duller to her ear;
> And quitting suddenly their gravelly toil,
> The wheels go spinning o'er the sandy soil.
> Here first the silence of the country seems
> To come about her with its listening dreams.
> And, full of anxious thoughts, half freed from pain,
> In downward musing she relapsed again,
> Leaving the others who had passed that way
> In careless spirits of the early day,
> To look about, and mark the reverend scene
> For awful tales renowned, and everlasting green.
> A heavy thirst the forest looks at first,
> To one grim shade condemned, and sandy thirst,
> Or only chequered, here and there, with bushes
> Dusty and sharp, or plashy pools with rushes,
> About whose sides the swarming insects fry,
> Opening with noisome din, as they go by.[58]

Although the congruence of inner and outer vision brings some measure of relief, Francesca is presented as falling out of consciousness once again—the adverbial "downward" suggesting as much a lapse of attention as it does the direction of a gaze or the cast of a thought. But even though she is "tuned out" of the poem—a fascinating and unconventional moment—surrogate observers move in to register the landscape, allowing it to continue its atmospheric work. The postilions and other riders, fresh from the noisy processional of Ravenna, now feel the sobering effect of a dim religious light (for why otherwise would Hunt apply the epithet, without biblical warrant, to pine trees?): "Much they admire that old religious tree / With shaft above the rest up-shooting free, / And shaking, when its dark locks feel the wind, / Its wealthy fruit with rough Mosaic rind." He no doubt means us to appreciate the tessellated ("mosaic") formation of the cones, but at the same time introduces a hint of Moses, of the Mosaic dispensation,[59] and thus of the stern prohibition against adultery in the Decalogue. That, however, is a detail so subtle in its resonance that I am prepared to concede that the resonance might not be there.

On the other hand, there can be no doubting the other, more tangible touches of atmosphere, as for instance the Doppler effect of insects' shrilling, which opens up and fades as the carriage passes—an effect that owes much more to the insect-attentiveness of Gray and Collins than it does to Chaucer. The detail would never have figured in medieval narrative: "About whose sides the swarming insects fry, / Opening with noisome din as they go by." That "frying" is aural—the sizzle of fat in a pan—but Hunt also uses it to evoke discomforting procreation and abundance. The insects have adapted to an inhumane environment, the inhumanity of which is further confirmed by their numerousness. I do not agree with L. R. M. Strachan when (s)he suggests that "instead of an obscure tautology, equivalent to 'the swarming insects swarm,' we have a reminiscence of Dryden's vocabulary."[60] Dryden's using "fry" to render the *sole... ardente* in Virgil's Second Eclogue creates a sense of hot exposure quite alien to the pine forest, and, since swarming and pullulation are quite distinct activities, we have no "obscure tautology" to "justify" in the first place.

Once we have passed through this forbidding landscape, there is a vivid sense of refreshment conveyed once again with a proto-Keatsian empathy. Who before Hunt and Keats would have thought to register the temperature of the horses' mouths, and the contrastive coolness of the grass they nuzzle: "Dip their warm mouths into the freshening grass."[61] And the fact that all this should transpire *outside* the consciousness of Francesca makes it all the more remarkable—modern, in fact. One is reminded of the rhythms of persistence and ignoration that Auden tracks so brilliantly in his *Musée de Beaux Arts* poem. The recurring pronoun "they" might seem to refer to a couple on their honeymoon, but in fact it is restricted to the riders outside the carriage. Again Hunt recalls, only to displace, the festive sounds of canto 2, and the congestion of the crowd is reversed and parodied by the dispersal of the rooks:

> At noisy intervals, the living cloud
> Of cawing rooks breaks over them, gathering loud
> Like a wild people at a stranger's coming;[62]

A plodding woodman (like the crepuscular insects and cattle, taken from Gray's *Elegy*) helps measure the separation of the bridal party from the ongoing rhythms of life. There is no epithalamium for Francesca—only the "shot-out raptures" of a nightingale, of Philomela, victim of sexual violence—and the canto ends with an anti- (rather than ante-) nuptial image of maidenhood. The noises on the sound track suggest that the bride has arrived at a prison rather than a wedding chamber. It is as though Hunt were anticipating *The Eve of St Agnes*, only that there there is noiseless escape, not noisy confinement:

> A hollow trample now,—a fall of chains,—
> The bride has entered,—not a voice remains;—
> Night, and a maiden silence, wrap the plains.[63]

Asyndeton throws each sound into jarring, discontinuous relief, the dashes functioning almost like a musical notation for long pauses, and then the figure of Francesca is enveloped with a sinister syllepsis blending the darkness of night with the radiance of maidenhood. Indeed, the dark wrapping of the plains functions as a displaced metaphor for still more distressing embraces.

In canto 3, Hunt introduces a *Verfremdungseffekt*, cutting from the time frame of his narrative into a compositional present, and referring specifically to his circumstances in Surrey Gaol. It is almost as if the "fall of chains" at the end of the preceding canto had functioned as a sort of Keatsian bell tolling the poet back to his "sole self." The phrasing itself is odd, for, given the circumstances of the narrative, the poet would in any case have been prevented from supplying "a dream of bliss"—a dream that would be forfeit the moment that Francesca married Giovanni by proxy:

> Now why must I disturb a dream of bliss,
> Or bring cold sorrow 'twixt the wedded kiss?
> Sad is the strain with which I cheer my long
> And caged hours, and try my native tongue;
> Now too, while rains autumnal, as I sing,
> Wash the dull bars, chilling my sicklied wing.[64]

This interruptive passage has several functions. Firstly, it follows the precedent of Milton's autobiographical excursus in *Paradise Lost*, book 3, which introduces a poignant lyric note into the impersonal epic mode:

> Taught by the heav'nly Muse to venture down
> The dark descent, and up to reascend,
> Though hard and rare: thee I revisit safe,
> And feel thy sovran vital Lamp; but thou
> Revisit'st not these eyes, that roll in vain
> To find thy piercing ray, and find no dawn.[65]

In the second place, the inset passage helps Hunt to establish his credentials as a romantic poet of empathy—someone able, through his own unhappy circumstances, to register the full extent of Francesca's tragedy from within. Finally, it also evokes—through the detail of rain-washed bars—a cold north to be set in opposition to the "warm south" of the poem, and so measures the strength of the imaginative flights that have gone into its creation. To offset charges of escapism, it is important that Hunt stress the fact he has to screw up his courage in order to proceed with the story. In courtroom dramas, witnesses frequently break down in their narratives, and, having composed themselves, proceed with the evidence, knowing full well that they have won the sympathy of the jury through a version of aposiopesis—breaking off not so much because words have failed, but rather because stoic self-control has been breached by emotion. Again, Hunt has to fight the "anthological" impulse so central to his philosophy of cheer—that desire to skim pleasure off the dross of suffering found even in such twentieth-century compilers as John Hadfield ("I realize that happiness has often to be sought. That it can be found by looking, and can be cultivated by those who know how, is the conviction in which I have compiled this anthology").[66] He does so through *occupatio*, which compresses the sufferings of Francesca into a cursory paragraph so as to be done with them:

> How bring the bitter disappointment in,—
> The holy cheat, the virtue-binding sin,—
> The shock, that told this lovely, trusting heart,
> That she had given, beyond all power to part,
> Her hope, belief, love, passion, to one brother,
> Possession (oh, the misery!) to another![67]

This reads like the contents summaries that start the chapters of eighteenth-century novels, and its cursorial speed is designed to gloss over material that Hunt otherwise finds unappealing. Yet, a few lines before, he has frankly admitted to an escapist motive behind the poem, but which the subject itself has made increasingly difficult to realize. We are accustomed to the improvisatory flavor of Hunt's verse, but it has an odd effect when, as here, he suggests that the poem is somehow writing itself, and forcing him almost against his will towards a tragic mode: "But thoughts it furnishes of things far hence, / And leafy dreams affords me, and a feeling / Which I should else disdain, tear-dipped and healing; / And shews me,—more than what it first designed,— / How little upon earth our home we find, / Or close the intended course of erring human-kind."[68]

The very gravity that seems to be bulldozing the poet into his solemn mode affects the quality of the verse. For the first time in the poem—and this may account for the fact that, of all the cantos, the third was the favorite of Lamb, Byron, and Haydon—Hunt attempts a detailed psychological analysis of the protagonists, shifting from a purely decorative to a semiotic concern with surfaces. He offers a fine diptych of the two brothers, quite as good as those oppositional portraits of siblings that Crabbe supplies in *Tales of the Hall*, and managed, moreover, without any loss of spirit. Sometimes that "spiritedness" forces itself on the reader in such "winsome" syntactic aberrations as "martialler," but the tone is more usually fingerprinted by subtler devices, as when Hunt moves from a dispassionate authorial vision located in the narrative past ("Some tastes there were"), to his own, declared as having a present-tense existence ("I think"):

> Some tastes there were indeed, that would prefer
> Giovanni's countenance as the martialler;
> And 'twas a soldier's truly, if an eye
> Ardent and cool at once, drawn-back and high,
> An eagle's nose, and a determined lip,
> Were the best marks of manly soldiership.
> Paulo's was fashioned in a different mould,
> And finer still, *I think*; [italics mine] for though 'twas bold,
> When boldness was required, and could put on
> A glowing frown, as if an angel shone,
> Yet there was nothing in it one might call
> A stamp exclusive or professional,—
> No courtier's face, and yet its smile was ready,—
> No scholar's, yet its look was deep and steady,—
> No soldier's, for its power was all of mind,
> Too true for violence, and too refined.
> A graceful nose was his, lightsomely brought

> Down from a forehead of clear-spirited thought;
> Wisdom looked sweet and inward from his eye;
> And round his mouth was sensibility:—
> It was a face, in short, seemed made for shew
> How far the genuine flesh and blood could go;—
> A morning glass of unaffected nature,
> Something that baffled every pompous feature,—
> The visage of a glorious human creature.[69]

An interesting struggle between Hunt the medieval narrator and Hunt the Regency Radical can be seen in his effort to recapture (and do justice to) martial values that he instinctively holds in contempt. Almost as if he were offering an ecphrasis of Piero's Montefeltro profile, the poet presents Giovanni's aquiline nose and jutting lip as emblems of highborn pride. ("Drawn back" suggests not only the slant of the canthus but also fastidious *withdrawal*, just as "cool" cancels "ardent" to restrict his ardor to abstract principles of rank and fortune.) Hunt's own rejection of these alien attitudes registers in his use of the provisional subjunctive ("if . . . were") and his sense that Paulo's martial prowess is a semblance brought out for ritual occasions.

Bound by the conventions of his narrative to offer a token nod towards conventions and values of an earlier time, he makes anachronistic use of Ophelia's speech in *Hamlet,* a speech that sets out some characteristic categories of Renaissance thought:

> The courtier's, soldier's, scholar's, eye, tongue, sword,
> Th'expectancy and rose of the fair state,
> The glass of fashion and the mould of form,[70]

The poet even recalls Ophelia's rhetoric in his own structure of symmetrical clauses (*metabole*) by which he comments, as if referring to a Renaissance checklist, on all the virtues that fulfill and yet transcend the limited construction that an earlier age might have put upon them. It is ironic therefore that, consciously or not, he should fall back on that Augustan *via media* set out in *Coopers Hill* as a cat's cradle of balancing concessives. The more things change—and Hunt's "system" was bent on changing the formulaic closure of the couplet—the more they stay the same. Yet even if in his effort to supply a moderated ideal he falls back on Denhamesque turns of phrase, he is wholly original in the way he reconstitutes the archetypal mirror we find in Shakespeare's "glass of fashion" as a Regency looking glass, a metaphor that enacts the ideal of unceremonious, unpompous behavior his verse is setting forth—"A morning glass of unaffected nature, / Something, that baffled every pompous feature."[71] It is in this spirit also that Hunt shakes off the cumbersome, ritual aspects of chivalry by employing bathos at the end of the portrait:

> And the decision of still knottier points,
> With knife in hand, of boar and peacock joints,—
> Things that might shake the fame that Tristan got,
> And bring a doubt on perfect Launcelot.
> But leave we knighthood to the former part;
> The tale I tell is of the human heart.[72]

Because it is a tale of the "human heart," *The Story of Rimini* becomes in effect a celebration of Huntian cheer, with Paulo the spokesperson for relaxed geniality and Giovanni the representative of neoclassic formalism. Hunt admits to being constrained by the historical demands of his narrative, but makes it clear that Paulo's participation in the rituals of chivalry is foreign to his temperament, which is altogether closer to the poet's own: "Not that he saw, or thought he saw, beyond / His general age, and could not be as fond / Of wars and creeds as any of his race,— / But most he loved a happy human face."[73] There (in a couplet nutshell) are the essential priorities of "Abou ben Adhem," many decades before Hunt wrote the poem.

It is also tempting to imagine that Browning, one of Hunt's last "discoveries," might have had Giovanni in mind when he came to characterize the duke in *My Last Duchess*, where the disparity of values between Hunt's brothers is recapitulated as a temperamental disparity between husband and wife. Indeed the influence of Hunt upon Browning is something that needs to be investigated at length, for in *Rimini* we often find Hunt versifying the phatic graph of conversation, with effects that anticipate the later poet's. Look for example at the casually adjusted emphasis and hesitation of the following lines, the relaxation of which is heightened by the *oratio obliqua* through which they are filtered (as so often in Browning): "Then almost angrier grown from self-repenting, / And hinting at the last, that some there were / Better perhaps than he, and tastefuller, / And these, for what he knew,—he little cared,— / Might please her, and be pleased, though he despaired."[74]

We have seen how Hunt anachronistically enters the poem as a way of coming to terms with the medieval attitudes he might otherwise find repulsive. The conversational tone of the narrative (glanced at above) provides a similar strategy of adjustment. Again and again Hunt relaxes his poetic demeanor to give the unpremeditatedness of human exchanges to a form more usually associated with judicious control. So it is that we find the intemperate claim that "conduct's only worth" is "The scattering of smiles on this uneasy earth,"[75] and, later in the same canto, "The two divinest things this world has got, / A lovely woman in a rural spot,"[76] a couplet that has been endlessly censured. I suspect the objections lodged against this unbuttoned diction are also covert objections against unbuttoned thought, a rococo extravagance of the moment that is hardly meant to be carried away and pondered. John Holloway suggests that the couplet embodies an Arabian epigram that Hunt might have taken from William Jones: "[T]he three most charming objects in nature are, a green meadow, a clear rivulet and a beautiful woman; and the view of these objects at the same time affords the greatest delight imaginable."[77] If he is right, then we must recall that the geophysical circumstances of Arabia make the utterance altogether less extravagant than it seems in the temperate setting into which the poet has transposed it—a setting where neither water nor greenness is quite so obviously the guarantor of life. Hunt's claim thus takes on the casual, throwaway effect that was later to be cultivated in the epigrams of the Aesthetic Movement.

Also, we ought not to take the reductio ad absurdum about "conduct's only worth" as a sober judgment, but rather as a nonce utterance designed to stress a *spur of the moment* impulsiveness in the writing of the poem. For while he sets up as the stern daughter of the voice of God, Hunt is preparing a defense on the basis of Paulo's good nature. His complaisance springs directly from his geniality, and it is from his complaisance that, in a prophetic aside, Hunt suggests that the adulterous yearnings will spring in turn:

> And wheresoe'er his fine, frank eyes were thrown,
> He struck with looks he wished for with his own.
> *His* danger was, lest, feeling as he did,
> Too lightly he might leap o'er means forbid,
> And in some tempting hour lose sight of crime
> O'er some sweet face too happy for the time;
> But fears like these he never entertained,
> And had they crossed him, would have been disdained.
> Warm was his youth, 'tis true,—nor had been free
> From lighter loves,—but virtue reverenced he,
> And had been kept from men of pleasure's cares
> By dint of feelings still more warm than theirs.[78]

Notice how Hunt is careful to differentiate in advance between a coarse sexuality (which he found in Sheridan, for example) and the kind of erotic candor that will ultimately lead to the affair between Francesca and Paulo. That aside about "men of pleasure" is an important moral grace note to the poem, and seldom (if ever) noted by those contemporaries who attacked the ethics of *Rimini*. Of course Paulo is no mere Regency rake, so the discrimination is made primarily to "inoculate" the congress of the lovers. Further condonation comes from our sense of Giovanni as another Angelo (*Measure for Measure*), altogether self-absorbed and incapable of the reciprocity that (importing his own view into the story) Hunt offers as the proper foundation of marriage. Here, for example, are Francesca's thoughts on the matter, couched in those optative infinitives we have come to associate with Keats—think of the sestet of "Bright Star." Infinitives are tenseless, and project a potential ideal rather than achieved reality—an ideal whose *spontaneous* transcription is further signaled by the improvisatory dashes used to notate it:

> She, who had been beguiled,—she, who was made
> Within a gentle bosom to be laid,—
> To bless and to be blessed,—to be heart-bare,
> To one who found his bettered likeness there,—
> To think forever with him, like a bride—
> To haunt his eye, like taste personified,—
> To double his delight, to share his sorrow,
> And like a morning beam, wake to him every morrow.[79]

This is written in the shadow of Goethe's *Ewig-Weibliche;* its vision of coequal mutuality (and even of the woman's ennobling role) makes no attempt to reproduce the standard medieval perceptions of marriage. Thus is the moral ground prepared before the climax of the narrative. There are numerous other extenuations as well. Paulo is the proponent of Watteauvian *fêtes champêtres,* and his association with the greenwood is opposed (in Hunt's moral color scheme) to the sanguinary red of Giovanni's temperament. Compare the following passages, the first of which carries the narrator's explicit endorsement, while in the second Francesca is attempting to please her husband with martial airs:

> Nor was there a court-day, or a sparkling feast,
> Or better still,—in my ideas, at least,—
> A summer party to the greenwood shade,
> With lutes prepared, and cloth on herbage laid,

> And ladies' laughter coming through the air,—
> He was the readiest and the blithest there.[80]

And here by, contrast, the green is made one red:

> Or when to please him, after martial play,
> She strained her lute to some old fiery lay
> Of fierce Orlando, or of Ferumbras,
> Or Ryan's cloak, or how by the red grass
> In battle you might know where Richard was.[81]

Also, by making Giovanni remote rather than deformed (as the historic Gianciotto was supposed to have been, and as d'Annuzio has him in his play and Zandonai in his opera), Hunt further subtracts animal passion from the equation. (Rather ludicrously and crassly, the *Blackwood's* critics argued the very opposite, and as Miller points out, claimed that the "changes from the historical version, an espousal by proxy instead of betrothal, the omission of deformity, the substitution of duel for murder, and the happy opening" were "wilful perversions for the furtherance of corruption.")[82] The sort of martial vigor and strength with which Hunt invests Giovanni have after all remained conventionally "attractive" masculine features even to this day, and the fact that a superficial attractiveness does not satisfy Francesca makes her sin somehow seem less venial than if relations with her husband had been complicated by deformity.

A peculiarly Huntian touch is supplied by Francesca's refuge from unhappy reality in interior design. We at once call to mind the painted clouds and rose trellises of the Surrey Gaol, and remember also how, immediately on being released, Hunt transformed his lodgings in the Edgware Road into a "box of lilies" by painting them white and green. Nowhere, perhaps, does the rococo sensibility of this and other poems declare itself in the stress on decorative setting. For Hunt, it is not enough simply to read a book or think a handsome thought. That book must be read and that idea conceived in a cozy study (a study embellished with casts, busts, flowers and wreaths), or in some arbor in the outskirts of a city. By exactly the same token Francesca carries her decorative setting into the new circumstances of the marriage. Jails seem less like jails for having clouded ceilings, and unhappy marriages the less unhappy for

> her private room
> Furnished, like magic, from her own at home;

> The very books and all transported there,
> The leafy tapestry, and the crimson chair,
> The lute, the glass that told the shedding hours,
> The little urn of silver for the flowers,
> The frame for broidering, with a piece half done,
> And the white falcon, basking in the sun,[83]

Never was a blazon more lovingly constructed, even if the subject was a room and not a woman. In Crabbe, the most circumstantial of the romantic poets, the spatial data of an interior are transcriptive, put there to fix and extend the detail of the characterization; in Hunt, on the other hand, they often seem rather to smack of romance, of daydream indulgence. As so often in his poetry, anaphora has the effect of creating a checklist of desiderata to ravish the imagination and fine-tune it for the idyll.

Despite the busy and self-conscious reformation of eighteenth-century diction that Hunt presented as part of his "system" in this poem, *The Story of Rimini* nowhere more declares its eighteenth-century heritage than in the anthropocentric bias that he persists in giving to his landscapes. There is always a figure to be seen: "The two divinest things this world has got, / A lovely woman in a rural spot!" So, as the idyll of canto 3 develops, Hunt increasingly stresses human participation in its pleasances. Let us compare the sort of garden that Coleridge projects in *Kubla Khan*:

> So twice five miles of fertile ground
> With walls and towers were girdled round:
> And there were gardens bright with sinuous rills,
> Where blossomed many an incense-bearing tree;
> And here were forests ancient as the hills,
> Enfolding sunny spots of greenery.[84]

Here the passive voice of "girdled" has the effect of deleting human agency, and the ancient forests seem pre-Adamic, evoking an image of uninhabited Earth. The garden, furthermore, has a Berkeleyan quality, as though it owed its existence to an encompassing, abstract omniscience. Not so the garden in *Rimini*, where again and again the poet cuts from natural detail to human consciousness. It is Hunt's interior decoration in reverse—beautiful things need to be complemented by poets and contemplatives, just as their composition and contemplation needs in turn to be encapsulated by a beautiful setting:

> So now you walked beside an odorous bed
> Of gorgeous hues, white, azure, golden, red,

> And now turned off into a leafy walk,
> Close and continuous, fit for lovers' talk;[85]

and

> A land of trees, which reaching round about,
> In shady blessing stretched their old arms out,
> With spots of sunny opening, and with nooks,
> To lie and read in, sloping into brooks.[86]

and

> And here and there, in every part, were seats,
> Some in the open walks, some in retreats;
> With bowering leaves o'erhead, to which the eye
> Looked up half sweetly and half awfully,—
> Places of nestling green, for poets made[87]

Even the metaphors and similes conscripted to anthropomorphize the land-scape take the chill off sublimity—"Betwixt the dark, wet green, a rill gushed out, / Whose low sweet talking seemed as if it said / Something eternal to that happy shade."[88] Here Hunt conceives eternity itself as a prolonged *fête champêtre*. In a setting such as this, who can blame the lovers for succumbing?—and that is a major intention behind it. Dante also creates a deliquescent atmosphere for the sin of Francesca and Paolo, but locates it (by contrast) within their sensibility—"We read of the smile, desired of lips long-thwarted, / Such a smile, by such a lover kissed away, / He that may never more from me be parted / Trembling all over, kissed my mouth."[89] At the heart of the matter is a theological discrimination that Hunt is not prepared to make, for, having espoused a philosophy of cheer (we might even go so far as to call it a religion), he has no very vivid sense of sin when abstinence supervenes upon pleasure and so impairs the happiness of the moment. Charles Williams provides a key to the essential difference between Dante and Hunt in this regard, the point at which Dante discriminates between shades of pleasure and Hunt scumbles the line of definition: "It is true that *lussuria* is to be distinguished from the *sollagia* of the *Convivio*. *Sollagia*, with all the rest of Pleasantness, is a moral duty—to oneself as to the other; eros itself is in that sense not only permissible, but enjoined. . . . But . . . they set up in the human organism a hunger for them which, from being mutual, becomes single. An appetite for the use of Image prevails; this is Gluttony and this is the next circle of Hell (VI)."[90]

Evidence of this kind of reduction is everywhere in Hunt, not least in his frequent objectification of women. These he often converts into benign but faceless luxuries, barely distinguishable from, and continuous with, his standard decor of bust-bedecked studies and leafy arbors—"A lovely woman in a rural spot." The way in which mutuality slides by slow gradations into self-concern is something altogether too subtle for the strategies of his poem. We might deplore the tone, but we are forced to concede the element of justice in Lockhart's sneer that the poem is a "genteel comedy of incest,"[91] for Hunt has tried to reproduce the moral vacuum in which comedy subsists. This vacuum, innocuous enough in stylized genres, becomes problematic in other contexts, for *Rimini* is no Restoration comedy, no elegant diagram. Hunt is predisposed to favor the lovers above all because they are impulsive and *human*, an impulsiveness and humanity he validates, as we have seen, through the heady improvisation and biographical asides of his narrative conduct.

For Hunt, the self-love of the wronged party has generated the wrong in the first instance, and he effectively crosses moral lines by suggesting that Giovanni's sense of right is almost a Lockean right to property rather than a moral faculty: "Secure in his self-love and sense of right."[92] While he tries to show that Paulo's arguments for drawing closer to Francesca are sophistical ("Concluding thus" feints his detachment from the premises), those arguments are so close to his own philosophy of cheer that we have no real sense of distance. He might not be a sensualist, but it is also clear that he has no sympathy with the stern Christian dictum that equates mental with physical sin:

> And as to thinking,—where could be the harm,
> If to his heart he kept its secret charm?
> He wished not to himself another's blessing,
> But then he might console for not possessing;
> And glorious things there were, which but to see
> And not admire, was mere stupidity:
> He might as well object to his own eyes
> For loving to behold the fields and skies,
> His neighbour's grove, or story-painted hall,
> 'Twas but the taste for what was natural;
> Only his fav'rite thought was loveliest of them all.
> Concluding thus, and happier that he knew
> His ground so well, near and more near he drew.[93]

We have seen how slight for Hunt the division between a sympathetic feminine presence and a green glade, and, given such attitudes, we can scarcely expect him to take the high moral ground.

He does, however, try for such a tone later on, chiefly to produce a
Verfremdungseffekt before the buildup to the tragedy. It is clear that he has
Gray's *Ode on a Distant Prospect of Eton College* in mind here, for in the latter
part of the story we have the same dooming prolepsis set over an apparently
carefree and innocent present. The "gentle pair" are Gray's "little victims" in
a marginally more adult guise:

> And now, ye gentle pair,—now think awhile,
> Now, while ye still can think, and still can smile;
> Now, while your generous hearts have not been grieved
> Perhaps with something not to be retrieved,
> And ye have still, within, the power of gladness,
> From self-resentment free, and retrospective madness![94]

It is possible that Hunt's "gladness"/"madness" rhyme originates in the
famous stanza from *Resolution and Independence* that also presents a doom-
laden view of happiness thwarted by circumstance.

Having noted the poet's bias to fanciful decoration at the expense of
integrated spatial commentary, we should not be surprised to find almost all
the remaining lines of the canto (and there are a good many of them) taken
up with a description of Francesca's garden and summerhouse. But whereas
the pageantry of the first Canto did have some sort of cumulative rhythm,
with a sequence of preparations deliberately geared to the anticlimax of the
proxy-wedding, here the rococo impulse to decorate all available space
obscures the larger design. There is certain charm in Hunt's hypertrophy—
one would be ungrateful to wish it wholly away—but, even so, there is no
denying that the emphases have been mismanaged. As John Hayden has
observed, "[T]he pleasure garden in which the tryst takes place in Canto III
seems to have been influenced by Spenser; in fact Hunt included an imitation of the Bower of Bliss from Book I of *The Faerie Queene* in his volume
of juvenilia in 1802 [actually 1801] ('The Pleasure Palace' [actually *The
Palace of Pleasure*]). The description in Hunt's hands in *The Story of Rimini*
is not well handled; he apparently succumbed to the temptation of vulgarity
inherent in the erotic imagery."[95]

I think the key to the congestion and confusion of this passage must be
sought once again in the self-indulgence they represent, and would like to
invoke C. Day-Lewis for a comment in this regard:

> Now I fear this will be an outrage to persons who close their eyes and
> genuflect before any piece by Hopkins, but I do not think *Harry Ploughman*

is at all a good poem. For me nothing emerges from this froth and flurry of images, neither a clear objective picture of Harry, nor a sense that I am apprehending the real inwardness of a ploughman. . . .

Why did so fine a writer fail to write a whole poem here? Why did the violent centrifugal force of his images disintegrate the poem? The answer, I suggest, is that the poem contains an unresolved conflict, between the poet's enthusiasm for the ploughman's physique (the reader may decide for himself in what proportion pure aesthetic pleasure and homosexual attraction were involved), and on the other hand the Jesuit's stern repression of such homosexual feeling.[96]

There is much the same "froth and flurry" in Hunt's bower of bliss, though obviously the terms of Lewis's diagnosis have to be revised to suit the issue in hand. It is not so much that Hunt feels any "unresolved conflict" between flesh and spirit—we know by now that he plumps firmly for the flesh—but rather a conflict between his sybaritic temperament and his narrative mandate. He attempts to defer the task of telling a tragic story for as long as he can. We have seen how the deferrals in canto 1 build up tension and create a meaningful anticlimax, but here the delay disintegrates the poem instead of focussing it. Look at this tissue of sensual pathetic fallacy:

> There was the pouting rose, both red and white,
> The flamy heart's-ease, flushed with purple light,
> Blush-hiding strawberry, sunny-coloured box,
> Hyacinth, handsome with his clustering locks,
> The lady lily, looking gently down,
> Pure lavender, to lay the bridal gown,
> The daisy, lovely to both sides,—in short,
> All the sweet cups to which the bees resort,[97]

Presented as a garland in an prothalamion, this would have proved very attractive—but here it has no function. We have not progressed beyond the rim of the garden yet, and already Hunt has become profuse. So when he needs to build to a climax as we move by concentric stages towards the spot where the love will be consummated, he has shot his bolt, and has nothing to aim with. As Clarice Short has observed, "[T]he whole remains as graphic but unmap[p]able as the landscape in a dream":[98]

> The ground within was lawn, with plots of flowers
> Heaped towards the centre, and with citron bowers;[99]

That unlexical "heaping" is symptomatic of the problem. Hunt is recalling his earlier profusions, and forgotten that growing flowers cannot be heaped in quite the same way. And how perfunctory this anticlimactic heaping is, how flat the "citron bowers," when earlier Hunt has taken us right into the grove, and parted the leaves of an orange tree. (He was a pioneer in restoring Marvell to grace, and almost certainly was writing with "Bermudas" in mind):

> With plots of grass, and perfumed walks between
> Of citron, honeysuckle and jessamine,
> With orange, whose warm leaves so finely suit,
> And look as it they'd shade a golden fruit;[100]

(Orange leaves, by the way, are no more "warm" to the eye than the box cited above is "sunny-coloured." What Hunt is doing here is transposing sense impressions in typically loose synaesthesia.) Having had its fire stolen by the lines above, the climax cannot work. Hunt's failure to take a long view (and that is perhaps the perennial failure of fancy) has spoiled the effect.

Something of the same fudging is apparent also in the architecture of the tempietto in which Francesca spends her time. Indulging the wish fulfillment of romance, Hunt presents a Bramantian design as a "real" classical vestige, and therefore a piece of pagan ground that has remained immune to Christianization:

> It was a beauteous piece of ancient skill,
> Spared from the rage of war, and perfect still;
> By most supposed the work of fairy hands,
> Famed for luxurious taste, and choice of lands,—
> Alcina, or Morgana—who from fights
> And errant fame inveigled amorous knights,
> And lived with them in a long round of blisses,
> Feasts, concerts, baths, and bower-enshaded kisses.
> It was a temple, as its sculpture told,
> Built to the Nymphs that haunted there of old.[101]

Those fairy hands enter Hunt's poem by courtesy of Collins, who, in his *Song from Shakespeare's Cymbeline*, also traces the work of mysterious agents in pagan folklore. As if further to endorse the values that ascetic Christianity has rejected, Hunt modulates from figurative to literal, and suggests that the nymphs *did* actually haunt the place in pagan times. He admits that

Ariosto's enchantresses were sirens, but at the same time leaves no doubt that his sympathy inclines (with Paulo's and away from Giovanni's) towards their unaspiring fleshliness. An ecphrasis of sculptures in the summerhouse furthers this line of neopagan thought. Here a curious pictorial obliquity—"Leaning at will"; "With sides half swelling forth"; "sidelong-eyed, pretending not to see"—projects a sidling coyness. In one of those displacements that characterize his pastiche, Hunt ends the idyll with the absolute formula romance reserves for its heroines, but which he oddly applies to the summerhouse itself: "Never, be sure, before or since was seen / A summer-house so fine in such a nest of green."[102]

It is usual for love poems to make correlations between human emotion and the cycle of the seasons, and in almost all medieval *reverdies* spring is the season chosen to body forth the buoyancy of love. Hunt's indolent sensibility chooses summer instead, an imaginative masterstroke that explains luxury's triumph over the rigorous will. Rococo art is recreational both in nature and in content, and it seems altogether fitting that, following Horace, Hunt should discard the working day (*solidus dies*) and conjure up a languorous trance. It sets the tone for the encounter:

> One day,—'twas on a summer afternoon.
> When airs and gurgling brooks are best in tune,
> And grasshoppers are loud, and day-work is done,
> And shades have heavy outlines in the sun,—
> The princess came to her accustomed bower
> To get her, if she could, a soothing hour,
> Trying, as she was used, to leave her cares
> Without, and slumberously enjoy the airs,
> And the low-talking leaves, and that cool light
> The vines let in, and all that hushing sight
> Of closing wood seen through the opening door,
> And distant plash of waters tumbling o'er,
> And smell of citron blooms, and fifty luxuries more.[103]

It goes without saying that grasshoppers have infinitely greater charm for Hunt than ants—indeed, in one of his sonnets he sets them in opposition to crickets and does away with the taint of idleness altogether. Here they are brought in as a *lourée* bass to provide an atmospheric hum of leisure, and they leave some doubt as to whether the airs that Francesca enjoys are ventilating airs or musical *arie*, like the melodies that haunt the landscape in *The Tempest*.

Hunt obviously intends to produce the dreamlike suspension of romance, where the "heavy outlines" of reality are crossed and blurred, and the consciousness hovers liminally between them. The effortless enjambment of the couplet supplies part of the spell, naturally, so that Francesca's cares are literally shed and dropped by the lineation of "to leave her cares / Without"; while, by a strange semantic blur, a "closing wood" is seen "through the opening door." On a sort of oneiric threshold, the wood seems to be advancing like the forest of Birnam, while the door would appear to be opening on its own to admit it—except that on inspection we realize that Hunt means "opening" in the architectural sense of "opening on" rather than the transitive sense of "swinging on its hinges." Into this atmosphere of reverie and suspension, Hunt's uneconomical genius cannot resist inserting the tale of Lancelot. As so often, the informal essayist gets tangled up with the poet, and, beset by the clutter, he almost loses the point of correlating two pairs of lovers.

The canto ends on a note of conscious or unconscious irony, for Hunt alludes to the world rather as though he were writing in the spirit of *contemptus mundi*, and so in a sense he is, except that he has inverted its meaning, offering "redemption" through indulgence rather than renunciation: "The world was all forgot, the struggle o'er."[104] An additional irony seems to inhere in the fact that "the struggle o'er" recalls the famous hymn *Finita iam sunt proelia*.

Having written canto 3, Hunt had clearly exhausted the material he found most attractive, but he still had the rest of the story to tell. It is not surprising therefore that the poem should fall off to a marked degree in the last canto, and, sensing in advance a poverty of inspiration, the poet inserts an apology in the form of an interlude. It has the effect of "knocking at the gate" after the rapt ellipsis at the end of canto 3 ("That day they read no more"), but it also shows the poet's determination to confront his subject matter and try, here at least, to write poetry that is not simply recreational. Yet even in spite of this resolute endeavor, Hunt cannot help falling back on his sense of poetry as a "charm"—a *carmen*, obviously enough, but more especially an analgesic to banish pain:

> And above all, the poet's task divine
> Of making tears themselves look up and shine,
> And turning to a charm the sorrow past,
> Have held me on, and shall do to the last.[105]

It is clear that Hunt here has Gray's *Progress of Poesy* in mind. The curious theodicy in that ode suggests that because art banishes evil, it therefore justifies that evil as being necessary to itself. In much the same way, Hunt regards sorrow as a sort of harmonic resource, a discord that heightens the resolution into sweetness. We are miles away from Johnson's Christian stoicism, on the one hand, and Keats's notion of soul-making, on the other:

> Sorrow, to him who has a true-touched ear,
> Is but a discord of a warbling sphere,
> A lurking contrast, which though harsh it be,
> Distils the next note more deliciously.
> E'en tales like this, founded on real woe,
> From bitter seed to balmy fruitage grow:
> The woe was earthly, fugitive, is past;
> The song that sweetens it, may always last.
> And even they, whose shattered hearts and frames
> Make them the unhappiest of poetic names,
> What are they, if they know their calling high,
> But crushed perfumes, exhaling to the sky?
> Or weeping clouds, that but a while are seen,
> Yet keep the earth they haste to, bright and green?[106]

Those weeping clouds will figure again in Keats's *Ode on Melancholy*, but how different the treatment there! The melancholy fit falling "Sudden from heaven like a weeping cloud, / That fosters the droop-headed flowers all, / And hides the green hill in an April shroud"[107] centers in the fact of transience, a mortality that has to be confronted through a heroic effort of will. Hunt, on the other hand, takes refuge in the *aere perennius* idea, finding consolation in the permanent sweetness of poetic form, which he sets against the passing bitterness of life.

Since in the first encounter of the lovers passion overrides guilt, the poet can afford an untrammeled largesse of feeling, and even borrows Dante's formula for consummation—"That day they read no more." However, in canto 4, Hunt has to deal with their guilt as it complicates and sours their relationship. Perhaps because he himself seems never to have felt guilt (he rejected the idea of damnation at an early age), the poem loses definition from this point onward. Indeed Hunt has to fall back on secondary sources to help himself out. On the one hand, Francesca's uncontrolled weepiness seems to derive from *Clarissa;* her tears gush so forcefully at one point that they "hide" her behind a curtain of water: "But a mute gush of tears from one / Clasped to the core of him, who yet shed none."[108] Paulo's distress, on the other hand, recalls the suffering of Aurelius in *The Franklin's Tale*. Since the latter's grief stems from a *want* of sexual fulfillment, it is clear that Hunt has inverted the courtly love convention:

> Sick thoughts of late had made his body sick,
> And this, in turn, to them grown strangely quick;
> And pale he stood, and seemed to burst all o'er
> Into a moist anguish never felt before,
> And with a dreadful certainty to know,
> His peace was gone, and all was come to woe.[109]

At the same time Hunt makes use of *procatalepsis* (the figure that anticipates objections) to soften the judgment of his readers. He is helped in this regard by the noble reproaches of Gray's *Elegy*. Half alluding to the indictments of scorn and pride we find there, Hunt "incriminates" all harsh, Dantesque pronouncements on the sin. Compare "Nor Grandeur hear, with a disdainful smile, / The short and simple annals of the poor"[110] with "Once, and but once,—nor with a scornful face / Tried worth will hear,—that scene again took place."[111] Further on still, Hunt attacks inflexible judgment as a "disease." He needs these rhetorical emollients, for he has a hard time applying his philosophy of cheer to a situation upon which it can barely find purchase. Nonetheless, there is something heroic about his insistence:

> It seemed as if such whelming thoughts must find
> Some props for them, or he should lose his mind,—
> And find he did, not what the worst disease
> Of want of charity calls sophistries,—
> Nor what can cure a generous heart of pain,—
> But humble guesses, helping to sustain.
> He thought, with quick philosophy, of things
> Rarely found out except through sufferings,—
> Of habit, circumstance, design, degree,
> Merit, and will, and thoughtful charity:
> And these, although they pushed down, as they rose,
> His self-respect, and all those morning shews
> Of true and perfect, which his youth had built,
> Pushed with them too the worst of others' guilt;
> And furnished him, at least, with something kind,
> On which to lean a sad and startled mind.[112]

Hunt is being deliberately vague, but it is clear from the context that Paulo's speculations center on the arbitrariness of marriage and the legitimacy of free love; this is hinted at by the juxtaposition of external constraint ("habit, circumstance, design, degree") and inner being ("merit, will, and thoughtful charity"). Here perhaps, there is an anticipatory whiff of Shelley in the air, for Paulo's philosophy is "quick" not only in the sense of being mercurial and deft, but also vital and responsive and challenging. It his *"thoughtful charity"* that finally absolves Francesca—"she he loved could have done nothing base"[113]—and those who differ will stand condemned (by Hunt's rhetorical maneuvers) as diseased, uncharitable, and unthoughtful. Since the philosophy of cheer must supply some consolation, we find that Paulo eventually modifies the stereotype of courtly love. Far from wasting away in hopeless passivity, he secures his health by exercise: "But thus, at least, he exercised his blood, / And kept it livelier than inaction could."[114]

However, Hunt does not allow this sort of adaptability to Francesca, perhaps because he needs a foil for her more resourceful, socially defiant lover. She is failed even by the otherwise unfailing Huntian resource of decor:

> The falcon reached in vain from off his stand;
> The flowers were not refreshed; the very light,
> The sunshine, seemed as if it shone at night;
> The least noise smote her like a sudden wound;
> And did she hear but the remotest sound
> Of song or instrument about the place,
> She hid with both her hands her streaming face.[115]

The anaphoric checklist of delights has become instead a list of deprivations, like the elegiac "no mores" that show that the forefathers in Gray's churchyard have been severed from their former lives. For, like Gray, Hunt is dealing here with the disruption of rhythm and recurrence, as witness the frequentative verb that opens the paragraph—"And oh, the morrow, how it used to rise!"—where for the moment we are uncertain how to hitch up the temporal reference ("used" in a pre- or postlapsarian sense?).

Hunt is not very happy with his task, and avails himself of *occupatio* (hitherto essentially a device of narrative tact) to speed up, if not altogether to evade, this unpleasant coda to the tale: "I pass the meetings Paulo had with her." Devising his own narrative here, he has Giovanni challenge his brother to a duel, whereas the historical Giaciotto is said to have killed the lovers in flagrante delicto. Finding the original events too brutal and abrupt, Hunt creates even greater artistic problems by his modification, and forces himself to fall back on memories of all the fustian duels he had seen on the London stage. He needs the men to confront each other, but rejects an armored medieval tournament as being too impersonal for his purpose. Even so, and even allowing for the shifting perspective of pastiche, this duel has a great deal in common with the cold, "honor"-preserving encounters of Regency England. (John Scott would lose his life to Lockhart over the infamous *Blackwood's* campaign against Hunt and his "school" and Hunt himself, according to Mary Cowden Clarke, was afraid that he would have to duel someone after the publication of *Lord Byron and Some of His Contemporaries*):[116]

> "May I request, sir," said the prince, and frowned,
> "Your ear a moment on the tilting ground?"
> "*There*, brother?" answered Paulo, with an air
> Surprised and shocked. "Yes, *brother*," cried he, "there."
> The word smote crushingly; and paler still,
> He bowed, and moved his lips, as waiting on his will.[117]

This belongs to the world of *The Rivals* and *Nicholas Nickleby* and *Eugene Onegin* rather than to that of medieval Italy.

James Thompson has drawn attention to the way in which *Rimini* is structured on static rather than dynamic principles: "[S]uch narrative action as exists is spasmodic and usually transitional. Hunt's chief preoccupation is with alternating descriptions of the characters' physical world and their emotional states. He is most comfortable when dealing with situations, and his descriptions evince obvious delight and perhaps relief."[118] This goes a long way towards explaining the barren patches that intervene between the interlusive episodes on which the poet lavishes the full range of his fancy (sometimes with congested results, as in the pavilion sequence). At the same time, Thompson's observation draws attention to the way the narrative blocks structurally balance and complement each other—the procession to Rimini counterpoised by the ride to Ravenna and the funeral procession that bears the bodies of the lovers back to Rimini at the end of the poem. There is also a very poignant inset before the duel—*nessun maggior dolore*— when Paulo hurries past the pavilion:

> It was a glimpse of the tall wooded mound,
> That screened Francesca's favourite spot of ground:
> Massy and dark in the clear twilight stood,
> As in a lingering sleep, the solemn wood;
> And through the bowering arch, which led inside,
> He almost fancied once, that he descried
> A marble gleam, where the pavilion lay;—
> Starting he turned, and looked another way.[119]

Here is a classic instance of the romantic epistemology that half-perceives, half-creates its data. Sorrow has turned a pleasance into a grove of initiation, not unlike the *lucus* in *Aeneid* VI. A seasonal shift from spring to autumn also contributes to the atmosphere, especially in the funeral cortège that closes the canto. Hunt has supplanted the *reverdie* of canto 1 with the sort of autumnal elegy we find in Shakespeare's seventy-third sonnet, where dusk, death, and autumn are correlated as logical extensions of each other:

> The days were then at close of autumn,—still,
> A little rainy, and towards night-fall chill;
> And ever and anon, over the road,
> The last few leaves came fluttering from the trees,
> Whose trunks now thronged to sight, in dark varieties.[120]

Again we find a characteristic originality in the way Hunt holds back on full-blown effects. He could have staged a Radcliffian storm; he opts instead for a little rain. He could have gnarled and deformed the trunks that have been bared by autumn; instead he simply paints their austere, minimalist beauty—"in dark varieties." The poem ends with an apparent obeisance to Donne. In *The Canonization* the lovers become patron saints of *eros*, invoked by future generations to give "A pattern of [their] love,"[121] while Hunt seems to ascribe the same benign patronage to Paulo and Francesca in turn:

> On that same night, those lovers silently
> Were buried in one grave, under a tree.
> There side by side, and hand in hand, they lay
> In the green ground:—and on fine nights in May
> Young hearts betrothed go there to pray.[122]

But a more obvious source for the poignant tableau is Collins's *Song from Shakespeare's Cymbeline:*

> To fair Fidele's grassy tomb
>   Soft maids and village hinds shall bring
> Each opening sweet of earliest bloom,
>   And rifle all the breathing spring.
>
> No wailing ghost shall dare appear
>   To vex with shrieks this quiet grove;

> But shepherd lads assemble here,
>   And melting virgins own their love.[123]

Like Collins's poem, and like the ending to *Wuthering Heights*, Hunt's lines are a kind of apotropaic charm, in this instance dispelling the idea of damnation and substituting one of peace—the lovers rest because their sorrows have made sufficient atonement. Earlier on in the canto he has raised the issue in his debate on situation ethics: "O, who that feels one godlike spark within, / Shall say that earthly suffering cancels not frail sin."[124] The force of these lines derives partly from the *quis est homo* topos so often associated with poems of *religious* compassion (such as the *Stabat Mater*):

> Quis est homo qui non fleret
> Matrem Christi si videret
> In tanto supplicio?
>
> Quis non posset contristari
> Christi Matrem contemplari
> Dolentem cum Filio?

The death of Francesca, in its quiet surrender of will, recalls the flesh-and-blood anguish of Hezekiah (who also turned to a wall) but encloses it in the shell of sepulchral effigy:

> There lay she praying, upwardly intent,
> Like a fair statue on a monument,
> With her two trembling hands together prest,
> Palm against palm, and pointing from her breast.
> She ceased, and turning slowly towards the wall,
> They saw her tremble sharply, feet and all,—
> And suddenly be still. . . .[125]

There is an echo of Viola's patience on a monument here, and a resonance of both the first encounter and final parting between Romeo and Juliet, but the artifice serves only to sharpen the real convulsions of death.

We have seen that *The Story of Rimini* takes liberties with its period, not only by using contemporary diction (the success of which is sometimes dubious) but also by importing contemporary attitudes and assumptions. Hunt's nostalgia directs itself only at the elaborate panoply of romance, never at medieval institutions per se. He might mention a hymn to the Virgin Mary for the delight of its period color (canto 3), but he would at the

same time have been appalled by the reactionary medievalism of a Hurrell
Froude that would eventually contribute to the Oxford Movement and to
Legitimism on the Continent—what Lukács has called "a pseudo-histori-
cism, an ideology of immobility, of return to the Middle Ages."[126] Nowhere
is this more apparent than in Hunt's rejected proem, discarded in favor of the
opening as we know it. Whereas the last begins festively *in medias res*, Hunt
started his first draft with an attack on tyrannical government. The poem is the
subtler for its omission, but its *pentimento* can be detected in the ideological
concerns that underlie the sometimes gaudy accumulation of period detail. The
rejected lines contain the authentic voice of *The Examiner*:

> And well indeed did all the gentle rays
> In that fair quarter [Francesca], gild the ev'ning gaze
> And justify, for once, the trusted fates,
> (That old credulity of dying states)
> For not by contrast loved was Guido's heir,
> Nor the mere dotage of the realm's despair,—
> No pampered prodigal, unshamed in waste,
> Whose childishness remains when youth is past,—
> No smirking ideot, trusting for its throne
> To custom and a worn-out race alone,—[127]

It is well for Hunt that he did not publish these lines on hereditary thrones,
for they might have embarrassed him when he fished for the laureateship in
the 1850s. As Short suggests, discretion "may have deterred him from
running the risk of jeopardizing the poem's success by beginning it with an
attack on inadequate rulers. Or his critical judgment may have suggested
that as a prelude the passage was disproportionately long."[128]

Also in this rejected opening is a blazon of Francesca's beauty, far more
detailed than the one eventually used. No doubt Hunt set it aside because
it seemed too sensual, moving as it does from shoulders to feet, but with
lecherous ellipses and token *occupatio*: "I may not trust the warm poetic
sense / To tell what beauties swelled from thence, / Nor how they wound
within the robe's retreat."[129] Nor does the "do-it-yourself" pertness achieve
the right sort of dignity, anticipating as it does the sketchiness and evasive-
ness to which Hunt is prone when his interest flags: "No brilliant pallets on
the dame I waste / But fairly leave to the good reader's guesses, / The colour
of her eyes and clust'ring tresses."[130]

It is clear than the poet felt the contemporary attacks on his diction
keenly enough to remove at least some of the *cruces* in his 1844 version.
Again and again he smoothes out characteristic wrinkles into facelessness:

the rich Titianesque impasto of "purple smearings" becomes a comparatively bland "heart's-ease purple"[131] and "backwarder" loses its characteristic hunch in the flat monosyllables of "in her grief."[132] These efforts at placating orthodoxy were not universally approved, and the reviewer in *Ainsworth's Magazine* regretted the demannerizing of *Rimini* as a loss of character.[133] More damaging was Hunt's decision to go back to a deformed historical Gianciotto and compromise the dignity of Giovanni (one of the more imaginative and innovative elements in the 1816 conception) with some altogether predictable Richard the Thirdery: "But on his secret soul the fiend still hung, / Darken'd his face, made sour and fierce his tongue, / And was preparing now a place for thee / In his wild heart, O murderous Jealousy."[134] Paulo's suicide on his brother's sword is likewise revoked in an alternative ending closer to Dante's, but incorporating a Melot figure who betrays the lovers to the husband. I think the revised ending preferable because it is more succinct, but Hunt felt fond enough of his first fruits to fashion a separate poem called *Corso and Emilia*, renaming the lovers to give the piece an independent life. Weak enough in its proper context, it is weaker still without it, and Milford leaves it out of the canon altogether.

The prefatory note in the 1860 edition is worth quoting, however. We are told that *Corso and Emilia* is the "fragment of the story of another victim to parental duplicity."[135] If *The Story of Rimini* had helped clarify Shelley's sexual ethics to himself, then perhaps *The Cenci*, dedicated to the author of *Rimini* in 1819, had led Hunt to reinterpret his own intentions apropos of Francesca and Guido. When he came to recast his 1814 version he subtitled it the *Fruits of a Parent's Falsehood*—a redaction that accounts for only a small part of a poem otherwise laden with fanciful baggage. If we read *The Story of Rimini* today, it is *for* those rich, loose outgrowths of the plot. As he grew older, however, Hunt seemed think that the poem had a much more important function to discharge. For whereas Shelley told Peacock that *The Cenci* had been divested of "peculiar feelings and opinions" of his own,[136] the author of *Rimini* made every effort to *introduce* such peculiarities and personal judgments. The result, as we have seen, was an innovative variety of pastiche, charged with anachronisms very different (in their self-consciousness) from the clocks and hats of *Julius Caesar*.

The phrasing of Hunt's later subtitle brings *Paradise Lost* to mind, and he no doubt means us to think of a "woman's first *obedience*" as the cause of the tragedy. He obviously could not have rewritten the poem to such an extent that Francesca's notions "on the marrying score" subverted the entire course of history, but it seemed to him in retrospect that this was where the moral and thematic energy of the poem was to be found.

3

Narrative Poems: II

The Hunt/Milford arrangement of the poetry dictates that this chapter be something of a catchall, for although all the poems that are marshaled into its compass are narrative poems to a greater or lesser degree, there are many generic differences separating the epyllia (*Hero and Leander* and *Bacchus and Ariadne*), the Hudibrastics and impassioned protest poetry of *Captain Sword and Captain Pen*, and the pastiche balladry of *Robin Hood*. Still, if we bear in mind that Hunt excels above all in celebrating the lyric moment, the odd assortment gathered under this roof will help us perceive a paradoxical truth, viz., that the more the narrative poems evade their narrative responsibilities, the more characteristically Huntian (and better) they become. There can be no denying the success of the slight, idyllic ballads into which Hunt has infused his fancy if we place them alongside the insipid verse of that overextended anecdote, *The Palfrey*, and the flat, undistinguished efficiency of the oriental parables. Only in *Captain Sword and Captain Pen*, his least characteristic poem, does Hunt succeed in matching length and intensity, and the key to his success in this hybrid poem must be sought in the looseness and miscellaneousness of a method that sets interlusive ballrooms and country hearths in the midst of war itself.

HERO AND LEANDER (1819)

When Bulwer-Lytton reviewed the 1832 edition of Hunt's poetry, he suggested that *Hero and Leander* is "Dryden himself, but . . . with a sentiment, a delicacy, not his own."[1] If that were so, one would need to add that a Dryden with the lingering sentiment and narrative arabesques we find in Hunt, would not be Dryden at all. Reading *Ceyx and Alcyone* as a tale comparable with *Hero and Leander*—both treat classical subjects—we find the imprint of an altogether different sensibility. Its narrative briskness and purposiveness prove that Dryden (like Ovid, whom he is translating) always has his destination in mind. This teleological drive gives it its perfection, perfection conceived both as finish and completedness. We get a hint of this sort of accomplished integrity in Byron's use of "perfect" when he comments on *Rimini*: "Hunt, who had powers to make the *Story of Rimini* as perfect as a fable of Dryden, has thought fit to sacrifice it to some unintelligible notion of Wordsworth, which I defy him to explain."[2] For *Rimini* is un-Drydenic not only in its diction but also in its tendency to dawdle, to finger and appreciate the minutiae of the story while the narrative as a whole is "put on hold." "Sentiment" and "delicacy" often entail stoppage and delay, something we can see in Hunt's reverse judgment on Byron—because *he* emulates the pace and purpose of Dryden's narrative mode, Hunt sometimes finds him "too melodramatic, hasty and vague."[3]

Huntian narrative often offers the circumstantiality that has made the novel so solid and accessible, but which the verse tale has seldom had the time nor the space to incorporate. In *Rimini* it manifests itself as a disproportion of decor to event, and a narrative rhythm that is either rushed or slowed to a lingering pace. Indeed, Hunt's narrative conduct occasionally suggests the piano playing of a gifted amateur (dare one think of Harold Skimpole in this regard?)—the parts that attract him, he dwells on and shapes quite pleasingly; those that fail to command his interest he hurries over or omits altogether. Donald Ericksen has suggested that when he was satirizing Hunt as Skimpole, Dickens might have been targeting the Pre-Raphaelites at the same time, sensing that they exalted detail over design (in the fullest sense of the word). In *Bleak House* Skimpole observes, "I can lie down in the grass—in fine weather—and float along an African river, embracing all the natives I meet, as sensible of the deep silence, and sketching the overhanging tropical growth as accurately as if I were there."[4] Ericksen comments that here "is the artistic equivalent of Mrs Pardiggle and Mrs Jellyby's long-distance philanthropy which Dickens detested. Not to be overlooked, however, is the likelihood that Dickens is thinking as well of one of the prominent qualities of Pre-Raphaelite art—its inordinate attention to detail."[5]

Attracted to luxurious, exfoliating detail, Hunt often so mismanages the tempo and emphasis of his narratives that the performance can seem incomplete or dilatory. He subordinates the neoclassical ideal of concinnity (a proportion of beginning to middle to end) and dwells on incidental delights of surface and texture. In *Ceyx and Alcyone*, by contrast, Dryden flanks the central catastrophe with an explanatory proem and a coda in which even the abruptness of suicide, yielding by gradation to the metamorphosis, receives a narrative "cushion." *Hero and Leander* exemplifies an altogether different sort of tale-telling. There is no contextualizing "Once upon a time," no formula of placement. Hunt is impatient to launch *in medias res*, moving swiftly to the religious materials that seem to have attracted him in the first place. Many years later, writing in *The Religion of the Heart*, he would observe that

> It was a great mistake of the nurturers of Christianity to preach contempt of the body, out of a notion of exalting the soul. Better and more piously was it said by the Heathen poet, that "We should pray for sound mind in sound body."

> But the Heathen world, generally speaking, had the advantage of the Christian in this respect, by reason of their gymnastics and sculpture, and the re-action of one kind of health on the other. Compare the melancholy and mortified looks of the Puritan and other divines with the busts of the Grecian philosophers, Plato, the man of the "broad shoulders" among them.[6]

In *Rimini* we sense no nostalgia for medieval institutions or habits of thought, and several authorial asides establish the narrator's remoteness from some of the values and norms he is forced by circumstance to handle. Not so the unembarrassed celebration of the flesh that in *Hero and Leander* informs the worship of Venus, even if a paradoxical chasteness presents the cult in terms more suited to a cathedral close:

> The hour of worship's over; and the flute
> And choral voices of the girls are mute;
> And by degrees the people have departed
> Homeward, with gentle step, and quiet-hearted;
> The jealous easy, the desponding healed;
> The timid, hopeful of their love concealed;
> The sprightlier maiden, sure of nuptial joys;
> And mothers, grateful for their rosy boys.[7]

To put this in perspective, we need first to consult an essay from *The Indicator* that Hunt wrote at roughly the same time as *Hero and Leander*. Its title is "Spirit of the Ancient Mythology."

> We take Apollo, and Mercury, and Venus, as shapes that existed in popular credulity, as the greater fairies of the ancient world: and we regard

them, at the same time, as personifications of all that is beautiful and
genial in the forms and tendencies of creation. But the result, coming as
it does, too, through the avenues of beautiful poetry, both ancient and
modern, is so entirely cheerful, that we are apt to think it must have
wanted gravity to more believing eyes. We fancy that the old world saw
nothing in religion but lively and graceful shapes, as remote from the more
obscure and awful hintings of the world unknown, as physics appear to be
from the metaphysical; as the eye of a beautiful woman from the inward
speculations of a Brahmin; or a lily at noon-day from the wide obscurity
of night-time.

Imagine Plutarch, a devout and yet a liberal believer, when he went to
study theology and philosophy at Delphi: with what feelings must he have
passed along the woody paths to the hill, approaching nearer every instant
to the divinity, and not sure that a glance of light through the trees was not
the lustre of the god himself going by! This is mere poetry to us, and very
fine it is; but to him it was poetry, and religion, and beauty, and gravity,
and hushing awe, and a path as from one world to another.[8]

The casual, unflurried opening of *Hero and Leander* likewise does justice to
the *reality* of ancient religion, treating the temple "service" as though it were
a familiar Anglican evensong. Like Matthew Arnold after him, Hunt perceived that the literary experience of religion and the religion itself are to
some extent dichotomous. Arnold, following Goethe, would later distinguish *Glaube* from *Aberglaube:*

It is exactly what is expressed by the German word "Aberglaube," *extra-
belief,* belief beyond what is certain and verifiable. Our word "superstition"
had by its derivation this same meaning, but it has come to be used merely
in a bad sense, and to mean a childish and craven religiosity. With the
German word it is not so; therefore Goethe can say with propriety and
truth: "*Aberglaube* is the poetry of life,—*der Aberglaube ist die Poesie des
Lebens.*" It is so. *Extra-belief,* that which we hope, augur, imagine, is the
poetry of life, and has the rights of poetry.[9]

Like Arnold, Hunt seems to have yearned after those very picturesque
elements to which his intellect would not assent, a yearning all the more
intense for the facelessness and abstraction of his own Deism, which recommends that God be called "the Great Beneficence (by which noblest of his
names it is comfortable to call him, since it has never been abused)."[10]

Behind *Hero and Leander,* then, we can detect the impulse to recreate a
religion as it might have been, as opposed to what it became in its literary

Nachleben. Even though Hunt concedes in his *Indicator* essay that ancient belief had "its portion of terror,"[11] he omits this entirely from his idyll. At the same time he takes care to redeem the myth from the province of "mere poetry" by domesticating and familiarizing its rituals. Since *Hero and Leander* tries in its way to recreate a vanished religious ethos, I cannot wholly agree with Douglas Bush when he claims that Hunt had "little thought of reproducing the antique."[12] Without attempting an archaeologically exact reproduction, he does try to project a plausible "might have been," rather like the "Christianism" Hunt proposed to Shelley shortly before the latter's death: "He assented warmly to an opinion which I expressed in the cathedral at Pisa, while the organ was playing, that a truly divine religion might yet be established, if charity were really made the principle of it, instead of faith."[13]

Returning to the start of the poem, we can see that Hunt has avoided all hints of licentiousness. He registers Venus-worship through a litany of fulfillment and blessing, incorporating all the decencies of bourgeois life—"mothers, grateful for their rosy boys." The decor might be Huntian in the extreme, but the poet has at the same time taken care not to clutter the narrative line with the bizarre details it received at the hands of other adaptors—Marlowe, who encrusted it with mock-Euphuism, and Chapman, who added a strange tract of *Marlowe moralisé*, and Thomas Hood, who, writing after Hunt, interpolated an encounter between Leander and a nymph. Hunt has in fact kept fairly close to Musaeus, though he seeks help from Ovid's *Heroides* here and there.

The Greek Orthodox ceremony of the *epiluchnion* (a formal salute to the evening) might or might not have been known to Hunt, and he might or might not have been familiar with the *Phos hilaron*, a famous hymn used for the occasion. Even so, he has caught something of its serenity and repose in his opening lines, which, in their atmospheric accumulation of data, also anticipate another *Indicator* essay entitled "A Now."[14] This account of a hot summer's day masses a series of paratactic sentences that fail to "go" anywhere, and so suggests a general immobility and indolence.[15] In exactly the same way, the start of *Hero and Leander* creates the stasis of late afternoon in its anaphoric run of clauses, measuring the peace by little grace notes of action:

> All, all is still about the odorous grove,
> That wraps the temple of the Queen of Love,
> All but the sparrows twittering from the eaves,
> And inward voice of doves among the leaves,
> And the cool, hiding noise of brooks in bowers,

And bees, that dart in bosoms of the flowers,
And now and then, a breath-increasing breeze
That comes amidst a world of tumbling trees,
And makes them pant, and shift against the light,
About the marble roof, solid and sunny bright.[16]

As Hunt himself admits in the *Indicator* essay, the "now" formula has a venerable heritage. He mentions *The Woman-Hater* by Beaumont and Fletcher as a source, but many others also come to mind—the anti-*epiluchnion* in *Macbeth* ("Now o'er the one half-world / Nature seems dead, and wicked dreams abuse / The curtain'd sleep")[17] and the "night piece" declaimed by Lorenzo and Jessica in *The Merchant of Venice*, which resembles Hunt's in the effort to project myth as historical reality: "In such a night / Stood Dido with a willow in her hand / Upon the wild sea banks."[18] It is also possible that the sparrows twittering in the temple eaves have entered Hunt's imagination by way of *Measure for Measure*, where, we are told, "Sparrows must not build in his [Angelo's] house-eaves, because they are lecherous."[19]

The very detail of the eaves, taken in conjunction with the homely sparrows, strikes a note of coziness that metopes and triglyphs would somehow have missed (had Hunt been pedantic enough to include them), though he substitutes fancy for fact by giving the temple a roof made from marble instead of from tiles. Even so, his "might have been" differs strikingly from the Marlovian extravagance that puts the priestess in seashell buskins and bedecks her with artificial birds. Unlike Marlowe, Hunt does not flout classical modes and *mores*—he simply adapts them to his nostalgia for a green, innocent world where the flesh and the spirit live in amity. Hero's temple is in the last resort a fancy like Francesca's *tempietto* in *The Story of Rimini*, and like the "tumbling trees" that Hunt has transplanted from a stock of rococo properties. Only deciduous trees "tumble" in this way, and since he is especially partial to greenwood trees—he missed them passionately during his Italian exile—Hunt is quite prepared to paint out the formal cypresses we might have expected so as to pastoralize the landscape. How otherwise could he project the atmosphere of a *fête champêtre?* This might seem irresponsible to the immediate facts of the situation, but it accords fully with his larger purpose of making ancient religion seem familiar and accessible. Viewed in such terms, Hero becomes a Regency diva adored by her fans at the "stage door" of the temple: "Only some stragglers loiter round the place / To catch a glimpse of Hero's heavenly face."[20]

Whereas Musaeus and Marlowe devote long sections to the courtship of the lovers, Hunt has little interest in the prelude to the love affair, and slips it into a brief contextual aside: "And yet 'twas he that in the porch but now, / Had held her, and had kissed, she scarce knew how; / And after months of mutual admiration / Felt more than told, and glancing inclination."[21] What does seem to interest him is the idea of a sexuality uncomplicated by guilt and "arbitrary" social ordinance. We must remember that Hunt espoused very Shelleyan ideals of marriage at the time that he was writing this, and Ann Blainey has suggested that he might even have put them into practice with his sister-in-law, whose attempted suicide was probably the sequel to an interlude of free love: "Hunt then was swimming in the seas of liberated love and Bess was struggling to keep afloat. In the light of the evidence one cannot automatically accept Haydon's view that they did not sleep together. Moreover, Thornton was worried enough about the affair to delete many passages in his father's letters when a generation later he prepared them for publication."[22]

In *The Eve of St Agnes*, Keats aligns the cult of the Virgin Mary with the cold ascesis of a beadsman, but in *Hero and Leander* Hunt creates a sort of pagan analogue to that cultus. The *seated* figure of Venus obviously transposes memories of the Virgin enthroned, but her smiling patronage endorses carnal love instead of rejecting it:

> At last, with twinkle o'er a distant tower,
> A star appeared that was to show the hour.
> The virgin saw; and going to a room
> Which held an altar burning with perfume,
> Cut off a lock of her dark solid hair,
> And laid it, with a little whispered prayer,
> Before a statue, that of marble bright
> Sat smiling downwards o'er the rosy light.[23]

This is a paean to the flesh, and to the cult that sanctions it—no penances here, only the surrender to the impulse of the moment. The *Stella Maris* has been secularized into a signal for the assignation; the sacrificial lock entails no corporal pain.

Hunt is heavily indebted to Musaeus for the erotic prelude to the lovers' tryst, even to the point of contrasting "rank" salt water (surely not a Huntian judgment) with the rosy oils with which Hero laves Leander's body:

> His glazy limbs she dried, and dripping locks,
> And emptied rosy essence from a box;
> And so restored him to himself again
> From the faint toil and rankness of the main.[24]

Compare Musaeus as translated by Chapman:

> Then brought she him into the inmost fair
> Of all, her virgin-chamber, that (at best)
> Was with her beauties ten times better drest.
> His body then she cleans'd; his body oil'd
> With rosy odours, and his bosom (soil'd
> With the unsavoury sea) she render'd sweet
> Then, in the high-made bed (ev'n panting yet)
> Herself she pour'd about her husband's breast,[25]

This has the effect of ritual solemnity not unlike that we find in the story the woman who anointed the feet of Christ—except, of course, that there is no salute to divinity, but rather a divinizing of the flesh. When the lovers go to bed, the love is once again ritualized and thus turned into something reverential, as though the courtesy of courtly love had colored and modified the lust:

> But looking up with glad yet reverent eyes,
> He breathed away the gentle self-disguise;
> And folding her, with doubled wish to bless,
> Strained to his heart the cordial shapeliness.
> Pleasure be with them, and affectionate sleep!
> I say no more; for foolish men still keep
> Their vice-creating ways, and still are blindest
> To what is happiest, loveliest, best and kindest.[26]

Hunt's characteristic use of *occupatio* takes on a somewhat different color here, for it is not out of distaste that the veil is being drawn, but out of reluctant deference to the prudishness in Regency England. Chapman's translation of Musaeus provides a graphic account of the consummation ("And now she took in Love's sweet-bitter sting, / Burn'd in a fire that cool'd her surfeiting"),[27] whereas Hunt seems instead to have adapted the circuitousness of the *Heroides*: "multaque praeterea linguae reticenda modestae, / quae fecisse iuvat, facta referre pudet" rendered by the Loeb translation as "many things else a modest tongue should say naught of, whose memory delights, but whose telling brings a blush."[28] This "enforced" veil-drawing prompts a polemical aside about sex and hypocrisy. (The line of thought is similar to that in Blake's "London," where the "vice-creating ways" of social bans create the oxymoron of a marriage hearse.)

Hunt allowed the lovers in *The Story of Rimini* only two sexual encoun-

ters, but in *Hero and Leander* the love lasts a season, and almost takes on the
rhythm of a natural cycle:

> Thus passed the summer shadows in delight:
> Leander came as surely as the night,
> And when the morning woke upon the sea,
> It saw him not, for back at home was he.
> . . . .
> The people round the country, who from far
> Used to behold the torch, thought it a star,
> Set there, perhaps, by Venus as a wonder,
> To mark the favourite maiden who slept under.
> Therefore they trod about the grounds by day
> Gently; and fishermen at night, they say,
> With reverence kept aloof, cutting their silent way.[29]

Once again, nostalgia for the *Aberglaube* of antiquity has impelled Hunt to
give the Sestians a reverence that, far from seeming misplaced in his eyes,
salutes the sanctity of mutual love. In a Christian worldview, those "summer
shadows" would signify the transience of the flesh, but for Hunt they are the
literal dapplings of the temple trees, or the gathered shades of evening.

Hunt's topic has forced him to confront the problem of evil, and he
cannot dwell on the recurrent happiness of summer love without taking its
tragic aftermath into account. As in the fourth canto of *Rimini*, he attempts
to present a "theodicy" of sorts—or rather theodicies, for he supplies three
independent arguments in quick succession. This is Huntian philosophy—
airy, undogmatic, couched in unassertive subjunctives. Firstly we are told
that unhappiness might be a condiment for the sharpening of joy; and
secondly, that a pagan providence might have ordained (as in Herbert's
"Pulley") that complete sublunary happiness would distract humankind
from its true vocation. But it is the third argument that seems to be most
closely related to Hunt's own vision, for here the blame is laid at the door of
society and the "vice-creating ways" of foolish men:

> Or lastly, whether, like distempered men,
> Who want the cure from nature's breast again,
> We talk of griefs and follies, yet lay claim
> To praise for both, and call it a good name,
> Hugging our thorns, and taking reverend measures
> To cut short all offenders who get pleasures,
> I know not; but if one true joy there spring,

> The world must have its speedy poisoning,—
> Must interfere, some way, to make it hard
> Of getting, or to blast it when not barred;[30]

This is a Shelleyan view of social bans that traces grief to the tyrannical nature of institutions. Hunt points out their tyranny by inverting the clichés that shore them up, so that a "good name" becomes folly and a grief, and, still more importantly, the "world" loses the taint it gets from its association (in Christianity) with the flesh and the devil. The world comes instead to stand for the flesh-denying nature of the Christian religion, bent on destroying the innocence of carnal love with doctrines of sin and guilt.

In the *Indicator* essay entitled "The Spirit of the Ancient Mythology," Hunt lauds the provisional paganism of *The World Is Too Much with Us* and at the same time derides the sort of dichotomous thinking that fragments the interrelatedness of life:

> It was a strong sense of this, which made a living poet, who is accounted very orthodox in his religious opinions, give vent, in that fine sonnet, to his impatience at seeing the beautiful planet we live upon, with all its starry wonders about it, so little thought of, compared with what is so ridiculously called *the world*.[31]

Hunt also ridicules this vision of the world in *Hero and Leander*, where it poisons the delights of the flesh, *compelled* to its Puritanism (as the repeated verbs of obligation suggest) by a sort of schadenfreude. Whereas the more conventional wisdom of *contemptus mundi* rejects worldly pleasures because they are fleeting, Hunt suggests they are fleeting *because* of the world's opposition:

> And thus it is, that happiest linked loves
> Glance and are gone sometimes, like passing doves;
> Or like two dancers gliding from a green;
> Or like two sky-streaks, filling with clouds between,
> All we can hope is, that so sweet a smile
> Goes somewhere to continue; and meanwhile,
> Hopes, joys and sorrows link our days together,
> Like spring, and summer-time and wintery weather.[32]

This cunningly recapitulates the interconnection of "linked loves" as the entanglement of "Hopes, joys and sorrows" in life itself, as though the one linkage issued inevitably in the other. At the same time it steers the poem back from a philosophical to a narrative mode, modulating through "wintery weather" to the season of Leander's death. The effect is masterly, like the arrival at the tonic key after a long symphonic development:

> Like spring, and summer-time, and wintery weather.
> For autumn now was over; and the crane
> Began to clang against the coming rain,
> And peevish winds ran cutting o'er the sea,
> Which at its best looked dark and slatily.[33]

A Huntian collocation of complementary adjective and adverb ("dark and slatily") produces a slew in the syntax, for while the adjective implies that an onlooker sees the baleful slaty color, "slatily" suggests that it is the ocean itself that is looking out through slats the winds are cutting on its surface. The disquiet created by the confusion helps justify this (and many another) neologism.

Hunt now finds himself once again with a distasteful narrative task in hand—Leander's drowning and Hero's suicide. He screws his courage to the sticking point by fading out idyllic elements and focusing sternly on the sublime:

> All noises by degrees
> Were hushed,— the fisher's call, the birds, the trees,
> All but the washing of the eternal seas.[34]

(The last, surely, is a line that stuck in Keats's mind when he came to write "Bright Star.") Good though that is, the verse from this point onwards lacks distinction; Hunt's material has deprived him of the sort of stimuli to which his imagination ordinarily responds—he is never at home with sublimity and terror. Although he tries to invest the sea with a malign energy, he succeeds only in making it seem spiteful ("ruffian waves"; "wilful wave"; "scornful sea"). Altogether more successful is his way of suggesting the process of thought as it forms and reforms in the contradictory flux of experience, something that Browning would later bring to perfection: "But what? the torch gone out! So long too! See, / He thinks it comes! Ah, yes,— 'tis she! 'tis she!"[35]

Another Huntian touch is the way the dying Leander's thoughts move in concentric circles from divine to human matters (anticipating the priorities of *Abou Ben Adhem*):

He thinks of prayers to Neptune and his daughters,
And Venus, Hero's queen, sprung from the waters;
Then of Hero only,—how she fares,
And what she'll feel, when the blank morn appears.[36]

Here Hunt anticipates the same memorable coupling of blankness and be-
reavement that Tennyson was to make in *In Memoriam* VII,[37] just as the
glimmering geometry of "the casement, at the dawn of light, / Began to
show a square of ghastly white" anticipates the moment in "Tears, Idle
Tears": "when unto dying eyes / The casement slowly grows a glimmering
square."[38] As in *Rimini*, he uses *occupatio* to hurry his narrative over Hero's
anxiety and grief ("I need not tell how Hero, when her light / Would burn
no longer, passed that dreadful night"),[39] and, by virtue of this speed, achieves
an abrupt sort of power. In this he had the example of Musaeus to follow,
who in his *Hero and Leander* (here translated by Chapman) also provides an
ending of sharp finality:

> Mangl'd with rocks, and all-embrued, she tore
> About her breast the curious weed she wore;
> And with a shriek from off her turret's height,
> Cast her fair body headlong, that fell right
> On her dead husband, spent with him her breath;
> And each won other in the worst of death.[40]

Hunt's stark ending, also stripped of a formal peroration, is impaired by the
metaphor of failed metamorphosis:

> On which such strength of passion and dismay
> Seized her, and such an impotence to stay,
> That from the turret, like a stricken dove,
> With fluttering arms she leaped, and joined her drowned love.[41]

Given the pervasive influence of Gray throughout his verse, Hunt might
also be remembering the finale of *The Bard*, where suicide also secures
closure—"He spoke, and headlong from the mountain's height / Deep in
the roaring tide he plunged to endless night."[42] (When he was at school,
Hunt "fell passionately in love with Collins and Gray,"[43] and because his
generous spirit honored the eighteenth-century achievement even while he
pioneered alternative modes of expression, we can hear their voices echo
and re-echo throughout his poetry.)

BACCHUS AND ARIADNE (1819)

Hunt did well to choose Bacchus and Ariadne for his next poem, for the
simple reason that the subject itself is comparatively static and makes few
demands for that narrative upkeep, that exigency of plot by which Hunt
sometimes appears to be embarrassed. The story of a woman who is deserted by a mortal and consoled by a god, lends itself to decorative anecdotal
paneling much more than the tales of *Rimini* or *Hero and Leander*. Musaeus
seems to have helped him with *Hero*, and it is clear that he worked closely
from *Heroides* when he came to write *Bacchus and Ariadne*, though he was no
doubt relieved that he could take the tale to the joyful end that Ovid leaves
unspoken. Hunt conjures up the aubade tradition (a tradition of contented,
consummated love) to highlight the pathos of Ariadne's plight, and might
have been prompted to his masterstroke by the fact that Ovid starts his
poem at sunrise. This the earlier poet correlates with Ariadne's dawning
awareness as she wakes up alone. The only major difference between the
two openings is that Hunt, showing a characteristic preference for what is
mild above what is harsh, substitutes dew for rime. Here is Ovid:

> Tempus erat, vitrea quo primum terra pruina
> spargitur et tectae fronde queruntur aves.
> incertum vigilans ac somno languida movi
> Thesea prensuras semisupina manus—
> nullus erat! referoque manus iterumque retempto,
> perque torum moveo bracchia—nullus erat!

('Twas the time when the earth is first besprinkled with crystal rime, and
songsters hid in the branch begin their plaint. Half waking only and
languid from sleep, I turned upon my side and put forth hands to clasp my
Theseus—he was not there! I drew back my hands, a second time made
essay, and o'er the whole couch moved my arms—he was not there!)[44]

And here is Hunt—using past continuous verbs in an unidiomatic but
mesmerizing way, as though he were writing not about events but a pro-
tracted state of being:

> The moist and quiet morn was breaking,
> When Ariadne in her bower was waking;
> Her eyelids still were closing and she heard
> But indistinctly yet a little bird,

> That in the leaves o'erhead, waiting the sun,
> Seemed answering another distant one.
>
> . . . .
>
> The sweet, self-willed content, conspired to keep
> Her sense lingering in the feel of sleep;
> And with a little smile she seemed to say,
> "I know my love is near me, and 'tis day."
>
> At length, not feeling the accustomed arm,
> That from all sense of fancied want and harm
> Used to enclose her, when she turned that way,
> She stretched her hand to feel where Theseus lay,
> Thinking to wake his mouth into a kiss;[45]

If this seems less impressive than Ovid, it is because Hunt has lowered the tension by amplifying something succinct. His laxity nonetheless brings its own reward—a sense of indolent half-wakefulness. Taken out of context, a line like "Seemed answering another distant one" seems excruciatingly nerveless, for the very syntax is in danger of disintegrating and meter and rhythm are so badly coordinated as to threaten cardiac arrest. Put back in the poem, however, its laziness becomes expressive. Whereas Ovid's verse is beautifully choreographed, with a formal reduplication of *nullus erat* to shape and control the disposition of limb and the nuance of gesture, Hunt's slack poetry comes closer to a real human waking. The mouth precedes the mind into consciousness.

We can also see the same temperamental difference between the poets in the way they handle Ariadne's panic when Theseus's absence strikes home. For Ovid, it is a case of balancing graceful antiphons; for Hunt, a convulsive calling, made intentionally graceless by *traductio*. Here is Ovid once again:

> interea toto clamavi in litore "Theseu!":
> reddebant nomen concava saxa tuum,
> et quotiens ego te, totiens locus ipse vocabat.

> (And all the while I cried out "Theseus!" along the entire shore, and the hollow rocks sent back your name to me; as often as I called out for you, so often did the place itself call out your name.)[46]

If Hunt were following Pope, he could have used the studied, formal symmetry we find in *Autumn* ("Thro' Rocks and Caves the Name of Delia sounds, / *Delia*, each Cave and ecchoing Rock rebounds["]),[47] but instead he sacrifices neoclassic order to romantic naturalism:

> But stops at last, her throat full-pulsed with fears,
> And calls convulsively with bursting tears;
> Then calls again; and then in the open air
> Rushes, and fiercely calls. He is not *there*.[48]

In *Rimini*, italics manipulate the stress in the melodramatic prelude to the duel scene; here they function much more successfully, giving a forceful downthrust to the rhythm that almost jams the line. The effect is a baffled, despondent finality, and it finds reinforcement from the caesura after "'Tis gone," when Ariadne realizes that Theseus has left. The line that records her fainting away serves structurally and thematically to reverse the aubadelike opening: "'Tis gone; and as a dead thing down falls she, / In the great eye of morn, then breaking quietly."[49] Compare this with "The moist and quiet morn was scarcely breaking, / When Ariadne in her bower was waking."

If *Bacchus and Ariadne* has fewer authorial asides than *Hero and Leander*, that is because Hunt has chosen not to contrast contemporary morals with classical. He does, however, express his contempt for the "caddishness" of Theseus by mocking the apologias that have been presented in his defense, each giving rise to a different versions of the legend. Robert Graves has listed some of these:

> Some days later, after disembarking on the island then named Dia, but now known as Naxos, Theseus left Ariadne asleep on the shore, and sailed away. Why he did so must remain a mystery. Some say that he deserted her in favour of a new mistress, Aegle, daughter of Panopeus; others that, while wind-bound on Dia, he reflected on the scandal which Ariadne's arrival in Athens would cause. Others again, that Dionysus, appearing to Theseus in a dream, threateningly demanded Ariadne for himself, and that, when Theseus awoke to see Dionysus's fleet bearing down on Dia, he weighed anchor in sudden terror, Dionysus having cast a spell which made him forget his promise to Ariadne and even her very existence.[50]

Hunt is more severe on Theseus. In his book, the vision of Bacchus is not a numinous reality but a self-justifying ploy, one all too familiar from the Regency government that claimed the sanction of God for its illiberal policies:

> Some say that Theseus took this selfish flight
> From common causes—a cloyed appetite;

> Others, that having brought her sister there
> As well, he turned his easy love to her;
> And others, who are sure to quote Heaven's orders
> For great men's crimes, though not for small disorders,
> Pretend that Bacchus in the true old way,
> A dream, advised him not to stay,
> But go and cut up nations limb by limb,
> And leave the lady and the bower to him.[51]

While Hunt rejects the selfish negligence that the "reasons" of boredom and fickleness imply, he reserves his full scorn for the hypocritical cloaking of those reasons in patriotic "duty." And by rejecting a value system that advances national above personal obligation, he seems to anticipate the famous credo of E. M. Forster—"I hate the idea of causes, and if I had to choose between betraying my country and betraying my friend, I hope I should have the guts to betray my country."[52] For Hunt, the end of duty is not the massacre of nations "limb by limb" but rather "the means of giving as much happiness as we can to others,"[53] and he goes on to offer the following counsel: "Rather be forsaken by a friend, than forsake one."[54]

Once he has done with Theseus, Hunt reverts to the descriptive mode he ordinarily finds so grateful, freed from any need to be sententious or thematically weighty. Ovid has helped him over the uncomfortable prelude to the story, and Titian is at hand to guide him to its climax. It is possible that very desire to versify Titian's picture prompted Hunt to the choose the topic in the first instance. That the picture figured in his print collection can be inferred from *Sleep and Poetry*. Here Keats describes the same Titian, recalling the "pleasant flow / Of words at opening a portfolio."[55] We need have no doubt that that portfolio was lodged in "a poet's house who keeps the keys / Of pleasure's temple."[56]

Before presenting yet another of his ideal topographies (full of "luxurious spots" and "leafy little hills"), Hunt shuts out the vista of the sea with a memorable line: "And wandering long beside the flat far sea."[57] Here and at a comparable point of *Hero and Leander* ("All but the washing of the eternal seas") and in *The Religion of the Heart* ("the fluctuating solitudes of the waters")[58] the poet achieves tragic plangency almost in spite of himself. *Because* he recoils from visions so open and unsheltering, he produces a memorable verbal spareness: the fancy flinches, and refuses to offer its usual decorative appliqué.

Hunt now inserts a lament for Ariadne cobbled together from the various other poems in the *Heroides*, although the "cento" does have some original strokes. The naturalistic hoarseness that we heard in Ariadne's terror once again modifies the formal rhetorical patterns, as when she allows her speech to stall in incredulous repetitions:

> And yet, for nothing worse, you have *left me*;
> *Left me—left* Ariadne, sleeping too
> Fast by your side; and yet *for you, for you*,
> She left her father, country, home, and all. [Italics mine][59]

This gracelessness helps offset the statuesque anaphora of "Bequeathed to death, while yet a living thing, / Bequeathed to death through every sharp distress" and the metabole that balances "father, country, home, and all" with "Homeless, and fatherless, and husbandless."

Hunt pacifies Ariadne (rather as one might a troubled baby) with a glittering artifact, and before long we find her "watching it, full-eyed."[60] According to more usual versions of the myth, this is the crown of Thetis that Theseus gave Ariadne. In Hunt's account, however, it comes from Europa, and is included for the sake of an ecphrasis: he loves nothing better than to linger over a decorative interlude and catch his breath. We see this also in the advent of Bacchus, conceived almost entirely in terms of the Titian painting:

> Suddenly from a wood his dancers rush,
> Leaping like wines that from the bottle gush;
> Bounding they come, and twirl, and thrust on high
> Their thyrsuses, as they would rouse the sky;
> And hurry here and there, in loosened bands,
> And trill above their heads their cymballed hands:
> Some, brawny males, that almost show from far
> Their forceful arms, cloudy and muscular;
> Some, smoother females, who have nevertheless
> Strong limbs, and hands, to fling with and to press;
> And shapes, which they can bend with heavenward glare.
> And tortuous wrists, and backward streaming hair.
> A troop of goat-foot shapes came trampling after,
> That seemed, with tickling, stung to frisks and laughter;
> Butting and mumming, they jumped here and there
> With backward knees, and a strange tottering air;
> And some eat grapes; some drank; and others chased
> The women, or with leering heat embraced;[61]

All Hunt has done here is amplify the picture by doubling up its elements, reduplicating the "brawny males" from the bearded figure to the right of the picture. His strange epithet ("cloudy") to describe their limbs might have been prompted by the clouds in the top left-hand corner of the Titian, since their bulbous shapes to some extent balance the line of thigh and buttock opposed to them. The satyr in the foreground also proliferates into a host of "goat-foot shapes," its leaning posture rendered as "a strange tottering air." We can account for the uncomfortable dislocation of "tortuous wrists" by Titian's having flexed both wrists of Bacchus and one of Ariadne's to enhance the mobility of his composition.

Had he simply transposed Titian into words, Hunt would have produced a succinct and impressive tableau, but he chooses to enlarge the picture, driven as always by the impulse to take his eye off the larger design and decorate *in loco*. As in *Rimini*, the luxuriating fancy tends to trip itself up in the very abundance of its invention, and, again as in *Rimini*, the effect seems congested and repetitive, and loses itself in a welter of contesting subclimaxes. It is easy to see how Hunt has gone about his task. At crucial points of the processional, he falls back on Titian, segments of whose picture can be identified from time to time. So at lines 212ff. we recognize the painterly origin of "a crimson vest / Slung by two clasps, reached half way up his breast. / His fruity cheek was rounded off, and bent / Just near the dimpled chin; his eye intent, / And liquid dark" and then, more than forty lines later, come across another Titianesque moment: "but the young gladsome power / Leaped from his car, like a frank paramour" (lines 258–59). Even details that are not explicitly in Titian can be traced back to the choreography of the painting. Following the tradition of temporal compression and narrative simultaneity that goes back at least as far as the trecento, Titian has painted in the crown of Thetis top left as a stellar circlet. Bacchus, leaping from his chariot, strikes the pose of the Discobolus, and Hunt, reading the coronet as a quoit, has fancifully linked the two features in a way that Titian never intended:

> Yet I must not forget, that just before
> The guests withdrew, and now its use was o'er,
> The grateful god took off from his love's hair
> Her fervid crown; and with a leap i' the air,
> As when a quoiter springs to his firm eye,
> Whirled it in buzzing swiftness to the sky.
> Starry already, and with heat within,
> It fired as it flew up with a fierce spin,

> And opening into grandeur round and even,
> Shook its immortal sparkles out of heaven.[62]

From this Hunt moves into his coda, trying, as Keats would later do, to "theologize" and apply the myth.

Bacchus and Ariadne being in many respects Hunt's own apotheosis of the *fête champêtre*, he is eager to establish a continuity between divine junkets and the picnics he enjoyed with the Cowden Clarkes, Haydon, and Novello. This elision of ancient and modern derives in part from a desire to popularize his material by making it accessible, for as he himself observes in *The True Story of Vertumnus and Pomona*: "Weak and uninitiated are they who talk of things modern as opposed to the idea of antiquity; who fancy that the Assyrian monarchy must have preceded tea-drinking; and that no Sims or Gregson walked in a round hat and trousers before the times of Inachus."[63] The proem that Hunt tacked on to the 1832 version of *Hero and Leander* also spells out his intention to rescue the myth from pedants and scholiasts by stressing its human content, and so making it available to the common reader:

> Old is the tale I tell, and yet as young
> And warm with life as ever minstrel sung:
> Two lovers fill it—two fair shapes—two souls
> Sweet as the last for whom the death-bell tolls:
> What matters it how long ago, or where
> They lived, of whether their young locks of hair,
> Like English hyacinths, or Greek, were curled?
> We hurt the stories of the antique world
> By thinking of our school-books, and the wrongs
> Done them by pedants and fantastic songs,
> Or sculptures, which from Roman "studios" thrown,
> Turn back Deucalion's flesh and blood to stone.
> Truth is forever truth, and love is love;[64]

Thus when at the end of *Bacchus and Ariadne* Hunt "floridizes" a new tutelary function for Ariadne's crown, he does so on the assumption that fancy can bridge the centuries and commandeer a myth for his own philosophy of cheer:

> These, when they issue from the unclouded seas
> Preside o'er all sweet things; all luxuries
> That come from odorous gardens; all the bowers

> That lovers sit in, and the princely flowers
> Attired the brightest; all the cordial graces
> Waiting on kind intentions and frank faces;
> Nay, even the true and better taste of dress,
> The easy wear of inward gracefulness.
> Beneath this star, this star, where'er she be,
> Sits the accomplished female womanly:
> Part of its light is round about her hair;
> And should her gentle cheek be wet with care,
> The tears shall be kissed off, as Ariadne's were.[65]

This adjustment of myth to current ends surely inspired the end of Keats's *Ode to Psyche*, where confident future verbs also assert the eternal truth of the legend: "And there shall be for thee all soft delight / That shadowy thought can win, / A bright torch, and a casement ope at night, / To let the warm Love in!"[66]

The Gentle Armour (1832)

The Panther and *Mahmoud*, the poems that follow the epyllia in Milford's edition, are parables in which the emphasis falls less on the narrative line than on the moral finishing point, the epimythium. Perhaps because the parable cannot function if it is freighted with detail, Hunt shows unusual economy in his handling of these pieces. The sort of oriental luxuriousness we might otherwise have expected from him figures in only a few atmospheric lines, lines all the more atmospheric for their concision: "And they said, as they lay in their carpeted rooms."[67] In *Caractacus* by contrast, Hunt cannot resist the invitation to "ecphrase" the Roman luxuries he professes to despise, so that even while celebrating a tribal democracy (imaged by "a rude hut built on the wild champaign"),[68] he succumbs to rhetoric à la Tamburlaine:

> Lord of a thousand victories he
> Concentred his empire's majesty;
> That empire which stretches from Afric's pyres
> To the icy North's impassive fires;
> While Iberia and Mesopotamia display
> The arc of its rising and setting day.
> Purple and gold was the robe he wore,
> With its rich folds piled on the marble floor.
> Perfumes in clouds of incense arose,

> Bearing the odours of amber and rose
> To the ceilings of fretwork and ribs of gold,
> And paintings rich that their wreaths enfold.[69]

Hunt has forged this description from memories of Marlowe, Enobarbus's speech in *Anthony and Cleopatra*, and the global ranging in such eighteenth-century poems as *The Progress of Poesy* and *The Vanity of Human Wishes*. Its function, that of demonstrating the pride of Rome, has been all but swallowed up in the accumulation of material. This in turn shows that fanciful disconnection, that lack of focus—Clarice Short has called it "unmapability"—that always seems to attend such moments. Hunt's Roman palace, for example, improbably combines Renaissance frescos and Gothic ribbed vaults. The result might lack the coherence and moral "leanness," say, of *The Panther*, but it nonetheless offers local rewards of texture. An immature "Speech of Caractacus to Claudius Caesar" in the *Juvenilia* makes the same point as the later poem—"Yes; they shall again be free, / And triumph in their liberty"[70]—but *because* makes it makes it more austerely, and with greater focus, it lacks distinctive Huntian color, and cannot be distinguished from all the odes to British liberty that Thomson's *Alfred* spawned.

Generally, however, Hunt does not admit rich textures into his fabular verse, eager as he is to arrive at his moral destination. While we might admire his self-discipline in lopping and trimming distractions from his path, the result is sometimes bleak and sometimes banal. It is in the oriental poems especially that Hunt has striven to exscind the play of fancy. Turning to the original material from which *The Panther* was crafted, we find that he has we even gone so far as to *impose* a fabular shape on a simple anecdote:

> And this animal had been for a time under the restraint of man, and would let you pat it with your hand and caress it; but when it was goaded to excitement by the springtime, for in that season the pards begin to rut, it would rush into the mountains from longing to meet the male. . . .[71]

In some cases parable fuses with informal essay, and, if were not for the metrification of *Mahmoud*, we might otherwise have expected Hunt to turn it into an item for the *Indicator* or *Seer* or *Liberal*, where indeed it was first published:

> I have just read a most amazing thing,
> A true and noble story of a king:
> And to show all men, by these presents, how

> Good kings can please a Liberal, even now
> I'll vent the warmth it gave me in a verse:[72]

This is the popularizer at work once again, introducing his readers to the great heritage of Islamic parable and story, which in *The Religion of the Heart* he would later describe as "the noblest as well as the most abundant sources of fiction in the world."[73] Although Hunt pretends to admire the sovereign in *Mahmoud* for a commitment to principle (which could have killed his son), one suspects that he wrote the poem for the sake of a dramatic denouement. His own morals were more usually casuistic, and he took fright at anything too stern and inflexible:

> The man who from his alleged love of truth should sacrifice a fugitive to the sword, or a patient to the terrors of a nervous fever, would assuredly, from pole to pole, be held to be nothing but a cruel bigot.
>
> It becomes a Religion of the Heart to proclaim such cases exceptional and privileged; for thus humanity is assured, and as little harm done to the opposing duty as possible.[74]

Abou ben Adhem lies altogether closer to his heart as a man ready to interpret religion as charity rather than faith. He is the subject of Hunt's most famous poem, and yet, when all is said and done, one of his least distinguished. Its strength lies in the fact that it popularized a moving item of Muslim lore; its weakness lies in its nerveless, sagging meter. In "Making it rich, and like a lily in bloom" the stress on "and" fractures the dactyls, but fails to establish an iambic force of its own. Only at one point does the meter rise to the challenge: the point where it rolls out its the great credal statement: "Write me as one that loves his fellow-men."[75] This provided an epitaph for Hunt's tomb—a suitable choice if we recall that "Abou ben Adhem" is indirectly about a "happy death." As Ernest Leisy has pointed out, its larger context can be found in "the Islamic belief that on the night of Nous Shaaban (the second month of the Islamic year) God takes the golden book of mankind and crosses off the names of those he is calling to him in the coming year (i.e., those whom he loves)."[76] One should also note in passing that although Milford lists the poem as having been printed for the first time in 1836, Joseph and Linda Wolfe have found an earlier version in *The Amulet* (1834).[77]

About the other oriental narratives little need be said. They are competent but entirely unmemorable, versified anecdotes to illustrate Hunt's humanistic Deism. They could be subjoined to the list of "Christianist scriptures" that he placed at the end of *The Religion of the Heart*. Sometimes he utters a perfunctory aside to bring the fable into focus, as in "The Bitter Gourd"—"(for wise / Is but sage good, seeing through final eyes),"[78] and sometimes, as in *The Panther*, he grafts a moral onto the anecdote, making sure that we too view it "through final eyes." In *The Trumpets of Doolkarnein* hr turns up the volume at the end of a mild little tale so as to create a finale on the *sic transit gloria* topos. The resolving cosmic "smile" invites two constructions—a smile that dismisses (in compassionate scorn) the frail enterprises of humankind, and a smile of pure benignity proceeding from what Hunt called the "Great Beneficence":

> O thou Doolkarnein, where is now thy wall?
> Where now thy voice divine and all thy forces?
> Great was thy cunning, but its wit was small,
> Compared with Nature's least and gentlest courses.
> Fears and false creeds may fright the realms awhile;
> But Heaven and Earth abide their time, and smile.[79]

There is mild interest in the fact that some of these poems ingest their dedications. In "Jaffàr" Hunt invokes Shelley, in "The Inevitable," John Forster. One is tempted to smile when one recalls that the dedicatee sat for the portrait of Podsnap in *Our Mutual Friend*: "Forster, whose voice can speak of awe so well, / And stern disclosures, new and terrible, / This were a tale, my friend, for thee to tell. / Seek for it then in some old book; but take / Meantime this version, for the writer's sake."[80] Hunt then proceeds without a stanza break into the narrative proper, and must try to generate awe in the face of this chattiness.

Forster had been instrumental in publishing *The Religion of the Heart*—he came from a Unitarian background—and Hunt might have intended the dedication of "The Inevitable" as a quid pro quo for *Abraham and the Fire-Worshipper*, which Forster had suggested he versify. James Davies describes the commission as having been "obediently" performed,[81] and, as in much "obedient" verse, its dutifulness saps its energy, although half-submerged allusions to *King Lear* ("think of his grey hairs, / Houseless, and cuffed by such a storm as this")[82] give it a little zest, as does the use of stage dialogue and blank verse. This is an unusual and innovative choice for the otherwise trim, editorial form of the parable. Even so, when Abraham pronounces the closing *sententia*, he speaks like Leigh Hunt rather than like a Middle Eastern patriarch, and we hear a ventriloquial version of that thought he expressed to Shelley, viz., "a truly divine religion might yet be established, if charity were really made the principle of it, instead of faith": "There's more in this than prophet yet has known, / And Faith, some day, will all in love be shown."[83]

Unlike the oriental poems, Hunt's medieval narratives are generally expansive and unhurried. Bearing in mind that the success of *Rimini* partly depends on its indulgent *rubati*, its perpetual adjustments of tempo to suit the impulse of the moment, we might expect a correlation of length and merit in these poems. This is not the case, however. Part of the problem inheres in the fact that in both *The Gentle Armour* and *The Palfrey* Hunt has adapted French fabliaux, poems that stand or fall by their story-lines. It is one thing to conjure up a four-canto narrative from some tercets by Dante, tercets that present a situation rather than a blow-by-blow history; it is another to make adjustments here and there to a self-contained tale. The fancy simply finds itself hamstrung. What issues from the adaptation therefore is neither the scrupulous "Chattertonian" reconstruction of *The Tapiser's Tale*, nor the topicality and refreshment of an Augustan-style imitation, nor even a transcription into sober contemporary verse such as we find in Hunt's "narrative modernizations." The material of the fabliaux often seems too thin for the space it has been attenuated to fill, and the verse too flat to conceal the bleak, underfurnished interior it has somehow to grace.

Although it begins by parodying the epic *cano* of the *Aeneid* ("Arms and a vest I sing"), *The Gentle Armour* is not a mock-heroic poem, and Hunt later revised the line to read "A Lady's gift I sing," aware that his first version had given off a false generic signal. For in mock-heroic, the validity of the epic mode is never called into question—if it were, it could not discharge its corrective function of supplying heroic norms for unheroic things. These heroic norms have no appeal for Hunt, however, since he recoils from the aggressiveness and the morbid honor-cult of chivalry, and inclines toward things domestic and intimate (those elements that enter the "mock" half of the mock-heroic equation). *The Gentle Armour* goes about its business in a different way—as though a Pope had written *The Rape of the Lock* to satirize Homer and not the values of Hampton Court. Hunt himself pointed out in a preface in the 1860 edition (omitted from Milford) that he deliberately modified the narrative and tone of the original fabliau to accord with his own values:

> The main circumstance of this story—a knight fighting against three, with no other coat of mail than the delicatest garment of his mistress—is

taken from one of the Fabliaux that were versified by the late Mr. Way. [A summary of the original narrative follows.]

Allowance is to be made for the opinions of a different age; and we see, even here, right and wrong principles struggling in the perplexities of custom. But the cultivation of brute force is uppermost; and nothing can reconcile us to the disposition of the woman who could speculate upon such a tribute to her vanity. It is hoped that the heroine in the following version of the story, without being wanting in self-love, is a little better, and not unsuited to any age.[84]

Such bowdlerism is incidental, however. Hunt is no prude, and the fabliau, after, all is licensed to be racy. His chief aim is rather to mock romance conventions, the precedent for which must be sought in Byron. (Such a model seems a little odd in view his bitter attack on the poet only four years earlier in *Lord Byron and Some of His Contemporaries*.) Just as Byron upends the improbable formulae of romance, so Hunt travesties its extravagant absolutes in *The Gentle Armour*. The casual, mocking obeisance to cliché in "Young, handsome, blithe, loyal and brave *of course*" [italics mine][85] is wholly Byronic, and so, too, the conversational stop and start, the midsentence qualifications, the spry ad libitum of a passage such as this:

> The knight looked troubled to the last degree,
> Turned pale, then red, but said it could not be.
> With many sighs he said it, many pray'rs
> To be well construed—nay, at last with tears:
> And owned a knight might possibly be better,
> Who read the truth less nicely to the letter;
> But 'twas his weakness—'twas his education,—
> A dying priest had taught him, his relation,
> A kind of saint, who meant him for the church,
> And thus had left his breeding in the lurch;
> The good old man! he loved him, and took blame,
> (He owned it) thus to mix his love with shame:[86]

Despite their derivativeness, such moments are wholly successful. The kind of stylistic undress attempted in *The Story of Rimini* comes into its own here, fully legitimized by the satire. Couching the knight's speech in *oratio obliqua*, Hunt manages to cool the impact of the rhetoric—what was meant as impassioned discourse turns into flustered self-justification, all the accidents and non sequiturs of a conversational moment are caught in a freeze-frame:

"A dying priest had taught him, his relation." Because the satire pervades the whole poem, pastiche updatings of detail and language present no problems of accommodation. We are thus amused rather than troubled when the shift arrives in a parcel that might have been sent by a nineteenth-century mantua-maker: "With trembling hands the string is cut, they lift / A lid of pasteboard, and behold—a shift!"[87]

Like the oriental narratives that precede it in the 1860 arrangement of the poems, *The Gentle Armour*'s spare texture shows that in a parable moral content must override the charm of period detail. While one might once again wish to applaud the economy and rigorous self-discipline of the poet, a great deal has been lost in the process. That dalliance that is at once Hunt's greatest charm and his weakness (in narrative verse, at any rate) has been sacrificed to a crisp, propulsive tempo. Gone is the pageantry of *Rimini* or the atmospheric idyll of Hero at her tower casement, and in its place there is a determination to get on with the job. It even means that Hunt has to screw his courage to the sticking point, for, although he deplored the "cultivation of brute force" in the original fabliau, his story nonetheless constrained him to mount a tournament. In *Rimini* as in *Hero*, he might have availed himself of airy *occupatio* to clear the boards with a skip and a jump; here he gives us blow by blow. He takes care, however, to trivialize and limit the contest—"bloody weather" in other contexts might signify a rainy day:

> The trumpets blew their blast of bloody weather,
> The swords are out, the warriors rush together,
> And with such bulk and tempest comes the knight,
> One of the three is overborne outright,
> Saddle and man, and snaps his wrist.[88]

Only in *Captain Sword and Captain Pen* would Hunt again force his imagination against its grain, but in that poem the vigor and swing of the balladry creates its own textural interest. The effect here is somewhat denuded and grey. Whereas the cortège in *Rimini* inspires Hunt to voluptuous pageants, *The Gentle Armour* reveals an entirely different set of priorities, as witness the way he shorthands the wedding celebrations: "'Tis June; 'tis lovers' month; in short, they wed. / But how? like other people, you suppose, / In silks and state, as all good story goes."[89] This is self-restrained, but it is also perfunctory. Hunt has produced a more shapely narrative by stripping away the surface encrustation, but the content of that story is neither subtle or searching enough to compensate. The result is a Crabbean austerity without any Crabbean acumen.

The Palfrey (1842)

The same holds true of the spatial texture of *The Palfrey*, which the poet seems to have conceived as a sort of amplified ballad. In that amplification lies its weakness. Hunt found the germ of his narrative in the same collection of fabliaux that gave him *The Gentle Armour*. In this case, however, he found only a "prose abridgement of M. Le Grand . . . and its imitation in verse by Messrs. Way and Ellis, inserted in the latter's notes to the select translations from Le Grand by the former of those gentlemen."[90] With only fragmentary materials at hand, and the slimmest anecdote by way of story, Hunt had to cobble up a poem long enough to warrant publication by itself. The result is a dilution of material, an endless eking out and padding, a narrative that ambles because it dares not arrive home ahead of schedule. In *The Palfrey* we encounter a ballad with elephantiasis.

But this is only one aspect of its weakness. Hunt has also misjudged his meter. The anapestic tetrameter of parts 1 and 2 soon outstays its welcome. Had its jovial, roistering rhythm been boxed and confined in ballad quatrains, and had the poem been one fifth of its length, there would have been little to blame, though proportionally little to praise. When, however, anapests gallop through long paragraphs of narrative verse, they seem to take on all the unwelcome energy and boisterousness of hyperactive children. We must in all fairness concede that the fault lies in initial choice rather than performance, for Hunt has tried hard to avoid mechanical versification. The paragraph below shows how flexible and varied his modulations are, and how he has here and there set disyllabic feet (which I have italicized in the text) to brake the pounding of the triple beat:

<pre>
      x   -   x   x   -   x   x   -   x   -
    "Ah, ha," / quoth Sir Grey, / with his twink/ling eyes:
      x -   x -   x   x   - x x   -
    "The lass, / I see, / is both mer/ry and wise;
    x -   x x -   x x -   x   -
    I call / her to mem'/ry, an ear/nest child,
    -    x x   -   x x   -   x   x   -
    Now looking / straight at you, / now laughing / wild:
        [dactyllic and catalectic]
      x   -   x x -   x   -   x   x -
    "Tis now / —let me see / —five long / years ago,
    x   -   x x   -   x -   x   x   -
    And that's / a good time / for such / buds to blow.
</pre>

<pre>
 x   - x x -   x - x x -
</pre>
Well, dry / your outside, / *and mois*/ten your in;
<pre>
 x   -   x x - x x - x -
</pre>
This wine / is a bud / of my old/*est bin*;
<pre>
 x   x   - x x - x x -   x x -
</pre>
And we'll talk / of the dow/ry, and talk / of the day,
<pre>
 x   - x x - x -   x -
</pre>
And see / if her bill / *be good*, / *boy, eh?* [91]

Only the penultimate line takes form as regular anapestic tetrameter; Hunt has graced all the others with free and easy modulations. Even when he allows the tune to glare out ("And we'll talk of the dowry, and talk of the day"), he is swift to follow it with a line in which there is only one anapest, the rhythm hobbled by a dominance of iambs. Touches like these are trampled underfoot, however: the poem's rhythmic monotony overwhelms any local effects and adjustments. Having written two parts of the poem, Hunt clearly came to realize his mistake, but seems to have blanched at the prospect of revision. So he arbitrarily changed gear, and wrote the remaining three sections in a roughshod iambic tetrameter. Although this is easier on the ear, it does not scale great heights. Hunt is sometimes like a composer who overharmonizes to disguise a banal tune—in certain circumstances banality might be preferred to fidgetiness.

One can only speculate as to why he made these errors of judgment. Perhaps he had a political motive. The Merrie Old Englishness of the meter (songs like *The Fine Old English Gentleman* have a similar rhythmic crudity even when they avoid trisyllabic feet) might be of a piece with his bow to Victoria in the opening paragraph. Hunt is not using *The Palfrey* (as he used *Rimini*) as a vehicle of protest, even though the motif of parental tyranny recurs; he is currying favor with the House of Hanover, and reshaping his *Liberal* persona with this end in mind. Blotted though it is with this servility, the first paragraph is worth quoting as a whole, since it constitutes one of the few idylls in a poem otherwise given over to the trudge of a tedious story. Like the evocative notations of "A Now," passages such as these might well have fed into those atmospheric paragraphs at the start of *Bleak House* and *Little Dorrit*, where the author develops a single leitmotif in sentence after sentence, and applies it to every feature of the landscape. While Hunt's might lack the imaginative weight of those Dickensian paragraphs, it reveals the full charm of his idyllic mode, and one wishes he had given more of the kind:

'Tis June, and a bright sun burneth all,
Sir William hath galloped from Hendon Hall
To Kensington, where in a thick old wood
(Now its fair Gardens) a mansion stood,
Half like a fortress, and half like a farm,
A house which had ceased to be threatened by harm.
The gates frowned still, for the dignity's sake,
With porter, portcullis, and a bit of lake;
But ivy caressed their warm old ease,
And the rooks chuckled across the trees,
And burning below went the golden bees.
The spot was the same, where on a May morn
The Rose that toppeth the world was born.[92]

Hunt complained that the original fabliau from which he had fashioned *The Gentle Armour* had values he found untenable: "[T]he cultivation of brute force is uppermost." His natural mildness and pacifism leads him here to set his poem during the reign of Edward I, who, with Henry III, had helped to curb baronial power. He signals the change toward a new order of peace by adapting the old prophetic metaphor of plowshares and swords, spears and pruning hooks: "Half like a fortress, and half like a farm." This generates one set of metaphors, so that ivy caresses the frowning gates, and a moat turns into a purely ornamental "bit of a lake." Summer heat provides the other image base: the replication of burning sun in burning bees, the tactual encounter with sun-drenched masonry: "But ivy caressed their warm old ease." Why, then, the intrusion of Queen Victoria (born in Kensington Palace on 24 May), a clumsiness made more clumsy still by the nature of the compliment? To be a *rosa mundi* in a medieval setting is to court comparison with Rosamond!

The answer must be sought in the date of composition. In 1842, as Stephen Fogle has pointed out, "Southey sank further and further into mental and physical decay but did not die. Hunt was to have further opportunities for taking over the duties if not the office of the laureate. . . . A further attempt to establish himself as royalty's bard came in April of 1842, with the publication of *The Palfrey*, to which Hunt prefixed an Envoy, printed just after the title page in elaborate type. It was sent to Queen Victoria via Lord Melbourne. . . ."[93]

At first sight this sort of maneuvering might seem merely naïve, but there are other aspects of *The Palfrey* that are far less venial than venal. Chief above all is Hunt's effort to project a conservative persona. In *Rimini* he had distanced himself from many dominant values of the Middle Ages; here he seems bent on adopting them—not out of conviction, but for tendentious reasons of his own, which he could camouflage in archaeological rather than renovating pastiche. Hence the jaunty violence of this characterizing vignette:

> Now for any deed else, in love or in war,
> Knight bolder was none than the knight De la Barre,
> (So styled by the king, from a traitor tall,
> Whom he pitched over barriers, armour and all);
> Short distance he made betwixt point and hilt;
> He was not a man that at tourney and tilt
> Sat bowing to every fair friend he could spy,[94]

In a word, Sir William is a version of Giovanni, who in *Rimini* Hunt condemned for his lack of ease and courtesy, his want of *sprezzatura*. The only difference is the manic energy with which he has been galvanized. Hunt furthermore allows his hero to voice illiberal sentiments without any demur: "Her father, no Christian like her, but a Jew, / Would make me disburse."[95] This from the Hunt who, in his *Autobiography,* records the instinctive sympathy with Judaism he felt as a boy:

> But identifying no such dogmas [of eternal punishment] with the Jews . . .
> and reverencing them for their ancient connection with the bible, I used
> to go with some of my companions to the synagogue in Duke's Place. . . .
>
> These visits to the synagogue did me, I conceive, a great deal of good.
> They served to universalize my notions of religion, and to keep them
> unbigoted. It never became necessary to remind me that Jesus was a Jew.
> I have also retained through life a respectful notion of the Jews as a body.[96]

Despite his efforts to think and write like Scott, it is hard for Hunt to slough off his habitual diction and quirks of phrase. So when he speaks of wine as though it were a rose, on the one hand, and a canary, on the other, the reader recognizes a distinctive voice "chirping" out from amid the fustian: "This wine is a bud of my oldest bin"[97] and "Serious the venison and chirping the wine."[98] But these rare moments of truth—whatever the absolute merit of Hunt's mannerisms, they are at least authentic—give way to the sort of archaism he had avoided throughout *Rimini*:

> Nathless, Sir Gray excepteth from blame
> His nephew Sir Will, and his youthful fame;

> And each soundeth t'other, to learn what hold
> The youth and the lady may have of his gold.[99]

And there are several "I wis-es" scattered through the text, and two "gramercies" in the 1842 version, which were later replaced by "Your pardon, your pardon."[100] Even so, the poem shambles between its options of a thoroughgoing medievalism à la Scott, to which the "gramercies" provide an index, and the renovative procedures that Hunt had tried out in *Rimini*. For example, he breaks his period illusion at several points of *The Palfrey*, as in this attack on the materialism and prudery of the Victorian era:

> This riding double was no crime
> In the first great Edward's time;
> No brave man thought himself disgraced
> By two fair arms about his waist;
> Nor did the lady blush vermilion,
> Dancing on the lover's pillion.
> Why? Because all modes and actions
> Bowed not then to Vulgar Fractions;
> Nor were tested all resources
> By the power to purchase horses.[101]

One cannot imagine Victoria's warming even to this purified libertinism. Hunt's problem is how to advertise a flexible outlook without compromising his belief in sexual decency, how to seem open-minded without seeming rakish. His characterization of Sir Grey's aunt is *fabula de se*:

> A dame of rank, a dame of honour,
> A dame (may earth lie green upon her!)
> That felt for nature, love, and truth,
> And hated old age pawing youth:
> One that at no time held wrong right,
> Yet somehow took a dear delight
> By secret measures, sweet and strong,
> In giving right the zest of wrong.[102]

Having been pilloried by *Blackwood's* as a voluptuary, Hunt clearly felt that a poet laureate-in-waiting ought to allay any fears on this score. The justifications are less than unequivocal. Finding credit in discredit, we can at least applaud Hunt's integrity in the midst of a venal exercise. He cannot for the life of him make a mealy mouth. If, however, these asides do not damage

Hunt's character, they assuredly damage the stylistic integrity of his poem. Cast in a racy, contemporary idiom, they wreck the half-hearted "medieval" verse the poet has elsewhere tried to set in place. *The Palfrey*'s chief fault, when all is said and done, lies in the fact that it has not been thought through and edited. It is as discontinuous in style as it is in meter, and where the discontinuity of *Captain Sword and Captain Pen* points to the barely disciplined vitality and energy of that enterprise, *The Palfrey* has neither the resourcefulness nor the passion to carry us over the breaks in texture. Indeed its mock-medieval epigraphs, all travel without arrival, sum it up to perfection. One of them is dragged into the main body of the poem to provide a coda:

> The palfrey; and full well he goes;
> Oh! merrily well the palfrey goes;
> Grief great as any there he knows,
> Yet merrily ever the palfrey goes.[103]

While the intended effect is *faux-naïf* charm, the actual result is a nightmarish walking on the spot.

If *The Palfrey* ranks among the least impressive poems in the canon, so too do the two medieval adaptations that follow it. *The Glove and the Lions* retells a story from St. Foix's *Essay sur Paris,* which Schiller had already versified as *Der Handschuh.* Its attraction for Hunt, like that of the oriental fables, lay in its moral, and it is to that culminating moral, away from any circumstantial texture, that he once again directs his energy. Where Schiller is subtle and reticent, Hunt prefers blatancy, offering statement for implication. Compare "Den Dank, Dame, begehr ich nicht" (which Bulwer-Lytton has fudged as "Nay, spare me the guerdon, at least")[104] with Hunt's "'No love,' quoth he, 'but vanity, sets love a task like that.'"[105] *Godiva* also turns historical anecdote into fable: "That step, that upon Duty's ear is growing more and more, / Though yet, alas! it hath to pass by many a scorner's door."[106]

Godiva thus comes close to symbolizing Hunt's "Christianism" because she has retrieved the spirit of Christ from the corruption of custom:

> No unaccustomed deed she did, in scorn of custom's self,
> She that but wished the daily bread upon the poor man's shelf.
> Naked she went, to clothe the naked. New she was, and bold,
> Only because she held the laws which Mercy preached of old.[107]

The prosopopoeia, while it is meant to give an antique medieval patina to the poem, also tries to renovate our perception of Christ as the historical embodiment, like Godiva, of a moral force.

CAPTAIN SWORD AND CAPTAIN PEN (1835)

If the medievalism of *The Palfrey* is tired and unembodied, that of *Captain Sword and Captain Pen*, charged with the indignation of a generous spirit, presents an entirely different aspect. Hunt once remarked that Shenstone's "somewhat effeminate reputation as a pastoral songster, and an idler in a country-nest" had "hindered justice from being done to his powers of observation,"[108] a comment that, mutatis mutandis, could apply to himself. For *Captain Sword*, even though it occupies a unique place in the canon, gives the lie to Hunt's own reputation as a "pastoral songster." Its vigorous beginning recalls the *chanson d'aventure*. Here, however, the writer is not trying to manufacture a conformity to medieval values, but rather making them an instrument of irony:

> Captain Sword got up one day,
> Over the hills to march away,
> Over the hills and through the towns,
> They heard him coming across the downs,
> Stepping in music and thunder sweet,
> Which his drums sent before him into the street.[109]

Captain Sword and Captain Pen is an inclusive poem, melding a variety of forms and a variety of materials. Because it opposes two embodied points of view, it invites classification as Menippean satire, with all the attendant range (and ranginess) of that form. Hunt has versified with extreme freedom and flexibility. His big, disorderly paragraphs and unheralded changes of line project the sort of improvisation we generally expect of him, except that here it is not at the service of rococo ease and amiable laxness. We should think rather of the angry, urgent tone associated with Skeltonic verse, as though the poet's indignation were too fierce to bother with niceties of form. At the same time, this indignation is modified by a cool, distancing mockery, possibly inspired by Samuel Butler. The opening four lines of *Captain Sword* make up a Hudibrastic quatrain if we detach them from their paragraph, and indeed whole sections, if we lineate them differently, suggest the half-disguised presence of this stanza, a generic signal for the fatuity of Captain Sword. As a further complication to an already complex texture, Hunt also recalls the innocence of the nursery by alluding to the Piper's son, whose only tune was "Over the hills and far away." This in turn recalls an air from the *Beggars' Opera* in which MacHeath converts criminal transportation into an idyll:

> *Were I sold on* Indian *Soil*
> *Soon as the burning Day was clos'd,*
> *I could mock the sultry Toil,*
> *When on my Charmer's Breast repos'd.*
> Mach. *And I would love you all the Day,*
> Polly. *Every Night would kiss and play,*
> Mach. *If with me you'd fondly stray*
> Polly. *Over the Hills and far away.*[110]

The poem therefore begins with a *faux-naïf* innocence, suggesting that the pageant of Captain Sword is as innocent as a nursery rhyme. "Over the hills and far away" has the effect of removing war from the lives of the people who hail it—thus endowing it with a misplaced prestige—and it also suggests that Captain Sword is as heartless as his ballad-opera prototype.

The fact that the phrase itself encases the whole first section (the figure *inclusio*) gives it additional importance in the design of the poem: "And Captain Sword went whistling gay, / 'Over the hills and far away.'"[111] In between these structural brackets Hunt has inserted a pageant in his most gorgeous manner. But whereas in *Rimini* the effect was genuinely festive, there are elements of unease in *Captain Sword* that turn the cortège into a *danse macabre*. Abstract nouns give a disquieting, spectral feel to horses and swords, and register massed cavalry as "a clustering sound, / Of shapely potency" and "a threatening charm, / With mortal sharpness at each right arm."[112] Although this stylistic quirk is not peculiar to the poem in hand, it rises here from being a mannerism to a genuinely expressive device. (It is more usual for Hunt to use it as an appliquéd ornament, one which he probably found in Chapman's late translations. For instance, in the "Homeric" *Ode to Pan* we find such extravagances as "cliffy highnesses" and "wat'ry softnesses.")[113]

Not only is Hunt menacingly vague about the furniture of war, but he also stresses the impersonality and will-lessness of the soldiers. In *Rimini* he repeatedly specifies individuals in the crowd, whereas in this poem only Captain Sword is foregrounded, presiding over the procession like *Mors* itself. "Indifferent-eyed," he mocks the Renaissance ideal of *sprezzatura* by being *really* indifferent and impassive, and in him Hunt consummates a line of characters going back to the figure of Giovanni, characters who confuse manliness with insensitivity:

> He nevertheless rode indifferent-eyed,
> As if pomp were a toy to his manly pride,
> Whilst ladies loved him the more for his scorn,

And thought him the noblest man ever born,
And tears came to the bravest eyes,
And hearts swelled after him double their size,
Seemed to think wrong's self in him could not be wrong,
Such love, though with bosom about to be gored,
Did sympathy get for brave Captain Sword.[114]

In *The Religion of the Heart*, Hunt deplores all moral and social perversions sanctioned by the heritage of custom. Writing about the Old Testament, for example, he remarks that civilization "has in fact outgrown it, and ought to be considerate and brave enough to say so; indeed is beginning to say so; and the oftener it is said, in no unkind manner, the better. . . ."[115] In *Captain Sword* he likewise urges that civilization should abandon its fatalistic belief in the necessity of war, and, as a first step, renounce its glorification in the military pageant. Captain Sword enjoys the prestige traditionally reserved for the soldier, a source of moral confusion: "Seemed to think wrong's self in him could not be wrong."

The poem's design thus presents a systematic oscillation between false ideals and the reality that gives them the lie. Viewed as a festive pageant, the army *seems* an organ of camaraderie and happiness, an illusion fostered by the Robin Hoodishness of "He and his merry men, all as one."[116] This is only the lull before the storm, however. To heighten still further the strength of his contrasts, Hunt presents the battlefield itself in his familiar idyllic mode:

It was a spot of rural peace,
Ripening with the year's increase,
And singing in the sun with birds,
Like a maiden with happy words—
With happy words she scarcely hears
In her own contented ears,
Such abundance feeleth she
Of all comfort carelessly.[117]

Like Gray in his *Eton College Ode*, Hunt sets the unconsciousness of present innocence against a grim futurity of violence and death. The preterit in "It *was* a spot" belongs not so much to the narrative as to the elegiac past tense, the tense of irrecoverable loss. This idyll is about to end; the sufficient, self-fulfilling cycle of nature about to be disrupted; the "spot" (Hunt's favorite noun for rural intimacy) about to lose its cozy circumscription. While it is not unusual for poets to hark back to violence that once transpired in a tranquil landscape (Southey's *The Battle of Blenheim* comes to mind), Hunt's reverse procedure achieves an altogether greater power—an effect of wounds opened rather than scars healed. It might well have inspired the opening paragraph of *The Battle of Life* four years later. Like Hunt, Dickens sets the battle in a ripening summer landscape, and displaces the rural crop with grapes of wrath:

> Once upon a time, it matters little when, and in stalwart England, it matters little where, a fierce battle was fought. It was fought upon a long summer day when the waving grass was green. Many a wild flower formed by the Almighty Hand to be a perfumed goblet for the dew, felt its enamelled cup filled high with blood that day, and shrinking dropped. Many an insect deriving its delicate colour from harmless leaves and herbs, was stained anew that day, and shrinking dropped. The painted butterfly took blood into the air upon the edges of its wings. The stream ran red. The trodden ground became a quagmire, whence, from sullen pools collected in the prints of human feet and horses' hoofs, the one prevailing hue still lowered and glimmered at the sun.[118]

This is impressive, but too stylized to convey the full horror of the battle—mutilation and violence are offstaged by the metonymy that converts blood to pigment, and chaos by the balance and poise of the *epiphora*.

Hunt, on the other hand, knows that this sort of distanced formality is not the stuff that protest poems are made of. He concedes that for as long as soldiers are marching or simply readying for battle, they present an awe-inspiring spectacle. He acknowledges their noble resignation and steady temperament with broad strokes of prosopopoeia ("Tranquil Necessity gracing Force"). But, like the abstract nouns in the marching sequence, these personifications tend also to depersonalize the protagonists. Even the simile that describes the massing of the troops reduces them to diagrams on a strategist's chart:

> Steady! steady! The masses of men
> Wheel and fall in, and wheel again,
> Softly as circles drawn with a pen. [119]

This tidy, abstracting procedure offsets the chaos of battle when finally Hunt unleashes it, since war can be glamorized only for as long as the fact of violence is effaced or suppressed. At this point the meter breaks into a slashing trochaic measure, with an insurgent anapest here and there to evoke the hoofs of chargers:

```
         -    x    -    x    -    x  -
       Death for / death! the / storm begins;
       -    x    -    x   x -   x   x   -
       Rush the / drums in / a tor/rent of dins;
       -    x    -  x    -     x    -
       Crash the / muskets, / gash the swords;
       -    x    -  x   x  -   x    -
       Shoes grow / red in / a thou/sand fords;[120]
```

In the midst of such chaos, Hunt's mannered manipulations of syntax and idiom take on a new expressiveness as emblems of forced displacement and violation. A phrase like "a torrent of dins" comes into its own because it gives a confusing numerousness to a abstract noun, and so do the subjectless verbs, half imperative, half indicative, which suggest that the instruments of death have an unmanageable animation of their own. Hunt's characteristic use of the transferred epithet (transferred often to the point of misapplication) also changes its mannered grace into power.

When we read of "plashing ears" we might think, "Oh, another loose confusion of sensuous object with sensory subject"—only to realize that the ears have indeed been ground to pulp, to a plashing mess of blood and tissue. When we read an utterance like "Trod on the ground are the tender cries" we might say, "Oh, another clumsy concretization"—only to perceive that real human heels are indeed pressing upon and bursting real human lips. This is brave stuff from a poet who would ordinarily shrink from images of violence, but he knows that, if the poem is to work, the reality of war must cancel the superficially attractive trappings of pageantry and heroism with which it has been clothed. Resorting to the rhetorical technique of *aversio*, which switches the line of address, Hunt confronts us in the very act of recoiling and withdrawing our imaginations from the material he has forced upon us:

> Oh! shrink not thou, reader! Thy part's in it too;
> Hast not thy praise made the thing they go through
> Shocking to read of, but noble to do?[121]

Hunt repeats the assault with even greater intensity in part 4 of the poem:

> A wound unutterable—O God!
> Mingles his being with the sod.

> "I'll read no more."—Thou must, thou must:
> In thine own pang doth wisdom trust.

His nails are in earth, his eyes in air
And "Water!" he crieth—he may not forbear.
Brave and good was he, yet now he dreams
The moon looks cruel; and he blasphemes.

"No more! no more!" Nay this is but one;
Were the whole tale told, it would not be done
From wonderful setting to rising sun.[122]

I find this colloquy both moving and original, something for which there seem to be only a few precedents. The same insistence of speaker and flinching reluctance of listener occurs in George Herbert's "Dialogue":

> *That is all, if that I could*
> *Get without repining;*
> *And my clay, my creature, would*
> *Follow my resigning:*
> *That as I did freely part*
> *   With my glorie and desert,*
> *Left all joyes to feel all smart— —*
> Ah! no more: thou break'st my heart.[123]

More impassioned and anguished still is the bedroom scene from *Hamlet*:

> *Ham.*   Nay, but to live
>   In the rank sweat of an enseamed bed,
>   Stew'd in corruption, honeying and making love
>   Over the nasty sty!
> *Queen.*   O speak to me no more!
>   These words like daggers enter my ears.
>   No more, sweet Hamlet.[124]

The forced confrontations and anguished reproaches in *Captain Sword* index an inner struggle within the poet himself, a poet who is doing violence to his idyllic cast of mind, rather as the champions of animal rights do violence to their natural sensitivity, and relay the horrors of vivisection to secure its abolition. When in the past the going got sticky, Hunt would almost inevitably turn to summary *occupatio*. This after all, is the option of which even Thackeray avails himself in *Vanity Fair*—and Thackeray's sensibility is altogether bluffer and more resilient than Hunt's:

We do not claim to rank among the military novelists. Our place is with the non-combatants. When the decks are cleared for action we go below and wait meekly. We should only be in the way of the manoeuvres that the gallant fellows are performing overhead. We shall go no further with the __th than to the city gate: and, leaving Major O'Dowd to his duty, come back to the major's wife, and the ladies and the baggage."[125]

Hunt, needless to say, remains on deck throughout *Captain Sword*, and so earns the right to reject the "gallantry" that, in the absence of firsthand experience, society attributes to war. He rejects out of court the sort of unthinking reflexes we find even in so gentle a poet as Keble: "'Tis so in war—the champion true / Loves victory more, when dim in view / He sees the glories gild afar / The dusky edge of stubborn war, / Than if th' untrodden bloodless field / The harvest of her laurels yield."[126] *Captain Sword* presents an actual bloody field, where the mud might even be the mud of the human body, ground to shapelessness by the press of war:

> To murder, and stab, and grow liquid with lives—
> Gasping, staring, treading red mud,
> Till the drunkenness's self makes us steady of blood?[127]

In such a context, the military "gallant" is disclosed for what he is, the rider of the pale horse in Revelation:

> And now there is one that hath won the crown;—
> One pale visage stands lord of the board—
> Joy to the trumpets of Captain Sword![128]

The assonant blending of "one" into "won" declares that the only victor in war is war itself, the principle of violence embodied in Captain Sword. Once again Hunt wrenches English idiom by making a visage *stand* as "lord of the board." Because they have been alienated from our usual habits of syntax, such moments seem disquieting, and that is precisely the effect Hunt intends. We need to remember similar slides and slippages in *Paradise Lost*, about which T. S. Eliot has said:

> I do not think that we should attempt to *see* very clearly any scene that Milton depicts: it should be accepted as a shifting phantasmagory. To complain, because we first find the arch-fiend "chain'd on the burning lake," is to expect a kind of consistency which the world to which Milton has introduced us does not require.[129]

A "shifting phantasmagory" is just the right phrase to apply to *Captain Sword*, with its *cacosyntheton* (violations of idiom), its syntactic "runniness," and its loose, amoebic structure.

In the next section, "Of the Ball That Was Given to Captain Sword," Hunt piles up Wardour Street archaisms to show that distance (whether temporal or spatial) is a necessary condition for glamorizing war. The romance "ladye," and the "eth" suffix of "floweth" and "holdeth" provide a sense not so much of "Over the hills and far away" as of "Over the hills and long ago":

> Boot, nor sword, nor stern look hath he,
> But holdeth the hand of a fair ladye,
> And floweth the dance a palace within
> Half the night to a golden din,[130]

The dance provides Hunt with an occasion to show his skill in programmatic metrics. There are lilting trisyllables to register the waltz, and incisive caesuras to mark off the components of a galop. But all the time the metric virtuosity is serving his theme, for the ball is simply an extension of the military order and pageantry that conceals the brutal facts of war:

> And the waltz, that loveth the lady's waist;
> And the galopade, strange agreeable tramp,
> Made of a scrape, a hobble, and stamp;
> And the high-stepping minuet, face to face,
> Mutual worship of conscious grace;[131]

Hunt's antiphon to the victory ball is a *danse macabre*—a ghoulish parody of the dance "whiche betokeneth concorde." Its figures are disorderly and graceless, its trampings mutilate, its hobblings are the hobblings of the maimed:

> The place where he writhes, hath up-beaten the ground.
> Like a mad horse hath he beaten the ground,
> And the feathers and music that litter it round,
> The gore, and the mud, and the golden sound.
> Come hither ye cities! ye ball-rooms take breath!
> See what a floor hath the Dance of Death![132]

The *epiphora* of "up-beaten the ground" / "beaten the ground" *formally* suggests the triumphant parallelisms of the psalms; *actually* it conveys a sufferer's thrashing impotently on the spot.

However, miseries like these have no effect on the wagers of war, and Captain Sword sets out again to repeat the cycle, a moment marked once more by archaic tense inflections and *cacosyntheton* ("sneering trumpets" and "stamping drums"). As before, Hunt puts war in the context of a pastoral landscape:

> Sneereth the trumpet, and stampeth the drum,
> And again Captain Sword in his pride doth come;
> He passeth the fields where his friends lie lorn,
> Feeding the flowers and the feeding corn,
> Where under the sunshine cold they lie,
> And he hasteth a tear from his old gray eye.[133]

Just as the trumpet and the drum seem to act intransitively, as though compelled by a demonic force of their own, so the corn, which ought to be feeding human beings, is stripped of its direct object, and left to dangle intransitively. Indeed it is human beings who are feeding *it* from beneath the ground.

After this upsetting episode, Hunt offers us respite and breaks off to cleanse both mind and soul. He does so by contemplating the sun as Keats had contemplated "the night's starr'd face"[134] to rid his soul of distress. Nature's eternal rightness measures the transitory wrongness of human actions. The respite is well earned, for never before had he written, and never again would he write, poetry of such graphic violence. George Gilfillan, nine years after the publication of *Captain Sword*, suggested that Hunt was incapable of anything beyond a fanciful and fragmentary lyricism: "His great want is not of fancy, nor of feeling, nor of language; it is that of sustained and masculine strength."[135] This fails to account for the inner parts of *Captain Sword*, which is the first antiwar poem in the language, or at least the first antiwar poem of the kind that Wilfred Owen would come to write—poems that directly address the issue of violence. Its horrors set it apart from all its predecessors. In *The Battle of Blenheim*, for example, a skull is barely recognized for what it is, so "large, and smooth, and round"[136] has it become in its conversion to symbol. *Captain Sword* is filled with atrocities altogether more immediate: "Another is mouthless, with eyes on cheek."[137]

Having gritted his teeth and forced himself through this purgatory, Hunt uses the last parts of *Captain Sword* to offer a pacifist solution. In James Thompson's words, it "concludes with a version of the Romantic apocalypse, the expression of which links Hunt not only to his friend Shelley,

but also to Wordsworth and Blake."[138] One might add that the poet also
seems to be recalling the great cosmic embrace of Schiller's *Ode to Joy*. But
of all these, it is Shelley who supplies the chief inspiration. Hunt was almost
certainly mindful of the choruses from *Hellas* when he wrote his millennial
coda. If in most of his verse he lacks Shelley's passion—that ability to
translate ideological fervor into tremulous, aspirant poetry—on this occasion the poetry does indeed take on a Shelleyan resonance. Hunt virtually
says as much when, in the 1849 preface, he claimed that it had been written
in his "later and more spiritual manner, which experience led him to adopt
after quitting the material school of Dryden"[139] (though I have not been able
to discover a substantive change between earlier and later poetry).

In the finale, Captain Sword, like all violent men, becomes prey to his
own megalomania, and takes the messianic titles of Revelation to himself:
"Captain Sword, like a witless thing, / Of all under heaven must needs be
king, / King of kings, and lord of lords, / Swayer of souls as well as of swords."[140]
This self-apotheosis turns him into a familiar compound ghost, compounded
of all military-minded people, no matter what their ideology. That is why
Hunt absorbs into him both Napoleon and Wellington—a continuity of
vision that blends even traditional adversaries. Captain Pen now enters the
poem, compounded in turn from all who believe in reason and peace:

> Then suddenly came he with gowned men,
> And said, "Now observe me—*I'm* Captain Pen:
> *I'll* lead all your changes—I'll write all your books—
> I'm everything—all things—I'm clergyman, cooks,
> Clerks, carpenters, hosiers,—I'm Pitt—I'm Lord Grey.[141]

The stage is thus set for a psychomachia, one waged not in the individual
but in the collective psyche of the human race. Whereas war has leveled by
death, knowledge levels by democracy.

Hunt even equates it with the principle that governs and harmonizes
the cosmos—"I'm everything—all things." Knowledge, indeed, is the
handmaid of the meliorism that lies at the heart of his creed. He believed so
fervently in progress that his mind refused to encompass even the eternal
stagnation and stasis of hell:

> Upon this innermost heart of man, God, the Great First Cause, in the
> mysterious graduality of his ways, imprinted those first sentiments of
> good and just, to grow with his growth of knowledge, and strengthen with

his strength in wisdom, which, however imperfectly read by conscience
for a time, were never wholly overlooked by it; which, however forgotten
or renounced by passion, have never been without some regret from passion; and which, however confused with local or other ordinances, or
refused participation in their authority, have never failed to prove their
sole and exclusive divineness, by remaining whole while others perished,
and by meeting with love and recognition in every corner of the earth,
instead of dispute and hatred.[142]

Just as Hunt turned to the sun in a self-cleansing gesture after the horrors of war,
so he conceives knowledge, the antitype of war as a second sun, one that takes
to the skies. Again a Shelleyan note sounds through the poetry, enriching it and
investing it with fervor. Some of the excitement and propulsiveness can be
traced to a repeated use of anadiplosis, the double thrust of which evokes the
centrifugal rush of the new science as it comes in being, born of itself:

> And at midnight the sound grew into a roll
> As the sound of all gatherings from pole to pole,
> From pole unto pole, and from clime to clime,
> Like the roll of the wheels of the coming of time;—
> A sound as of cities, and sound as of swords
> Sharpening, and solemn and terrible words,
> And laughter as solemn, and thunderous drumming
> A tread as if all the world were coming.
> And then was a lull, and soft voices sweet
> Called into music those terrible feet,
> Which rising on wings, lo! the earth went round
> To burn of their speed with a golden sound;
> With a golden sound, and a swift repose,
> Such as the blood in the young heart knows;[143]

In contrast to this weighty, cumulative progression, Captain Sword sticks in
the past, outmoded by his own unyieldingness. Like a bizarre protagonist in
a John Crowe Ransom poem, he turns to the wall and rusts to death: "And
so, like the tool of a disused art, / He stood at his wall and rusted apart"[144]—
a whimper justly supplanting all his bangs. Hunt said of Carlyle that "it is
better to contemplate the dark side of things in his pages than in most; for
behind all, like the sun behind the tempest, is a warm and even smiling
heart."[145] The same could be said of this disturbing but finally affirmative
war poem.

THE BALLADS OF ROBIN HOOD (1820; 1855)

From the dark and energetic protest of *Captain Sword and Captain Pen* we turn to some of the sunniest of all the narrative poems, *The Ballads of Robin Hood*. Although Hunt's subtitle specifies these ballads as having been written "for children," they seem not to have established themselves in the nursery. One reason for this might lie in the absence of any memorable incantatory passage—Hunt offers nothing comparable to the catalog of rats in *The Pied Piper of Hamelin* or the driving refrain of Noyes's *Highwayman*. Then again, the anticlerical cast of the ballads might also have served to marginalize them in orthodox Victorian families. Hunt seems to have had a shrewd idea of what children *do* enjoy as opposed to what they ought, and must have sensed that the antinomianism of the Robin Hood legend is a major part of its appeal. We would surely not be wrong to speculate that children who from infancy had been dosed with the starchy, moralizing poems of Isaac Watts might have been attracted to an amoral life in the greenwood, a prospect altogether more pleasant than that of improving each shining hour. After he had launched the first two ballads (*Robin Hood a Child* and *Robin Hood's Flight*) in 1820, Hunt produced another two in 1855—*Robin Hood as Outlaw* and *How Robin Hood and His Outlaws Lived in the Woods*. Clearly the sequels were written to fill a felt gap in children's literature. In the intervening years Mrs. Alexander had published her *Hymns for Little Children*, hymns that consolidated the Wattsian tradition of the paragon poem. Such poems urge the child's obedience, conformity, and submission to the edicts of an adult world ("Christian children all must be, / Mild, obedient, good as he")[146] and are miles removed from the anticlericalism of the *Robin Hood Ballads*. The antagonism between church and outlaw was at least as old as the legend itself, as the following lines from *Piers Plowman* attest: "But I can rymes of Robyn Hood . and Randolf erle of Chestre / Ac neither of owre lorde ne of owre lady . the leste that euere was made."[147]

Honoring the subversiveness implicit in the ballads, Hunt banished the cautionary tale from their confines. There are no gruesome denouements to cow children into submission, but rather a celebration of freedom and anarchy. Hunt was an unusually liberal parent for his time, and brought up his children—with varying success—on principles culled from Rousseau. Not wanting to crib, cabin, and confine their spirits, he might well have erred in the other direction, or so at least Byron thought when he denounced the young Hunts as "Yahoos."[148] Thus, far from punishing the young Robin for his pranks and merriment, Hunt invites his readers to applaud him. The following quatrains seem deliberately to "set up" and knock down the formulas of the paragon poem, in which children were certainly not invited to be bold, nor—one imagines—were defiant curls generally appreciated. (Longfellow, indeed, once suggested a connection between a little girl's curl and her schizophrenic behavior!)

> Robin was a gentle boy,
>   And therewithal as bold;
> To say he was his mother's joy,
>   It were a phrase too cold.
>
> His hair upon his thoughtful brow
>   Came smoothly clipped, and sleek,
> But ran into a curl somehow
>   Beside his merrier cheek.[149]

Because he rejects the world of adult disapproval, Hunt comes close to recreating Robin Hood as Robin Goodfellow:

> Merriest was he of merry boys,
>   And would set the old helmets bobbing
> If his uncle asked about the noise,
>   'Twas "If you please, sir, Robin."[150]

No hint of corporal punishment here; no supperless exile to the nursery. Even so, Robin is not wholly wild. Hunt seems to imply that precisely because his "animal spirits" have been channeled into pranks, he can quieten into docility: "And yet if the old man wished no noise, / He'd come and sit at his knee, / And be the gravest of grave-eyed boys, / And not a word spoke he." Perhaps this is the voice a busy author, begging his offspring for at least some peace and quiet.

Having thus, in the "bildungsroman" of the suite, shown no mindless submission to authority, the grown Robin adopts an outlook akin to those of *The Examiner* and *The Liberal*. In a skillful adaptation of ballad procedure (the antithetic use of metonymy), Hunt connects parental influence with these social attitudes. His model is a quatrain in *Sir Patrick Spens* ("The first line that Sir Patrick read, / A loud laugh laughèd he; / The neist line that Sir Patrick read, / A tear blinded his ee"),[151] which he applies to a dual view of mother's grave and usurping abbey:

> Often when Robin looked that way,
>> He looked through a sweet thin tear;
> But he looked in a different manner, they say,
>> Towards the Abbey of Vere.
>
> He cared not for its ill-got wealth,
>> He felt not for its pride;
> He had youth, and strength, and health,
>> And enough for one beside.[152]

This sense of personal wrong is soon generalized and applied to medieval society as a whole. Here Hunt perceives the church to be as imperious and oppressive as royalty, and, to make this point, dovetails tonsure (disclosing physical crowns) with the crowns of kings: "And he thought him then of the friars again, / Who rode jingling up and down, / With their trappings and things as fine as the king's, / Though they wore but a shaven crown."[153] But while he might have agreed with Robin Hood in his social judgments, he must surely have felt some unease about the violence of his methods. He gets round this crux by objectifying the victims. In other contexts, his spirit would have revolted at the killing of a deer, but here it is forced upon him by the exigencies of his chosen myth. All he can do is to sanitize the moment of slaughter by extending the vitality of the animal's leap into a death throe—"And a leaping deer, with one leap higher, / Lies motionless in the fern."[154] In much the same way, he clothes the murder of the abbot in similes that reduce it to a household prank. The human body is denatured into an unglamorous artifact, and the arrow accordingly pierces an inanimate texture:

> As in a leathern butt of wine,
>> Or dough, a household lump,
> Or a pumpkin, or a good beef chine,
>> Stuck that arrow with a dump.[155]

Hunt also turns Robin Hood's subsequent murders into innocent feasts, the similes of carving knife and gravy displacing the actual sword and the blood it lets:

> A monk to him was a toad in the hole,
>> And a priest was a pig in grain,
> But a bishop was a baron of beef.
>> To cut and come again.[156]

Since he clearly conceived the ballads as a feast of misrule, he must have felt such tactics were in order.

Violence of one sort or another has a central place in the ballad tradition, and Hunt also has to confront the issue in his "adult" ballads—*Wallace and Fawdon* and "Kilspindie." His solution in one instance is to resort to a kind of solemn parody, making a "screech" rather than a head the object of decapitation, a screech he jauntily prolongs by anadiplosis:

> Wallace with his dreadful sword,
> Without further speech,
> Clean cut off dark Fawdon's head,
> Through its stifled screech:
>
> Through its stifled screech, and through
> The arm that fenced his brow;[157]

As romantic ballads go, these two are certainly quite creditable, conscientious in the way *The Tapiser's Tale* is conscientious. However, unlike *La Belle Dame Sans Merci* or *The Rime of the Ancient Mariner*, they remain marginal for the simple reason that Hunt has undertaken the reconstruction with an "academic" rather than a personal motive. *Wallace and Fawdon* and "Kilspindie" have no vehicular function; they are contained by their own careful research.

Not so the *Robin Hood* suite, into which the poet's own ideology and expressive mannerisms have entered. So instead of trying to reproduce the austere heroics of border warfare, he taps his unique idyllic vein, admitting greenwood luxury and delicate effects of diction. *Robin Hood a Child* begins as a *reverdie*, written in a style quite different from the ballad "manliness" we find in *Wallace and Fawdon*. Only rococo art can convert showers to silver and birdsong to droplets:

> It was the pleasant season yet,
> When the stones at cottage doors
> Dry quickly while the roads are wet,
> After the silver showers.
>
> The green leaves they looked greener still,
> And the thrush, renewing his tune,
> Shook a loud note from his gladsome bill
> Into the bright blue noon.[158]

This might not be vintage balladry, but, without question, it is vintage Hunt, and presents *in parvo* the strength and weakness of his narrative verse. It is a paradoxical strength in weakness, for it is when he breaks the "rules"—when he idyllizes the heathy bleakness of the ballad tradition, or when he lets his tales bulge with digressions and incidental detail—that he comes into his own. In those idylls and digressive bulges of the tales we find the best poetry; they are the nodes at which the fancy shoots forth and flourishes. Hunt was not on the whole suited to narrative verse. He lacked the rigor to keep up the pace and get to the goal. And when he tried to do this, the verse invariably went grey and flat. Rococo, after all, is more an art of leisure than of strenuous purpose.

4

Political and
Critical Poems

The tag "Political and Critical Poems" would seem at first to banish any ideas of idyll and rococo pleasance, but even though the material of this chapter tends not to foster the atmosphere of Hunt's recreational verse, the relaxation and looseness of his structures, the graceful way in which he levels reproach and criticism, and the relative absence of *saeva indignatio*—all these features suggest that satire and fancy are indeed capable of lying down together as lion with lamb. Satiric verse, after all, derives from the Latin *lanx satura*, and the metaphors of crammed plate or indeterminate stew have invariably sanctioned structural license and variety in the form. And even though satire is popularly associated with bitterness, it has its milder strain. Horace's temperate, companionable persona, delighting in the idyll of the Sabine farm, comes close enough to Hunt's. However, this is not to say that Hunt was incapable of malice. As he himself admitted, some of his early critical efforts had a touch of arrogance, and he later became ungenerous when, after the disappointment of Italy, he wrote *Lord Byron and Some of His Contemporaries*. On the whole, though, he was a kindly person, and wrote an essentially kind form of satire. Hobbes had defined laughter as "nothing else but sudden glory arising from a sudden conception of some eminency in ourselves by comparison with the infirmity of others, or with our own formerly: for men laugh at the follies of themselves past, when they come suddenly to remembrance, except they bring with them any present dishonour." In *Wit and Humour* Hunt takes issue with that:

> Hobbes refers all laughter to a sense of triumph and "glory;" and upon the principle here expressed, his opinion seems to be justifiable; though I cannot think it entirely so on the scornful ground implied by him. His limitation of the cause of laughter looks like a saturnine self-sufficiency. There are numerous occasions, undoubtedly, when we laugh out of a

contemptuous sense of superiority, or at least when we think we do. But
on occasions of pure mirth and fancy, we only feel superior to the pleasant
defiance which is given to our wit and comprehension; we triumph, not
insolently but congenially; not to any one's disadvantage, but simply to our
own joy and reassurance.[1]

In view of such pronouncements, and in view of the fact that his prose essays
(like most of his verse satire) show next to no bitterness and spleen, Stuart
Tave has suggested that we regard Hunt as a leader amongst the pioneers of
"amiable humour":

> In the early nineteenth century it was Leigh Hunt in particular who made
> good humor an ideal and the cultivation of cheerfulness his "avowed
> doctrine." He is forever reminding us of the relationship between wit and
> good nature, or that raillery requires the exquisite handling of candor and
> benevolence. . . . With him cheerfulness and good humor have arrived at
> their relaxed and nostalgic period, the Merry England, Christmas-and-
> fireside sort of thing.[2]

By connecting relaxation and nostalgia to the notion of "Merry England,"
Tave implies a direct continuity between Hunt's idyllic vision and the tone
of his satire, a continuity which also has its impact on the form and conduct
of the "political and critical poems." In a poem of Hunt's early maturity—
Politics and Poetics—he sets the idyll apart from the world of human affairs,
but in such a way as to suggest that each depends on the other in a reluctant
symbiosis. He is forced to reject the escapism of pastoral visions as long as
real human suffering calls him to arms, but moments of escape replenish an
exhausted soul and fire a jaded imagination.

POLITICS AND POETICS (1811)

Hunt's subtitle for *Politics and Poetics*—*The Desperate Situation of a Journalist Unhappily Smitten with the Love of Rhyme*—encapsulates its rationale.
For, its playfulness notwithstanding, *Politics* belongs to a tradition of rebel-
lion poems, poems in which the speakers feel thwarted by their life's work
and pause to take stock of their vocations. On the one hand we have the
example of Herbert's *The Collar* (the resistant gestures of which are altogether more angry than Hunt's), and, on the other, *An Epistle from Mr.
Pope, to Dr. Arbuthnot*. Hunt begins by flumping down at his desk, and so

recalls the exhausted start to Pope's poem: "Shut, shut the door, good *John!* fatigu'd I said, / Tye up the knocker, say I'm sick, I'm dead":[3]

> Again I stop;—again the toil refuse!
> Away, for pity's sake, distracting Muse,
> Nor thus come smiling with thy bridal tricks
> Between my studious face and politics.
> Is it for thee to mock the frowns of fate?
> Look round, look round, and mark my desperate state.
> Cannot thy gifted eyes a sight behold,
> That might have quelled the Lesbian bard of old,
> And made the blood of Dante's self run cold?[4]

In *Arbuthnot* Pope deplores the pass to which his vocation as a poet has brought him, so much so that he wonders whether by writing he is doing penance—"Why did I write, what sin to me unknown, / Dipt me in ink, my Parents', or my own?"[5] In much the same way, Hunt conceives his political writing as a vocation so hellish that it might have "made the blood of Dante's self run cold." He is immured in his study as in a tomb ("Look around, look around" calls up the epitaph of Sir Christopher Wren—*si monumentum requiris, circumspice*). As comic foil for these "sepulchral" horrors, Hunt also draws on *The Rape of the Lock*, subverting and adapting famous episodes and topoi from that poem.

In a note added to *Politics* when it was republished four years later, Hunt wrote that "These lines were omitted in the first edition, on account of the general indifference of the versification; but, as they have been thought to resemble that mixture of fancy and familiarity, which the public have approved in the 'Feast of the Poets', . . . they are for the greater part reprinted."[6] What better way to activate the fancy, therefore, than by recalling the chaos of Belinda's toilette table, and displacing all its items (themselves mock-heroic displacements of ritual furniture) with political works as ephemeral and confused as her cosmetics:

> Lo, first the table spread with fearful books,
> In which, whoe'er can help it, never looks;
> Letters to Lords, Remarks, Reflections, Hints,
> Lives, snatched a moment from the public prints;
> Pamphlets to prove, on pain of our undoing,
> That rags are wealth, and reformation ruin,
> Journals, and briefs, and bills, and laws of libel,
> And, bloated and blood-red, the placeman's annual Bible.[7]

Just as Pope uses asyndetic catalogs to convey a disorder of values both in the toilette scene and in the apotheosis of *The Rape of the Lock*, so Hunt heaps up a conjunctionless pile of Tory publications to indicate the confused thought behind them. By converting the Red Book to a leech gorged with the blood of commons, he furthermore conveys his contempt for the claims of a nobility and for the social parasitism it entails.

In the introduction of *Wit and Humour*, Hunt tabulates the different kinds of comic effect. One of these is the enthymeme or suppressed premise, which he calls the "*Poetical Process*, the *Leap to a Conclusion*, or the *Omission of Intermediate Particulars in order to bring the Two Ends of a Thought or Circumstance together*," striking "the mind with a lively sense of truth abridged, in guise of a fiction and an impossibility."[8] He employs just such a "truth abridged" at this point of *Politics and Poetics*, equating books with writers, and burying them beneath illiberal materials that, as a liberal apologist, he has been forced to read:

> Scarce from the load, as from a heap of dead,
> My poor old Homer shows his living head;
> Milton, in sullen darkness, yields to fate,
> And Tasso groans beneath the courtly weight;
> Horace alone (the rogue!) his doom has missed,
> And lies at ease upon the Pension List.[9]

This might owe something to *The Library*, for Crabbe also animates books as authors, and makes a parable of their relations to each other. The theological bookshelves, for example, present the very image of ecumenical peace:

> An Athanasian here, in deep repose,
> Sleeps with fiercest of his Arian Foes;
> Socinians here with Calvinists abide,
> And thin Partitions angry Chiefs divide;
> Here wily Jesuits simple Quakers meet,
> And *Bellarmine* has rest at *Luther*'s feet.[10]

Hunt has included Homer in his list as the *fons et origo* of imaginative literature, but the references to Milton and Tasso have additional weight, both writers having suffered from reversals of political circumstance. The Tory tracts exclude the light and recall Milton's blindness after the Restoration; while, by pinning Tasso to the table, they also represent his imprisonment at the whim of a despot. Horace alone enjoys the *otium* of his Sabine farm, having given up his republican ideals to make peace with the Augustan order. He therefore rests emblematically on the government lackeys that fill out the pension list. Given his temperament, Hunt envies the idyllic life this poet has secured, but he qualifies that envy with judgment ("the rogue"), knowing that he himself could never renounce his liberal position, no matter what attractions an alternative lifestyle might offer.

As it is, he must continue laboring in a study that, with help from the Cave of Spleen in *The Rape of the Lock*, he proceeds to reinvent as a comic Tartarus. Like Pope, he couches his description in verbs of the habitual present to suggest an eternity of torment; and (again like Pope) he personifies the trivial disorders of "Distaste, delays, dislikings to begin," the blue devils of depression (comically platonized as "the Blue Daemon") and "Headache." All these owe their inspiration to Pain, Ill-nature and Megrim in canto 4 of *The Rape of the Lock*. By reducing a man to a domestic artifact (barometer), Hunt also recalls the "living *Teapots*" and the "Maids turn'd Bottels" of Pope's phantasmagoria:[11]

> Round these, in tall imaginary chairs,
> Imps ever grinning, sit my daily cares;
> Distaste, delays, dislikings to begin,
> Gnawings of pen, and kneadings of the chin.
> Here the Blue Daemon keeps his constant stir,
> Who makes a man his own barometer.[12]

While fancies of this order remain rooted in Pope, they also look forward to the goblins and grotesques we find in the early fiction of Dickens. When Hunt synthesizes "a harpy shape" with "jaws of parchment, and long hairs of tape,"[13] he is mediating a tradition of "jolly" gothic that seems to have begun with Gray's *Lines Spoken by the Ghost of John Dennis at the Devil Tavern*, and to have ended in W. S. Gilbert's *Ruddigore* ("With a kiss, perhaps, on her lantern chaps, and a grisly grim 'good-night'").[14] En route it passes through early Dickens, as witness this excerpt from *The Pickwick Papers*:

> Tom gazed at the chair; and, suddenly as he looked at it, a most extraordinary change seemed to come over it. The carving of the back gradually assumed the lineaments and expression of an old shrivelled human face; the damask cushion became an antique, flapped waistcoat; the round knobs grew into a couple of feet, encased in red cloth slippers; and the old

chair looked like a very ugly old man, of the previous century, with his
arms a-kimbo.[15]

This rollicking macabre, designed to evoke a smile instead of a frisson, has
the effect of belittling and "cozifying" the sublimity of terror. Thus Hunt
alludes to Poor Tom and his distresses in *King Lear* ("Away! the foul fiend
follows me! Through the sharp hawthorn blow the winds")[16] only to over-
extend the catalog into mindless weather-talk. He also impishly reincar-
nates Edgar's fiend in a printer's devil:

> Last, but not least, (methinks I see him now!)
> With stare expectant, and with ragged brow,
> Comes the foul fiend, who—let it rain or shine,
> Let it be clear or cloudy, foul or fine,
> Or freezing, thawing, drizzling, hailing, snowing,
> Or mild, or warm, or hot, or sharp, or sloppy,
> Is sure to come,—the Devil, who comes for copy,[17]

At this point the first version of *Politics* contained a seventeen-line *ad
hominem* attack on Tory reviewers. That Hunt should have deleted it from
the 1815 reprint is proof of his desire to detoxify satire and preach his gospel
of good humor. This purge of spleen is all the more touching if we look at
some of the "offending" lines: "Enchanter Scott, who in black-letter read, /
Gains a rank life by raising of the dead"[18]—entirely mild when they are set
against the spiteful crudities, say, of *Blackwood's*.

Having spent the first fifty-odd lines on the miserable plight of a political journalist *malgré lui*, Hunt banishes the gloom with a sunburst, a great
irruption of light and festivity into the ordinary confines of a room. Dickens
might or might not have remembered this effect when the Ghost of Christmas Present arrives in *A Christmas Carol*—"all this time he lay upon his bed,
the very core and centre of a blaze of ruddy light":[19]

> That instant, as the hindmost shuts the door,
> The bursting sunshine smites the windowed floor;
> Bursts too on every side the sparkling sound
> Of birds abroad; th' elastic spirits bound;
> And the fresh mirth of morning breathes around:
> Away, ye clouds; dull politics, give place;
> Off, cares, and wants, and threats, and all the race
> Of foes to freedom and to laurelled leisure!—
> To-day is for the Muse, and dancing Pleasure.[20]

For the idea of poetry as a light that banishes darkness, we must go back to Gray's *Progress of Poesy*:

> Night and all her sickly dews,
> Her spectres wan and birds of boding cry,
> He gives to range the dreary sky:
> Till down the eastern cliffs afar
> Hyperion's march they spy and glittering shafts of war.[21]

But what Gray conceives of as a sublime allegorical tableau, Hunt reduces to pastoral *fête champêtre*, invoking "Dancing Pleasure" and exorcizing "cares, wants and threats" in the manner of Milton's *L'Allegro*. By now we should be thoroughly familiar with the clauses of his contract for the good life:

> Oh for a seat in some poetic nook,
> Just hid with trees, and sparkling with a brook,
> Where through the quivering boughs the sunbeams shoot
> Their arrowy diamonds upon flower and fruit,
> While stealing airs come fuming o'er the stream,
> And lull the fancy to a waking dream!
> There shouldst thou come, O first of my desires,
> What time the noon had spent its fiercer fires,
> And all the bow'r, with chequered shadows strewn,
> Glowed with a mellow twilight of its own.
> There shouldst thou come, and there sometimes with thee
> Might deign repair the staid Philosophy,
> To taste thy fresh'ning brook, and trim thy groves,
> And tell us what good task true glory loves.
>
> I see it now!—I pierce the fairy glade,
> And feel th' enclosing influence of the shade.
> A thousand forms, that sport on summer eves,
> Glance through the light and whisper in the leaves,
> While every bough seems nodding with a sprite,
> And every air seems hushing the delight,
> And the calm bliss, fixed on itself awhile,
> Dimples the unconscious lips into a smile.[22]

While it is clear that the tradition of the *beatus ille* poem informs this sequence, one is struck more by differences than by similarities. It is certainly possible that some of the topographic details—brook, fruit, flowers—were suggested by *The Garden*, since Hunt pioneered the reinstatement of

Marvell's "strong and grave talent for poetry."[23] But, unlike Marvell, he entertains no Puritan misgivings about the flesh. In *The Garden* the speaker moves up hierarchically from "pleasure less" so as to create "transcending these, / Far other Worlds and other Seas,"[24] whereas in *Politics* the terms of this ascent are inverted, and Hunt shifts *from* the strenuous mental effort of journalism *to* a state of physical satiety.

Another possible influence on the idyll in *Politics* can be found in Gray's *Ode on the Spring*, which also explores the notion of beatific retirement. Here, however, Gray satirizes his own detachment by presenting his muse as someone prim and censorious:

> Where'er the oak's thick branches stretch
> A broader browner shade;
> Where'er the rude and moss-grown beech
> O'er-canopies the glade,
> Beside some water's rushy brink
> With me the Muse shall sit, and think
> (At ease reclined in rustic state)
> How vain the ardour of the crowd,
> How low, how little are the proud,
> How indigent the great![25]

Hunt cuts his muse from very different cloth. Bridget Allworthy makes way for a voluptuary, and the directives of time and place turn the encounter into an erotic assignation, rather like that of Shelley's "I Arise from Dreams of Thee" and Tennyson's "Fatima." Instead therefore of endorsing the "staid Philosophy" of Gray, Hunt "repairs" and reforms it, recasting the traditional worldly priorities of "glory." His muse makes love where Gray's condemned, but like Gray's in another poem—*The Progress of Poesy*—she also privileges the poet with moments of vision. Speaking of his early vocation to poetry, Gray claims "Yet oft before his infant eyes would run / Such forms as glitter in the Muse's ray / With orient hues, unborrowed of the sun."[26] The sublimity of these Platonic forms resides in their unspecified nature, something that Hunt takes over and domesticates as a glimmering fairy lore: "A thousand forms, that sport on summer eves, / Glance through the light, and whisper in the leaves." (His immature *Progress of Painting*, in which we hear Gray's ode through the resonant blur of an echo chamber, contains another such reference—"before his sparkling sight / Fair forms of Joy, and panting Pleasures shine.")[27] These forms pass through Hunt's early verse to Keats, whose *Sleep and Poetry* presents "Shapes of delight, of mystery, and fear."[28]

These are the precedents for, and *Nachleben* of, the poetic "shapes," which Hunt has linked to an equally distinctive and recurrent metric pattern:

> A thousand forms, that sport on summer eves,
>
>   –   –   x –   x   – x –   x –
> Glance through / the light, // / and whisp/er in / the leaves,

In the second line of the couplet, a spondee accentuates and slows the action of the first foot, and a strong caesura prevents the iamb that follows from making contact across the break. Only in the remaining three feet does the meter establish its regulatory tune. The rhythm of this structure thus follows momentary arrest with swift dispersal, as in a comparable line from Pope's "Summer":

>   –   –   x –   x –   x – x –
> Trees, where / you sit, // / shall crowd / into / a Shade,[29]

and from Gray's "[Lines on Beech Trees]":

>   –   – x   –   x   –   x –   x –
> Cling to / each leaf // / and swarm / on ev/ery bough.[30]

While both of these coincidentally relate the metric pattern to a wooded landscape, Tennyson adapts the pattern of concentration and release to an entirely different situation in *The Princess*:

>   –   –   x –   x   – x –   x –
> Rise in / the heart, // / and gath/er to / the eyes.[31]

Hunt thus keeps distinguished company with these distinguished lines. Indeed, he liked the tune well enough to use it again for a valediction later in the poem—"Where the trim shapes, that bathe in moonlight eves, / Glance through the light, and whisper in the leaves."[32] This valediction, by returning the poet to the world of political journalism, balances and reinstates the mock-despondency of the start.

Hunt uses the section in between to describe his flight to a world of recreation, one that has no place for miseries of Tory policy, and that thus exempts him from exposing them. If by cutting away the digressive matter we reduce this part of *Politics* to its bare bones, a much greater poem comes into view. (I have italicized some phrases to throw them into prominence): "Look round, look round, and mark my desperate state . . . Oh for a seat in some poetic nook, / Just hid with trees, and sparkling with a brook . . . While stealing airs come fuming o'er the stream, / And lull the fancy to a *waking dream* . . . I see it now!—I pierce the fairy glade, / And feel th' enclosing influence of shade . . . Anon strange music breathes;—the fairies show / Their pranksome crowd . . . I turn to them, and listen with fixed eyes, and feel my spirits mount on winged *ecstasies*. / In vain.—For now, with looks that doubly burn, / Shamed of their late defeat, my foes return; / They know their foil is short;—and shorter still, / The bliss that waits upon the Muse's will . . . Farewell, for gentler times, ye laurelled shades, / Farewell, ye sparkling brooks and haunted glades." This anticipates not only the general contour but also occasional words and phrases of *Ode to a Nightingale*, while the *doubling* of Hunt's sorrow as it flows back into an imaginative vacuum also looks ahead to *Sleep and Poetry*:

> The visions all are fled—the car is fled
> Into the light of heaven, and in their stead
> A sense of real things comes doubly strong,
> And like a muddy stream, would bear along
> My soul to nothingness: . . .[33]

Like Keats, Hunt wrestles with temptations to escape from suffering into art, a temptation to which he succumbed after his release from prison, and which turned him into an unwitting co-instigator of the Aesthetic Movement.[34] Indeed he *began* his withdrawal when he turned his jail cell into a Venetian palazzo.

At the time of *Politics*, however, his spirit was unbroken, and he conceived himself as a Spenserian knight who had to resist the enchanted bower threatening to deflect his quest:

> At that dread sight the Muse at last turns pale,
> Freedom and Fiction's self no more avail,
> And lo! my Bower of Bliss is turned into a jail![35]

These are subtle and prophetic lines. In book 2 of *The Faerie Queene* Sir Guyon destroys Acrasia's bower; here the world of politics destroys the idyll by irrupting into its confines. "Freedom," which during the fanciful interlude had been narrowed to an analgesic "freedom from care," thus comes into its own as a nobler, disinterested vision of liberty. And since it can be secured only by liberal policies, a reluctant Hunt once more embraces his study-prison, knowing full well that, after two narrow escapes, *The Examiner* would again collide with the establishment, and that a *real* prison sentence might follow. Even so, to abandon his political vocation in the knowledge that so much had still to be done would turn art itself into the prison of the better self, as inimical to the quest as Spenser's Bower of Bliss. That is why the poem moves so vigorously and rousingly to its final *sententia*, one of the most memorable couplets that Hunt ever wrote. The lyric intimacy of the first line is typically his own, but in the second he forges a wise, compact epigram, one that discriminates between ease (self-indulgent evasion) and leisure (the fulfillment of reward): "Farewell, farewell, dear Muse, and all thy pleasure! / He conquers ease, who would be crowned with leisure."[36]

THE FEAST OF THE POETS (1811; REVISED 1815)

Hunt made frank acknowledgment of his debt to Suckling in *The Feast of the Poets*, a debt evident not only in what Blunden has called "the 'sessional' device of provocation,"[37] but also in its rollicking anapestic meter. Having chosen to write in couplets rather than in the bob-yoked quatrains of his source, he runs the danger of the kind of monotony that years later would damage *The Palfrey*. Nonetheless, the anapests help generate the amiable tone of the satire. To have written in the staider tradition of the heroic couplet would have been to court the memory of Pope's elegant, compacted malice, so Hunt chose to stick with Suckling's measure, as happy-go-lucky and as generous as the satire it relays. Where Pope is merciless, Suckling is conciliatory, and often half-revokes his satiric raps after having administered them. For example, although he did not care for Jonson, he is nonetheless ready to admit him to the feast:

> *Apollo* stopt him there, and bid him not go on,
> 'Twas merit, he said, and not presumption
> Must carry it; at which *Ben* turned about,
> And in great choler offer'd to go out:
> But
> Those that were there thought it not fit
> To discontent so ancient a wit;
> And therefore *Apollo* call'd him back agen,
> And made him mine host of his own new Inne.[38]

That reference to an inn also alerts us to another important tradition feeding the work both of Suckling and Hunt—that of Lucianic satire. Lucian's
satire is good-natured but thoroughly irreverent. He delights especially in
demystifying the gods of Olympus into a gaggle of ordinary mortals gossip-
ing about ordinary things. Here, for example, is his Apollo, as querulous as
any failed Don Juan of the suburbs:

> I'm generally unlucky in love; at least I lost my two special sweethearts,
> Daphne and Hyacinthus. Daphne so loathes and shuns me that she's
> chosen to turn into a tree rather than share my company, and Hyacinthus
> was killed by that quoit. All that's left of them for me is wreaths.[39]

On another occasion Lucian suggests that Neptune makes whirlpools by
using his trident as an oceanic egg-whisk.
    Both sorts of irreverence (leveled at "godly" diction on the one hand and
"godly" deportment on the other) come together at the start of *The Feast of
the Poets*: ·

> T'other day, as Apollo sat pitching his darts
> Through the clouds of November, by fits and by starts,
> He began to consider how long it had been
> Since the bards of Old England had all been rung in.
> "I think," said the God, recollecting, (and then
> He fell twiddling a sunbeam as I may a pen,)
> "I think—let me see—yes, it is, I declare,
> As long ago now as that Buckingham there
> And yet I can't see why I've been so remiss,
> Unless it may be—and it certainly is,
> That since Dryden's fine verses, and Milton's sublime,
> I have fairly been sick of their sing-song and rhyme.[40]

Like Lucian, Hunt had an aversion to excessive formality. In the *Poetical
Works* (p. 45), for example, he says of Kemble's manner of solemn declama-
tion, "I'd as soon have gone down to see Kemble in love," and he took quite
naturally to the sort of dishabille affected by his two sources. Apollo (as
Hunt conceives him) is a wastrel playing darts, and is making straight for
Gordon's when he decides to call a latter-day session. His speech, full of
ruminative pauses and self-revising patterns, bears no resemblance to the
dignified monologues of seventeenth-century masques. Instead of godly
omniscience, we find memory-jogging ("Unless it may be—and it certainly
is"); in place of magisterial will, casual velleity ("I'll e'en go and give them a

lesson or two"). These are the words of Mercury rather than the songs of Apollo. Also, if we recall the customary grandeur of a deus ex machina, and set it against the god's arrival in *The Feast of the Poets*, we feel as though we are witnessing the failed effect of a pantomime: "and as Gods who drop in do, / Came smack on his legs through the drawing-room window."[41] This joke, like so many of its kind, literalizes an idiomatic expression and converts an informal visit to startling vertical descent. (Its longevity is attested by the writers of the 1978 *Superman*, who used it again in a context rather similar to Hunt's.)

The playfully mixed register is further enhanced by Hunt's half-onomatopoeic use of a verb as an adverb, something we find also in the informal verse of the eighteenth century. To parallel the energetic "smack" with which those all too corporeal legs make contact with the ground, we must go back to Gray's *Long Story*, where the heroines "[r]apped at the door, nor stayed to ask / But bounce into the parlour entered."[41] The rhyme scheme supplies another source of fun. As so often in comic verse, the challenge of rhyme resembles the impossible situations of a farce, and requires the same deft escape-artistry. Hunt sets himself outrageous rhyming tasks ("in do") and accomplishes them with outrageous deftness ("window"). Sometimes he avoids obvious rhymes to generate the humor of surprise—we would not ordinarily expect a slurred "pop in" to rhyme with "stopping," but Hunt supplies it simply *because* we do not expect it. The same holiday spirit leads him to sport with the very process of composition, and set up a veritable fitting room of similes in which to strut the part of a literary fop, trying on and rejecting at whim. Here we see the idyllic spirit shape and contain the energy of satire by giving it rein in party games:

> Apollo, arrived, had no sooner embodied
> His essence ethereal, than quenching his godhead,
> He changed his appearance—to—what shall I say?
> To a young gallant soldier returning in May?
> No—that's a resemblance too vapid and low:—
> Let's see—to a finished young traveller?—No:
> To a graceful young lord just stept out of his carriage?
> Or handsome young poet, the day of his marriage?
> No,—nobody's likeness will help me, I see,
> To afford you a notion of what he could be,
> Not though I collected one pattern victorious
> Of all that was good, and accomplished, and glorious,
> From deeds in the daylight, or books on the shelf,
> And called up the shape of young Alfred himself.

> Imagine, however, if shape there must be,
> A figure sublimed above mortal degree,
> His limbs the perfection of elegant strength,—
> A fine flowing roundness inclining to length,—
> A back dropping in,—an expansion of chest,
> (For the God, you'll observe, like his statues was drest)
> . . . .
> I wouldn't say more, lest my climax I lose;—
> Yet now I have mentioned those lamps of the Muse,
> I can't but observe what a spendour they shed,
> When a thought more than common came into his head:
> Then they leaped in their frankness, uncommonly bright,
> And shot round about them an arrowy light;
> . . . .
> A sprinkle of gold through the duskiness came,
> Like the sun through a tree, when he's setting in flame.
> The God, then, no sooner had taken a chair,
> And rung for the landlord to order the fare,[42]

The description of the god can scarcely be said to further the satire, but that is neither here nor there. In almost all his poetry, Hunt shows himself a poet of impulse, seldom taking stock of the larger shape if his fancy has been seized by incidentals. Having confessed the inadequacy of his repertoire of similes, he then recalls the formula of failed comparison ("Shall I compare thee to a summer's day? / Thou art more lovely and more temperate")[43]— recalling it in order to send it up. With this in mind, he overextends the topos, and deliberately flattens his comparisons (soldiers on the town, fops).

We have already seen from passages in *Rimini* that Hunt felt quite at ease in supplying accounts of male beauty, an ease he anticipates here in his blazon of Apollo. He itemizes the physique in an oddly sensuous way, pausing appreciatively (as it were) at every dash. But he reverses the mischievous *descent* of the physical person in poems such as *Love's Progress* (Donne) and moves towards a climax in the eyes, at which point he breaks off. This aposiopesis is especially interesting for its hint of self-knowledge. In many poems written after *The Feast*, Hunt was to blur the sharpness and soften the impact of certain climactic scenes—the pavilion of Francesca, the advent of Bacchus—by letting his fancy riot over the data and confuse them. Here he seems to be aware of the problem, albeit in a poem where mismanaged climaxes do not matter at all. Indeed, there is comedy in their very mismanagement. The unsatiric celebration of Apollo's beauty sets up a level from which the poetry can fall into bathos. For example, having stressed that we should keep the Apollo Belvedere in mind, ("For the God, you'll observe, like his statues was drest"), Hunt takes a puckish delight in plumping the god on an armchair.

From this point on *The Feast* takes up the roll-call formula of the session poem. In Suckling's hands the catalog seems a little random, but there is nothing arbitrary about Hunt's sequence, where he has paired and balanced his candidates. He begins with the hack dramatists of the London stage. Their reaction when they are mistaken for waiters suggests that Hunt was writing with Gray's *Candidate* in mind. This variant of the session poem, in which Lord Sandwich angles for the high stewardship of Cambridge, is also written in anapestic measure, and Hunt seems to have echoed some of its lines: "When sly Jemmy Twitcher had smugged up his face / With a lick of court whitewash and pious grimace" and "'Lord! Sister,' says Physic to Law, 'I declare.[']"[44] Compare: "But lord! to see all the great dramatists' faces! / They looked at each other, and made such grimaces!"[45] Hunt's alignment of hack dramatist and waiter carries a special satiric weight, for in other contexts he claims that the vocation of a waiter centers on the word "yes." There is this essay from *The Seer*, for example:

> If you told him that, in Shakespeare's time, waiters said "Anon, anon, Sir," he would be astonished at the repetition of the same word in one answer, and at the use of three words instead of two; . . . He would drop one of the two syllables of his "Yes, Sir," if he could; but business and civility will not allow it; and therefore he does what he can by running them together with the swift sufficiency of "Yezzir."
> "Thomas!"
> "Yezzir."
> "Is my steak coming?"
> "Yezzir."
> "And the pint of port?"
> "Yezzir."
> "And you'll not forget the postman?"
> "Yezzir."
>
> For in the habit of his acquiescence Thomas not seldom says "Yes, Sir," for "No, Sir," the habit itself rendering him unintelligible.[46]

If waiters are proverbial "yes-people" whose assent becomes mindless through habit, then, Hunt implies, popular dramatists figure as their literary analogues, pandering to public taste with just as little independence. (In a satiric attack on the poet laureate, *The Extraordinary Case of the Late Mr.*

Southey, he seems to intend much the same slur on John Murray—"Murrain said, "Yes, Sir," as usual, and then turned pale.")[47] Furthermore, by making one of the Dibdin set wait on the feasters, Hunt is simply replicating a joke in the Suckling poem, where Carew is tolerated only as a steward.[48]

Spencer, Rogers, and Montgomery suffer a fate marginally less wounding than that inflicted on the theater hacks—Apollo hints his sense of their slightness by inviting them to tea instead of to the session. We find Crabbe occupying a slightly higher place in his scheme of things, although he is banished to the inn kitchen on grounds that once commanded wide assent, viz., the "kitchen-sink" quality of his imagination. Nonetheless, Hunt is generous enough to allow him some scraps from the feast ("And let him have part of what goes from the table."[49] The putative "coarseness" of Crabbe he at once balances with the "refaynment" of Hayley, as though to set up an Aristotelian medium between two related distortions of his ideal. At this point the verse texture takes on an almost novelistic flexibility to reproduce Hayley's silken, deferential cadences. Hunt has italicized some words to tilt the voice across them with all the unction of insincerity, and he also parodies the forms of polite speech by applying them to a noun ("god") they were never meant to serve:

> And then, with a sort of a look of a blush,
> Came in Mr. Hayley, all polished confusion,
> And said, "*Will* Apollo excuse this intrusion?
> I might have kept back,—but I thought 'twould look odd,—
> And friendship, you know,—pray how *is* my dear God?"[50]

Hunt sets off these stylized self-abasements with the strutting self-importance of William Gifford. Gifford was a man whom he confesses in his *Autobiography* to having loathed above all others. Yet, even with a fund of hatred to empower the thrust of the satire, he is not unduly harsh. If Pope had been presented with a comparable opportunity, he would have let his guns blaze—but then Pope, greater poet though he was, fell short of Hunt in his store of humanity. In this characterization of Gifford we once again see meter taking on the phatic shape of conversation—Hunt catches all the bluster and venom of Gifford in congested caesuras (suggesting incredulous pauses), and in a syntax virtually incoherent with indignation:

> "And pray, my frank visitor, who may you be?"
> "Who be?" cried the other; "why really—this tone—
> William Gifford's a name, I think, pretty well known!"[51]

The phrase that introduced Gifford—"a sour little gentleman"—also ushers him out, which use of *inclusio* suggests the character's entrapment in his own malicious selfhood.

Having thus excluded the versifying rabble, Hunt now turns his attention to poets of substance, and Walter Scott makes an appearance amid a gaggle of fans. Hunt implies that this literary pop star, like the hack dramatists, has been guilty of pandering to popular taste: "Well, Mr. Scott, you have managed the town; / Now pray, copy less,—have a little temerity,— / Try if you can't also manage posterity."[52] Each of the three succeeding poets also receives a mild rebuke—Campbell for faults of versification, Moore for the trivial eroticism of his early verse (though Hunt acknowledges the "higher" vocation of the *Irish Melodies*) and Byron for his misanthropy. Hunt's treatment of Southey, Coleridge and Wordsworth is very severe, though by the time he came to revise the text in 1815, his growing appreciation of Wordsworth led him not so much to retract his attack on the *Lyrical Ballads* as to acknowledge the achievements that followed. (All versions of *The Feast* fail to record the fact that by the 1850s Hunt had come to regard Coleridge as the most gifted of all the romantic poets, Wordsworth included.)

The reservations that Hunt voices about each writer can be traced back to the format of his model, for Suckling's session also reveals a pattern of salute and countervailing rebuke; but they also map out (in negative profile) his ideas on the mission of the poet. When Moore writes merely sensual verse, he is accused of betraying the ethical side of his calling: "And never should poet, so gifted and rare, / Pollute the bright Eden Jove gives to his care, / But love the fair Virtue, for whom it is given, / And keep the spot pure for the visits of Heaven."[53] Byron likewise falls short of the ennobling function of poetry as Hunt defines it—"You owe some relief to our hearts and your own; / For poets, earth's heav'n-linking spirits, were born, / What they can, to amend—what they can't, to adorn; / And you hide the best proof of your office and right, / If you make not as I do a contrast with night, / And help to shed round you a gladness and light."[54] When one considers the modest compass of Hunt's own verse, these Shelleyan yardsticks come as something of a surprise. Still, by omitting himself from the guest list, he has cleared the way to this stringent Platonism, which also underpins the notorious attack on Wordsworth:

> And Wordsworth, one day, made his very hairs bristle,
> By going and changing his harp for a whistle.
> The bards, for a moment, stood making a pause,
> And looked rather awkward, and lax round the jaws,

When one began spouting the cream of orations
In praise of bombarding one's friends and relations;
And t'other some lines he had made on a straw,
Showing how he had found it, and what it was for,
And how, when 'twas balanced, it stood like a spell!—
And how, when 'twas balanced no longer, it fell!—
. . . .
Apollo half laughed betwixt anger and mirth,
And cried, "Was there ever such trifling on earth?
What! think ye a bard's a mere gossip, who tells
Of the ev'ry-day feelings of every one else,
And that poetry lies, not in something select
But in gath'ring the refuse that others reject?
Must a ballad doled out by a spectacled nurse
About Two-shoes or Thumb, be your model of verse;[55]

It is clear that Hunt conceives the poet as a prophetic intermediary between earth and heaven, and writers who deal exclusively in human misery and failure, whether they be Byron or Wordsworth, have betrayed their function. No wonder that when Shelley burst on to the horizon a few years later, he so completely overwhelmed Hunt: in almost every respect he conformed to the beau ideal set up in *The Feast*. Although he rejected the Christian notion of a fall, Hunt to all intents and purposes suggests that the poet must seek out divinity in a fallen world—poetry by his definition is something "select"—and, by the instrumentality of this good, lift the world to the heaven from which it has been exiled. This as an ethical mandate went hand in hand with an aesthetic one—the ideal poet should search for ideal forms. We can see the breadth of Hunt's definition in the range of his rebukes. He takes Campbell to task on the technical issue of poor versification; he trounces Moore for his moral laxity; and he takes the Wordsworth of the *Lyrical Ballads* to task for erring on *both* aesthetic and ethical counts. The latter's chosen form (the "dole," the unflighted singsong of the nursery rhyme; the homophonic, unample capability of the rustic flute above the chordal possibilities of a harp) matches his chosen content ("gossip" and "refuse").

Paul Dawson has remarked that "Hunt admired Wordsworth's poetry more than he liked it; his preference for the sunny side of things (a preference based on principle as well as temperament) made it hard for him to relish the more sombre aspects of Wordsworth's genius, and he disliked his poems about mad mothers and idiot sons, which he found morbid and distressing. But his reservations about Wordsworth's poetry were no obstacle to setting him up as a figurehead of the new school."[56] Largely true though this is, it needs to be qualified. That Hunt disliked and ridiculed the *Lyrical Ballads* can be gathered from his parodic lapallisade about the straw. Such lines measure the extent to which he mistook the transparent innocence, say, of *We Are Seven*, for commonplace and tautology. And, like most of us, having had one bad experience with an author, he was chary of courting another. We can be fairly sure that he read nothing more by Wordsworth before he mounted his 1811 attack, and can speculate further that, once the injustice of this onslaught had been pointed out to him, he only then condescended to read the 1807 poems and perhaps *The Excursion*. These impressed him so favorably that, without revising his assessment of the *Lyrical Ballads*, he composed the additional passage praising Wordsworth in the 1815 version of *The Feast*. Since the passage in question offers a *generous* salute to the later verse, we need not infer, as Dawson does, that it was mere lip service and ideological expedience. Hunt's anaphoric paean provides a checklist of all the "Huntian" delights he has since been able to uncover in the greater poet. *Daffodils*, after all, is the sort of idyllic poem that he himself could have written with his powers at full stretch:

> Of nature, it told, and of simple delights
> On days of green sunshine, and eye-lifting nights;
> Of summer-sweet isles and their noon-shaded bowers,
> Of hearts, young and happy, and all that they show
> For the home that we came from and whither we go;
> Of wisdom in age by this feeling renewed,
> Of hopes that stand smiling o'er passions subdued,
> Of the springs of sweet waters in evil that lie;—
> Of all, which, in short, meets the soul's better eye
> When we go to meek nature our hearts to restore,
> And bring down the Gods to walk with us once more.[57]

Hunt has to some degree been guilty of recreating Wordsworth in his own image—no question whence the synaesthesia of "green sunshine" derives—and his editorial emphases have privileged light at the expense of shade. Even so, it is easy to see what poems in the 1807 collection struck a chord with him—the priorities of *The World Is Too Much With Us* would have commanded his full assent ("And bring down the Gods to walk with us once more") and so would the philosophical celebration of childhood in the *Intimations Ode* ("For the home that we came from and whither we go")— much more universal than the interrogations of *We Are Seven* and *Anecdote for Fathers*. It is was the absence of *range*, after all, that Hunt deplored in the *Lyrical Ballads*, a range encompassed and fully explored by such passages as that in *The Excursion* which describes the stargazing Chaldeans ("eye-lifting night"?).

The Feast of the Poets has virtually completed its business once it has hailed Wordsworth (in 1815) as "the Prince of the Bards of his Time." All that remains is a fanciful and decorative postlude. First of all, Apollo banishes the unworthy by revealing the unbearable fullness of his godhead. Hunt handles this theophany in a sumptuous passage based (it would seem) on an acquaintance with the baroque. Certainly the "fiery rods" recall the metal rays so beloved of Bernini, and the "clouds, burning inward" recall the luminous vortices of Andrea Pozzo. Hunt confers additional sublimity on the passage with a prophetic *also sprach*:

> He said; and the place all seemed swelling with light,
> While his locks and his visage grew awfully bright;
> And clouds, burning inward, rolled round on each side,
> To encircle his state, as he stood in his pride;
> Till at last the full Deity put on his rays,
> And burst on the sight in the pomp of his blaze!
> Then a glory beamed round, as of fiery rods,
> With the sound of deep organs and chorister gods;
> And the faces of bards, glowing fresh from their skies,
> Came thronging about with intentness of eyes,—
> And the Nine were all heard, as the harmony swelled,—
> And all things, above, and beneath, and around,
> Seemed a world of bright vision, set floating in sound.[58]

Even though the rollicking anapests impair the majesty of this vision, Hunt has clearly suspended his satiric intention and tried to write seriously. We would be wrong to read it as a parody of the descent and self-revelation of gods in epic verse. Remembering the *vera incessu patuit dea* of the *Aeneid*, he presents his own variant as a sort of *vero carmine patuit deus*. Apollo's apotheosis is attended by that commingling of heaven and earth, that integration of the ordinary and the sublime, which Hunt repeatedly specified as the true end of poetry. Floating in the *sound* as much as the sight of an idealizing poetry (i.e., combining both ideal form with ideal matter), the world is transfigured, and the poets themselves participate in its transfiguration.

The tone of the following banquet is different yet again, for here Hunt has dispensed with his solemn high baroque. It is impossible to imagine that most material of entities—food—in a sublimated form. The Commendatore in *Don Giovanni* claims that "non si pasce di cibo mortale, / chi si pasce di cibo celeste" and the Gospels maintain a fitting silence about the menu of the messianic banquet. Shakespeare and Herrick, on the other hand, present fanciful speculations about fairy diets, and, as soon as they do, sacrifice dignity to charm. Here are some of the dishes in *Oberon's Feast*:

> His kitling eyes begin to runne
> Quite through the table, where he spies
> The hornes of paperie Butterflies,
> Of which he eates, and tastes a little
> Of that we call the Cuckoes spittle.[59]

Whereas Herrick etherealizes by diminutives, Hunt chooses to sublimate by magnification when he opens a vein of comparable whimsy. *His* heavenly feast boasts platonized apples, greengages, and table furniture:

> Then as for the fruits, you might garden for ages,
> Before you could raise me such apples and gages;
> And all on the table no sooner were spread,
> Than their cheeks next the God blushed a beautiful red.
> 'Twas magic, in short, and deliciousness all;—
> The very men-servants grew handsome and tall,
> To velvet-hung ivory the furniture turned,
> The service with opal and adamant burned,
> Each candlestick changed to a pillar of gold,
> While a bundle of beams took the place of the mould,
> The decanters and glasses pure diamond became,
> And the corkscrew ran solidly round into flame:—[60]

There is a faint note of satire here, but it remains very muted. While a fiery corkscrew might recall *The Rape of the Lock* (the tortures of negligent sylphs, say, or the phantasmagoria of the Cave of Spleen), Hunt intends no belittlement of heavenly fire by linking it to tableware. Rather, it is the fancifulness of *Oberon's Feast* put in reverse, and, like Herrick's poem, a simple display of fanciful invention. The same sort of improvisation underlies the earlier crowning of the bards, where instead of relying on conventional laurel wreathes, Hunt plaits his own from a repertory of ad hoc emblems. Even though one can detect strokes of mischief in his wreathing a sycophantic "creeper" into Scott's thistle crown and his implying the venality of the laureate by putting a crown of pennyroyal on Southey's head, such strokes are incidental to the "straight" pleasures of the flower-catalog convention he has taken over from pastoral.

The Feast of the Poets ends in a series of toasts, a conspectus of the great poets of the past (newly defined by an anticlassical canon). Then, returning to the jovial mock-heroic tone of the opening, Hunt suggests that Apollo's godhead depends on his keeping "good hours"[61] and despatches him on a Lucianic comet-tandem to the "inn" of Ursa Major. *The Feast* is an entirely pleasant poem, free and relaxed in its conduct, but never so digressive as to lose its way. Whatever variations of tone and level there are find their sanction in the genre. But when all is said and done, these pleasures remain incidental to the poem's interest as a document of taste, as the response of an important critic towards important contemporaries.

BLUE-STOCKING REVELS (1837)

Our sense of substance in *The Feast* is bound up with the substance of the writers invited to the banquet, something that becomes apparent the moment we turn to *Blue-Stocking Revels*. In this companion poem written twenty-six years later, there are some biggish names on the guest list (Fanny Burney, Elizabeth Barrett, Maria Edgeworth, Mary Mitford), but they are crowded out by a host of minor ones. Hunt himself confesses that some of the names mean nothing to him and tries to milk comedy from the very flatness of his catalog and the vacancy of his comment: "Betham, Blackwood, Bowles, Bray, and Miss Browne too, were there; / What a sweet load of B's! But then what a despair! / For I know not their writings. (I'm tearing my hair!)." Even though scholars such as Stuart Curran are pioneering a new, more inclusive romantic canon, most of us, like Hunt, "know not the writings" of the women on Apollo's guest list. The *Revels* thus poses a problem similar to that posed by *The Dunciad*—having to dip systematically from poem to footnote and back again in order to fill out blank names. In the case of the *Dunciad* such labor is its own reward, for we are reading the greatest Juvenalian satire in the language. The *Revels*, by contrast, is nothing more than a *rechauffée* of what is in itself a minor poem. Although it has some of *The Feast*'s exhilaration and bounce, and although Hunt proves quite as adept in its fanciful passages, it is hamstrung by the obscurity of its subject and by the banal, unsystematic nature of its criticism. Hunt on Wordsworth is interesting even when he is wrong; Hunt on a minor novelist is wholly unmemorable:

> Cary Burney came next, so precise yet so trusting,
> Her heroines are perfect, and yet not disgusting.

> "However," said Phoebus, "I can't quite approve them:
> Conceit follows close on the mere right to love them."[62]

Readers might be forgiven their impulse to break a butterfly upon a wheel, and enquire what concessive connection there can be between precision and trust, or whether the entire line about conceit and the right to love means anything at all.

It would, however, be unfair to dismiss the poem because these longueurs clog up most of its second canto. Canto 1, in which Apollo assumes the role of interior decorator, and canto 3, an account of the transcendental feast, provide Hunt with occasions to which his fancy can rise with aplomb. His verse texture, moreover, is extremely free and easy, so much so, indeed, that some lines read like jottings that have still to be amplified and cast in metrical form:

> He said; and some messages giving those daughters
> Of Ocean,—arch-eyed—buxom dancers in waters,—
> They gave him some answer (I never heard what)
> Which they paid for, i'faith, with a dance on the spot.[63]

Then, building on the Lucianic elements of *The Feast*, Hunt has Apollo furnish an empty Hyde Park mansion in a sort of *style olympique*. The fashionable designers displaced by this godly house-making are hustled into a couplet of apostrophe, all the funnier for being as meaningless to the modern reader as many of the authors listed in canto 2: "O Seddon! O Gillow! O Mr. Morrell! / O Taprell and Holland! O Minter! O Snell." The repeated vocative "O's," jostling with people less classical than those they are used to hail, have the effect of turning the couplet into a compendium of Irish surnames. Once they have been shooed out of the poem, Hunt's fancy sublimates human decor into heavenly—a technique he had already pioneered in the banquet scene of *The Feast*:

> Then the drawing-room—What, think ye, hung the walls there?
> Cloth of gold? No, of sunbeams. 'Twas made of his hair.
> The immense window-curtains, Calypso's own woollen,
> Like clouds to the sunset, hung gorgeously sullen.[64]

We have seen in *Rimini* how important setting is to Hunt, setting conceived not as an index to character, but as a bower of luxuries that seal off the idyllic self from the outside world. It all goes back to his stint in the Surrey Gaol, and the imaginative screen that decor provided throughout that ordeal.

When, as here, that talent for interior design is liberated from the constraints of the real, Hunt seems as happy as a sand-boy. Part of the prettiness and the tricksiness of such moments springs from his habit of turning metaphor back into "fact." For example, while words like "comet" suggest that light has often been associated with the fall and radiance of human hair, Hunt recasts that association as a literal "truth." A conceit becomes a fixture of the room when he commandeers the comparison of cloud to tester curtain in Collins's *Ode to Evening* ("while now the bright-haired sun / Sits in yon western tent, whose cloudy skirts / With brede ethereal wove, / O'erhang his wavy bed")[65] and hangs it at a window.

In *Bacchus and Ariadne* we saw Hunt furnish forth the first of several transcendental feasts in his poetry. Then he had only the elfin fancies of Herrick to inspire him, but at the time of *Revels* there was the additional inspiration of *The Eve of St Agnes* to work from. Developing Keats's "jellies soother than the creamy curd,"[66] he comes close to achieving a comparable delicacy and richness in his viands:

> And betwixt the fair couches were services small
> Of ices, and creams, and clear jellies, smooth-souled,
> The very tip-ends of refreshment and cold.[67]

Rather more vulgar, but nonetheless compelling, is the unveiling of a banquet, not by the removal of a cloth but by the lifting of mist. Here the dominant influence would seem be the Technicolor luxuriousness of Thomas Moore, though there is also perhaps a hint of Marvell in the pendant peach:

> Very beauteous the mist was,—thin, white, with a bloom;
> An odour of violets filled the whole room;
> Ever trembled the music; and as the mist cleared,
> First, bunches of violets gently appeared,—
> Then silver,—then gold,—then the tops of decanters
> Of diamond,—then peaches, those cheek-like enchanters,
> And other fruit, some in white baskets and some
> Enleafed on the bough, with a dew on the plum,
> Then dishes, half seen, fit to make a physician
> Turn glutton, from pastures and dairies Elysian;
> The peaches hung over them, ready to drip;
> And now the guests sat, and the mirth was let slip,
> And white went the fingers from foliage to lip.[68]

Moore and Marvell might have fed the fancy informing these lines, but only Hunt could have written them—the sensibility, the pattern of focus, and the verbal nuance are all distinctively his. Who else would half-personify peaches as "cheek-like enchanters" or stress the contrast of white flesh against green leaves? And who else would burden a poem ostensibly about the state of women's writing with incidentals so beguiling and distracting? If *The Blue-Stocking Revels* remains in the memory, it is because of its occasional pretty lanes and side roads, not because of its highway. As so often, a rococo concern with surface has effaced the shape of the whole.

Having made these reservations on point of form, however, I need to acknowledge the social significance of the poem. Hunt clearly saw parallels between the emphases and procedures of women's verse and his own modus operandi. He had fallen foul of a brutal male establishment, and had been reproached for "unmanly" habits of diction and "unmanly" choices of topic. He knew, furthermore, that this same establishment had, over the centuries, sidelined gifted woman to make space for ungifted men. It was hardly to the credit of the British reading public "when it is considered what stuff it has put up with in collections of 'British Poets,' and how far superior such verse-writers as Lady Winchelsea, Mrs. Barbauld and Charlotte Smith were to the Sprats, and Halifaxes, and Stepneys and Wattses that were re-edited by Chalmers, Anderson and Dr. Johnson; to say nothing of the women of genius that have since appeared."[69] Hunt was also shrewd enough to realize that the aesthetic values of the patriarchy were so entrenched as to affect the originality and independence of earlier women poets who, against great odds, had managed to appear in print. Striving for self-expression, they were nonetheless forced on occasion into expedient replications of the dominant mode:

> When they did write, they condescended, in return, to put on the earthly feminine likeness of some favourite of the other sex. Lady Winchelsea formed herself on Cowley and Dryden; Vittoria Colonna, on Petrarch and Michael Angelo. Sappho is the exception that proves the rule (if she was an exception). Even Miss Barrett, whom we take to be the most imaginative poetess that has appeared in England, perhaps in Europe, and who will attain to great eminence if the fineness of her vein can but outgrow a certain morbidity, reminds her readers of the peculiarities of contemporary genius. She is like an ultra-sensitive sister of Alfred Tennyson.[70]

Viewed in the light of such pronouncements, and in the light of Hunt's own experiments with a domestic mode of poetry, *Blue-Stocking Revels* must be seen as compensatory exercise, public reparation for the masculinist bias of which he (as much as any woman poet) had fallen foul.

ULTRA-CREPIDARIUS (1823)

Since Hunt seems to have connected Suckling's anapestic galop with amiable satire, I find it strange that he should have chosen this measure for his most vengeful poem—*Ultra-Crepidarius*. Its subject is William Gifford, who, Hunt proclaims in his *Autobiography*, was "the only man [he] ever attacked, respecting whom [he had] felt no regret,"[71] and its title alone ("Super-Cobbler") declares that it is to be an attack with no holds barred. Gifford, the editor of the *Quarterly Review*, had taken umbrage at his treatment in *The Feast of the Poets*, and had appointed himself Hunt's Tory nemesis. Unlike John Wolcot, who had taunted Gifford with his humble apprenticeship in *A Cut at a Cobbler*, Hunt was ordinarily above such undemocratic sneers, but he probably felt impelled to spell out some central contradictions in Gifford's role as Tory lickspittle. Furthermore, he took pains, as satirists often do, to imply that he had been stung into satire by repeated provocation, to which, for as long as his charity lasted, he had turned a deaf ear. In the same year that *Ultra-Crepidarius* appeared, Hunt had published *To a Spider Running Across a Room*, in which he states that he had long had a punitive satire on Gifford in hand, but had withheld publication out of kindness:

> Have I, these five years, spared the dog a stick,
> Cut for his special use, and reasonably thick,
> Now, because prose had felled him just before;
> Then, to oblige the very heart he tore;
> Then, from conniving to suppose him human,
> Two-legged, and one that had a serving-woman;
> Then, because some one saw him in a shiver,
> Which shewed, if not a heart, he had a liver;
> And then, because they said the dog was dying,
> His very symptoms being given to lying.[72]

The whole strategy of the spider poem lies in its ostentatious parade of restraint, and the *occupatio* that Hunt had used to hurry unsympathetic material from his narrative verse is now put to a different use—successive Tory bugbears are displayed and loftily exempted from the attack they deserve. Hunt's mercy to the spider, like Burns's to a field mouse in the poem that seems to have inspired it, exalts a feeling brute creature above an unfeeling human.

Having thus advertised his innate kindliness and self-restraint, the poet could afford to let his guns blaze in *Ultra-Crepidarius* without opening himself to charges of unprovoked malice or personal revenge. His preface reminds the reader that his forbearing conduct towards Gifford has borne no fruit— "The following *jeu d'esprit* is the 'stick' which is mentioned in the third number of the *Liberal* as having been cut for Mr. Gifford's special use"[73]—although, given the dominant metaphor of *Ultra-Crepidarius*, he might have substituted "shoe" for "stick," since it was also with a shoe that he threatened his spider: "Dost shrink with all thine eyes to view / The shadowing threat of mine avenging shoe?"[74]

But even in circumstances as bitter as these, Hunt's good nature repeatedly triumphs over malice. A fragmentary spin-off entitled *Talari Innamorati* admits to the fact with a sort of indolent complacency: "Take a story that came in my head t'other day, / As writing a libel, all careless I lay, / So good-natured am I, and soon caried away."[75] In the first part of *Ultra-Crepidarius* he keeps up the spry Lucianic bounce familiar from *The Feast of the Poets*, and, alongside the irreverence that reduces a god to a lay-abed and demythologizes a king to "a charming old boy of a Prince,"[76] we find distracting interpolations of fancy that blur and diffuse the force of the attack. For instance, Hunt cannot resist some fanciful asides on the *talaria*, the winged sandals of Hermes:

> The latter indeed were as famous as Love's,
> And they rivalled in hue even Venus's doves;
> For at every fresh turn, and least touch into light,
> Which the clear God of Eloquence took in his flight,
> They varied their colours in fifty directions,
> And perfectly dazzled with brilliant reflections.[77]

Those varied colors are not solely visual. Hunt would have known the rhetorical meaning of "color" from *The Franklin's Prologue*, and he seems, moreover, to continue the pun in "brilliant reflections," signifying both mental effort and play of light. Such prettiness and playfulness are altogether unexpected in a poem of revenge—it is as though the fairy lore of *The Rape of the Lock* had strayed into *The Dunciad*. As *Ultra-Crepidarius* moves toward its climax, however, Hunt dispenses with joviality and fanciful asides, and pronounces a curse of Juvenalian intensity on his victim. No longer do the anapests seem to rollick, but, weighed down by the heaviness of the attack, appear to club out the sentences with a relentless force much closer to the trisyllabic meter of Skelton:

> Thus, edit no authors but such as unite
> With their talents a good deal of dirt or of spite;
> Ben Jonson, because he was beastly and bluff;
> And Massinger,—mince through his loathsomer stuff;
> And Persius,—"let him be writ down" Imitated,
> And say to poor Juvenal, "Thou art translated."
> These Latins will help too the fondest of penchants,
> And swell thy large hate with the hates of the ancients.[78]

Recalling Quince's horror-struck cry in *A Midsummer Night's Dream* ("Bless thee, Bottom, bless thee! Thou art translated"),[79] Hunt implies that Gifford's translation of Juvenal has recreated the Roman satirist in the asinine image of himself. Not only his Juvenal indeed, but all his literary scholarship (Hunt implies), is simply a ventriloquial projection of his spleen.

The Juvenalian hatred in Gifford provokes an unwonted passion in Hunt, so much so that, failing on his own turn to write with sufficient virulence, he highjacks the *Dunciad* and updates its ad hominems. It is a stroke as startling as it is unique. In the seventeenth and eighteenth centuries, poets used the imitation to modernize the references of classical satire, but never with so bald and efficient a pattern of displacements as we find in *Ultra-Crepidarius*:

> But office shall then be shop so entire
> For any dull fellow to keep that can serve.
> While Britons, turned beggars, are told to go starve,
> That a whole set of dunces,—yes, Pope, thine own band,
> Thy *Dunciad* itself, shall rule over the land!
> As gutters dive down to re-issue in ditches,
> Thy divers for pay shall emerge with new riches.
> Then quality's fools, long be-libelled in vain,
> In the Stuarts, the Georges, and "Jenkies" shall reign:
> Then Cymons (not Greek, nor yet mended by Cupid)
> Shall lord it with faces triumphant as stupid:
> Happy Page shall be Best, well aware of his fury,
> Cocanen be Croker, and Lintot be Murray:
> In Southey poor Blackmore, beginning to doat,
> Shall not only turn a new stave, but his coat:
> The Wards and the Welsteds shall pamper their spleens,

And club in Scotch papers and Scotch Magazines:
And finally, thou, my old soul of the tritical,
Noting, translating, high slavish, hot critical,
Quarterly-scutcheoned, great heir to each dunce,
Be Tibbald, Cook, Arnall, and Dennis at once.[80]

Never before has a poem been appropriated so neatly, and its meaning retained by a deft reallocation of references.

THE BOOK OF BEGINNINGS (1823)

The full-blown Juvenalianism of *Ultra-Crepidarius* (at least of its latter part) is hardly sustained in *The Book of Beginnings*, also published in *The Liberal* during 1823. Milford would have been better advised to hold the piece over for the division of "Miscellaneous Poems," for it is in itself a miscellany, versifying the free-associative flow of an informal essay. We know that Hunt was pressed to supply copy for *The Liberal*, and the enterprise does indeed have a faint air of desperation, of being spun out to meet a preordained length. Even so, ad hoc doodle though it might in some respects seem, in others it is startlingly original. While the earlier tradition of the critical verse-essay tended to prescribe (the imperative mood prevails both in the *Ars Poetica* and *An Essay on Criticism*), the romantics chose the prose essay for their prescriptive "decalogues" and reserved verse measure for a new but related genre, the poem of critical response. Keats's obiter dicta on Spenser in the epistle *To Charles Cowden Clarke*, or his encounter with Chapman's Homer, or his bracing himself to re-read *King Lear* are all of them poems about poetry, but they do not attempt to be systematic, nor do they profess objectivity, translating their critical perceptions as they do into colorful metaphor. Hunt's *Book of Beginnings* mediates between these two models. It is an essay, half academic, half personal, on the way poems start—not unlike more recent critical efforts such as Barbara Smith's investigation of "how poems end":[81]

Exordiums are my theme.—Thou great "O thou!"
Whoe'er thou art, whom poets thou by thousands,
Whether thou sit'st upon the Olympian brow
Of epic bard, or wonderest at the cow's hands
Of rude invoker, rhyming any how
Allow me to be clerk for both advowsons;

> For if my own rhyme's nothing of itself,
> It sings of others worthy of thy shelf.[82]

Such a stanza is an exordium in itself, like the opening paragraphs of Hunt's familiar essays, and the poem as a whole shows further conformity to this pattern. Taking "A Now" (published in *The Indicator*) as typically Huntian in its form, we find the essayist flying solo with his topic for as long as he can. After a while, however, he senses the need to "imp his wing" and falls back on a large hunk of Beaumont and Fletcher's *Woman-Hater*.

In many other essays, "unaided" personal discourse also gives way to make-weight materials from other sources, and the essayist turns introducer or anthologist. The same structure supports *Coaches* (also in *The Indicator*) and *A Human Being in a Crowd* (*The Seer*): a general disquisition followed in the first instance by lengthy quotations from Prior, and in the second by an excerpt from Lewis's *Monk*. And so Hunt ekes out the length of his *Book of Beginnings* by interpolating a run of stanzas he has translated from Forteguerri. The essay influence is not restricted to this aspect alone; its contents likewise follow an essayistic line of association as Hunt moves gracefully and randomly (it is rococo criticism, after all) from the sort of prescriptions we associate with Horace—"The opening, like the ending, must be settled / By nature and the occasion"[83]—to the dreamy metaphoric conversions we find in Keats's "critical" poetry:

> I give up that. But not the breathing wood,
> Entered, with hat off, after sun and dust;
> Not going to sleep in smiling gratitude;
> Nor meal that we approach, as walkers must;
> Not cutting string from books; nor subject good,
> Hit on by fingered pencil; nor the gust
> Of Philharmonic winds, waked all at once,
> Touch like a bard's pen, tilted for the nonce.[84]

Simply to have assembled these disparate elements into a coherent essay is a small feat in itself, but the real originality of the poem lies in its having *versified* them to create a critical poem sui generis.

THE POLITICAL SATIRES

Even though *The Book of Beginnings* presents itself as a critical poem, no easy divorce between poetics and politics was possible in the early nineteenth century. Hunt seems to recollect at the very end that his verse-essay needs some ideological color, and dabs it on in a witty but unrelated coda:

> But I digress; so here I stop; for *Finis*
> *Coronat opus*,—"a good end's a crown";
> A maxim, that in my mind so divine is,
> That heartily, and with "devocioun,"
> As Chaucer says, I wish that every Highness
> And Majesty (but ours) may soon lie down,
> And treat their realms with the sole coronations
> That give a perfect finish to their stations.[85]

By the same token, even though the attack on Gifford in *Crepidarius* centers primarily on the critic's creative pretensions, Hunt cannot help targeting his political allegiance at the same time. Indeed, it is Gifford's politics as much as anything else that sharpens his satire to a trenchancy more cutting than his creed of good humor would otherwise have allowed. Hunt seems to have indulged this bitterness on the assumption that attack prompted by political injustice will spring not from self-love but from altruism. Hence any lampoon on the regent, no matter how harshly directed ad hominem, is an attack launched on behalf of disenfranchised and suffering people, not a satisfaction of personal animus. Edmund Blunden has taken care to stress this disinterestedness in his account of *The Examiner*: "The Hunts were determined to use their entire resources in order to relieve the country from rulers whose bad habits infected the general welfare."[86]

In *The St. James's Phenomenon* Hunt turns the prince regent into an exhibit for a freak show, and writes what purports to be a broadside "puff," complete with a broadside summons like Goldsmith's in *An Elegy on the Death of a Mad Dog*—"Good people all, of every sort, / Give ear unto my song":[87]

> Good people all, attend now,
>   And I'll tell ye of such a monster,
> As shall make your eyes
> Be double their size,
>   And the hats that ye have on stir.
>
> I'm aware there've been before this
>   As pretty frights as may be,
> Two sisters in one,
> And babes like a tun,
>   And much worse things than they be.

> . . . .
> But Lord! all these were handsome
>   To the one I'm going to mention;
> To whom a shark
> Is a perfect spark,
>   And an ogre deserves a pension.[88]

This is *faux-naïveté* of this first water, a parody of popular verse that conjures up the sweat and orange-peel of the fairground and, by its own shambling monstrosity, prepares to draw the veil on the poor "deformed" prince. While at first glance *The St. James's Phenomenon* might seem like an attack on "the crooked nose" that Swift had the tact and humanity to spare, it is not wholly ungenerous. The detail becomes so grotesque that it soars past the realm of ad hominem into the realm of fable. When, for example, George takes two hours to put on his stockings, he becomes the impersonal embodiment of indolence and vanity, as impersonal as the personifications of sin in *Piers Plowman*; and when his bowels clank, we are flung forward into the world of the Futurists—the gestures seem too extravagant to be hurtful. That the poet himself connected hyperbole with "animal spirits" can be gathered from his remarks on Marvell: "The exaggerations, no doubt, are extremely far-fetched, but they are not forced; Marvel [*sic*] could have talked such by the hundred ad libitum; and it is this easiness and flow of extravagance, as well as the relative truth lurking in it, that renders it delightful to those who have animal spirits enough to join in the merriment."[89] Animal spirits likewise make for merriment in the poem under scrutiny:

> His organs of digestion
>   Make a noise like the wheels of mangles;
> His tongue's a skin,
> And hollow within;
>   And his teeth are dice at angles.[90]

Yet even though the satire detoxifies itself by Rabelaisian overstatement, a remonstrance from a friend (Lamb?) caused Hunt to doubt its efficacy and taste, and he abandoned the promised sequel to the poem. Many years later he would say that the bitterness of Garth's poem on Queen Anne "must have had double effect, coming from so good-natured a man"[91]—a judgment that applies quite as fully to the bitter poems of his own "committed" phase of writing.

The uncharacteristic mordancy of Hunt's political poems springs from his passionate belief in reform and impatience with reactionary thought. Also uncharacteristic is their crisp, clean outline, which we can trace to the circumstances of their composition—there is little time for "floridizing" if a printer's devil is at hand to demand copy. The poems that result from this combined sharpness and economy are often telling, though their topicality has tended to "date" them. *The Lord Mayor and the Butcher* versifies an incident that had earlier been reported in *The Examiner*. This story of a butcher who met criticism with violence no doubt struck Hunt as a parable for the state of the nation. Yet, parable though the poem might be, there is nothing remote or stylized about its materials. Hunt has invested them with a verbal energy and acumen that turn the butcher into a prototype for Ned Dennis, the hangman in *Barnaby Rudge*. Look at the way he relays second-hand insults, comically indifferent to the feelings of their object, and the way in which his attention-seizing expletive bursts through the meter like a shout:

> "Oh, blood and wounds!" the butcher he cried,
>   "I don't know what I may do;
> For they not only call your Lordship an ass,
>   But a damned old scoundrel too!
>
> "Think o' that—hey—think of that!"
>   And the butcher like Falstaff puffed;
> "I couldn't bear the vagabonds,
>   So I kicked 'em and I cuffed;
>
> ["]I kicked their shins, and I cuffed their skins,
>   Both back and eke belly;
> And I told 'em, damme, once and for all,
>   You were no more fool than I."[92]

Nothing in the dialect poems of Barnes or Tennyson can match that for vigor, and we have to wait for Kipling before demotic speech is once again funneled through a formal meter.

Other political poems also attest the galvanizing influence of popular forms. Because the *Lawyer's Lament, or the Fees in Danger* takes off Catullus in its invocation—compare "Mourn, all ye Graces, Loves and Sports" with *Lugete, o Veneres Cupidinesque*[93]—it seems comparatively effete and bookish alongside *Reverend Magistracy* and *An Excellent Scotch Parody* and *Coronation Soliloquy*, which seize the diction of popular songs and ride on the back of its vigor. While the stanza of *Reverend Magistracy* has a Sapphic outline, that "classical" impression is all but effaced by the content it relays and by the distortions imposed by a rhyme scheme that mimics the magistrate's own inflexibility:

> For he's the fist of Justices;
> And nothing but mere dust he sees
> In those who eat dry *crustises*   `
>   And 'tatoes.[94]

Hunt exposes the Church's guilt in failing to speak out against oppression (and sometimes actively abetting it)[95] in *A New Chaunt*. This he has cast in a highly original measure—the rhyme can barely hold these decameter (?) couplets together, and the strain and sag of the ten feet between them images a society as rotten as its rotten boroughs, and yet smoothed into a semblance of order by sluggish and arbitrary rhyme.

Just as in psalm chant the unpredictable variant of each Hebrew clause is *made* to fit the graph of the melody by hurryings here (Hunt's dactylic feet) and slowings there (the trochees), so the Church has sanctioned the "Holy" Alliance's "adjustments" of liberty:

> First of all, in order to give a convenient finish to our
>   impudence and collusion,
> We'll buy and sell seats so openly, that it shall put no true
>   gentleman to confusion,
> And we'll put soldiers all about instead of constables, like our
>   good promise making friend the Prussian;
> And keep all good and knowing things to ourselves, like a close
>   Rosicrucian.[96]

A different kind of musical parody gives point to the macaronic poem about Caroline's accuser, *Memory or Want of Memory*. Hunt would have known Masetto's ironic response in *Don Giovanni* to the Don's "protection" of Zerlina (*Ho capito, signor, si*)[97] as well as the *concertato* in act 2 of *Il Barbiere di Siviglia*, where the phrase "Si, signor" reinforces widely differing responses to the same event, viz., Almaviva's attempt to billet himself on Dr. Bartolo ("In allogio quel briccone / Non me volle qui accettar / Si, signor, si, signor" as opposed to "Questa bestia di soldato, / Mio signor, m'ha maltrattato, / Si, signor, si, signor, si, signor").[98] With all these dramatic precedents ringing through the phrase, Hunt is able to imply his contempt

for the charges brought against the queen. Just as the waiter in the *Indicator*
essay chants a mindless assent to the commands of the patron, so too does
Maiocchi in Hunt's lampoon. By mechanizing the response, Hunt turns him
into a Bergsonian automaton. Additional humor flows from the fact that by his
desperate attachment to a single signifier, the speaker jams it against signifieds
it was never meant to serve, and threatens a comic disruption of language itself.
It is just possible that Dickens had Hunt's comic formula in mind when he
characterized a group of American travelers in *American Notes*:

> STRAW HAT. Warm weather, Judge.
> BROWN HAT. Yes, Sir.
> STRAW HAT. There was a snap of cold, last week.
> BROWN HAT. Yes, Sir.
>
> A pause. They look at each other, very seriously.
>
> STRAW HAT. I calculate you'll have got through that case of the
>   corporation, Judge, by this time, now?
> BROWN HAT. Yes, Sir.
> STRAW HAT. How did the verdict go, Sir?
> BROWN HAT. For the defendant, Sir.
> STRAW HAT. (Interrogatively.) Yes, Sir?
> BROWN HAT. Yes, Sir.
> BOTH. (Musingly, as each gazes down the street.) Yes, Sir.[99]

The macaronic form of the *Coronation Soliloquy* derives from a popular
song onto which Hunt has "contrafacted" the thoughts of George IV during
his coronation. By turning the event into splendid feast of misrule, Hunt
also turns the monarch himself into a King of Fools. Here is a specimen of
its "animal spirits":

> What a *dies*!
> How it fri-es!
>   Handkerchiefs for sixty.
> *Approbatio*!
> *Sibilatio*!
>   How I feel betwixt ye!
> Curlies, burlies,
> Dukes and earlies,
>   Bangs and clangs of band O!
> Shouty, flouty, heavy rig, and gouty.
> When shall I come to a stand O![100]

Hunt has the form of a Latin word bully an English monosyllable into rhyming with it, and furthermore blends a hint of the *Dies Irae* into the heat of an English summer—heat which implies that it is sweat rather than popular approval that has prompted the unpocketing of handkerchiefs. Even the peers are addressed with a roly-poly diminutive from the nursery ("earlies") and can offer no protection from the hisses of popular discontent from which George IV has hitherto been screened. Like all great comedy, the farce of this poem trenches on pathos. We can apply Hunt's own words post factum: "[E]xtremes meet; excess of laughter runs into tears, and mirth becomes heaviness. Mirth itself is too often but melancholy in disguise. The jests of the fool in *Lear* are the sighs of knowledge."[101]

I have noted how, by steering satire in the direction of the grotesque, Hunt often draws the sting of malice and offers good-natured romping and roistering in its place. However, there are occasions when, with a reality grotesque in itself, the spirited treatment proves more hurtful than it was meant to be. The corpulence of George IV provides a case in point. Hunt might have held fire had he known the king's morbid sensitivity about his weight and how he avoided public appearances in London towards the end of his life, fearing "the ridicule which might be excited by his dropsical bulk."[102]

By far the most substantial of the topical satires is *The Dogs*, published in 1822. Hunt's choice of stanza (ottava rima) makes it clear that he has taken Byron as his model, and Byron's influence is apparent also in its "outrageous" management. The loppings and enjambments, while they pretend to make servile adjustments of language to form, actually deride that form by suggesting that its challenges can be met by shameless expediency. Again like Byron, Hunt "wears" his learning to create a foil for slangy contemporary matter. The result of this mix is a stanza like the one below, a stanza so charged by anarchic energy that it barely holds together. Speech stress defies the conforming pressure of meter and expletive asides block the passage of the syntax:

> Herodotus says only that there were
> Four villages allotted for their dog's-meat;
> A handsome pension, I allow: but here
> Warriors stand by, wanting, like proper rogues, meat,
> Bread being even for a few too dear,
> While the Duke's hounds to their respective progs meet.
> Warriors, mind—hollow squares—without whom, marry! an
> Arbiter I could name had now been carrion.[103]

Hunt has also imitated that Byronic ability to sideswipe other targets en passant, so that for a moment a military formation becomes a hungry man with square shoulders.

Although Byron is the chief inspiration behind the poem, we ought not to forget that Hunt also had a special affection for Rabelais, whose "combination of work and play, of merriment and study, of excessive animal spirits with prodigious learning, would be perpetual marvel, if we did not reflect that nothing is more likely to make a man happy, particularly a Frenchman, than his being able to indulge his genius, and cultivate the task he is fit for."[104] The influence of Rabelais is most palpable in the exuberant listings and heapings-up, the riotous adaptations of *acervatio*. In the catalog of Tory dogs, for example, the stanza perpetually threatens to disintegrate into unmetrical atoms:

> The names of their Canine-nesses—Prince, Jowler,
> Jolly, and Folly, Tippler, Fop, and Tough,
> Duke, Dundeed, Slim, Fang, Whistler, Gamester, Growler,
> Standfast, and Steady, Waterloo, Chance, Rough,
> Charge, Trooper, Glutton, Hollo-boy, Old Towler,
> Blucher, Spot, Shriek, Jump, Victor, Old Boy, Puff,
> Rascal, Force, Bourbon, Throat, Spite, Promise, Viper,
> Moonshine, and Betty, Riot, Rage, and Piper:
>
> Hungry, Old England, Hot, Shot, Scot, and Lot,
> Old Soldier, Gaunt, and Grim, Seize-him-boy, Eat-'em,
> Tally-ho, Thief, Fool, Devil, Brute, and Sot.
> A pretty list. Ovid has one (see *Metam.*
> *Lib. Ter.*) but Ovid's pack of hounds was not
> The moral, order-loving, plumb, legitim-
> Ate hounds, that these are. These, to run the faster,
> Eat but one's men, but those eat up their master.[105]

Hunt uses his stanza and its rebellious contents as an image of Tory government in 1822. There are ingredients of disruption—Riot, Rage and Hungry—but they are balanced (and therefore neutralized) by answering elements of repression (Force, Shot, Seize-him-boy). Random fragments of the Holy Alliance also find their way into the stew (Blucher and Bourbon) and so too do the insentient foolishness and squalor and unreality of the king's circle (Tippler, Fop, and Tough). It is government without vision or purpose, government intent on preserving an inherited notion of order, which it forces in all its meaninglessness onto situations it cannot control.

Here the stanza comes into its own as political icon of repressive force, so much so that even words are mangled to furnish forth the rhyme: "legitim- / Ate." The arbitrary fracture of "legitimate" releases the word "ate" into a poem pitting gluttonous aristocracy against starving populace, and also (with the *e* sounded) the Greek word for folly and delusion. This macaronic punning is also evident in other parts of the poem, as when, in parody of Wilson's *Noctes Ambrosianae*, the crisis in Ireland is waved off during a symposium more Scotch than Greek:

> All eyes for the moment, even on that day,
> Turn at the name of Ireland, to look at
> The nation whom a king's nod made so gay:
> Even some certain members cry "What's that?"
> "Only the Irish,"—"Oh—the Irish—eh?
> What do *they* want? I's thank ye for some fat."
> "The Irish, eh? Send 'em some soldiery
> And eighteen pence. Hock, if you please for me."[106]

Hunt no doubt remembered all the jibes that *Blackwood's* had leveled against tea-drinking Cockneys, and how Christopher North, after making some heartless Tory pronouncement, would ask for lemons to be passed in the ostentatious mixing of his drink. This is the sort of "stage direction" he has in mind when the speaker (ignorant and unfeeling) requests the carver for some fat—an obvious enough irony—and the wine steward for some hock. But "hock" also suggests *ad hoc*, the crude legislative patching and piecemeal of unprogressive government. In much the same way, Hunt has the bishops of a collaborative church sing "the psalm beginning 'Cur, domine.'"[107] The psalm in question, part of the ninth in the Vulgate (but the tenth *secundum Hebraeos*) reads:

> Why standest thou so far off, O Lord: and hidest thy face in the needful time of trouble?
> 2 The ungodly for his own lust doth persecute the poor: let them be taken in the crafty wiliness that they have imagined.
> 3 For the ungodly hath made boast of his own heart's desire: and speaketh good of the covetous, whom God abhorreth.[108]

The irony does not stop here, however, for Hunt has altered the Latin of St. Jerome from "Ut quid, Domine, recessisti longe" to "Cur, Domine"—with the express purpose of making a cross-lingual pun on the English "cur."

In the mock-apotheosis that enskies the regent's ministers, Hunt reads a massive cosmic allegory into the disposition of the stars, so that the constellations of Lupus and Ara dramatize the predatory unholiness of the Holy Alliance, blockish both in its stupidity and in its reactionary desire to block all progress—"Nay, things are there which absolute blocks produce. / The Altar's next the Wolf." And Wellington also figures as the Dog Star by virtue of another dash across linguistic frontiers: "Canis the Major too, by which it's clear / That army-rank with dogs is of old use."

The Dogs is a good poem, but it is complicated by Hunt's admiration for dogs (as for all creatures, including Giffordian spiders) and by his having at the same time to use them as images of satiric belittlement. The result is too much hemming and hawing, too many revisionary asides that try to redeem the animals at the same time as they damn the people thus imaged—"You wouldn't see them come, through thick and thin, / Leaping and panting at you, all a-grin."[109] If dogs are endearingly faithful and cordial, have they been wisely chosen as the vehicle for a satiric apologue? Furthermore, while the poem has zest and momentum, there are moments when Hunt lets his "animal spirits" congest it with so many satiric targets that we lose sight of shape and form. James Thompson has suggested that the "weakness of Hunt's satire results not so much from this esthetic shift of interest as from his very nature. Despite his wit and his youthful zeal and enthusiasm, his tolerant, cheerful character largely incapacitated him for literary warfare."[110] There is a great deal of truth in this, though I do not wholly agree with Thompson's assessment of the satire. Lockhart, after all, had much the same opinion: "You, Leigh Hunt, are without exception, the weakest and wishy-washiest satirist whose pen ever dribbled,"[111] an insult that, coming from the most intemperate of men, is a compliment indeed. Hunt's temperamental sunniness might not furnish him with a armory of barbs and brickbats, but I think that what Thompson calls "youthful zeal" can often develop an arms programme of its own. We have seen how indignation of a truly *disinterested* political nature heightens the tone and sharpens the attack in Hunt's topical satires. But it was there to be tapped only for so long as Hunt was politically active. The moment he retired, he virtually abandoned satire, returning to the form only for *Captain Sword and Captain Pen*. After the demise of *The Liberal* and up to his death, he chose for the most part to ring endless lyric changes on the idyll.

5

Miscellaneous Verse

In earlier chapters we have seen how Hunt's fanciful impulses worked often against the grain of his narrative and satiric poetry (however attractive and characteristic the fruit they bear). In this chapter we shall see them rising gratefully to the occasion in his familiar essayistic verse, the form in which, after all, the assumptions and attitudes of rococo art are best accommodated.

EPISTLES

Tucked in among the "Miscellaneous Poems" in Hunt's arrangement of the 1860 edition were several verse epistles that Milford, with good reason, presents in a separate component. The poems assembled here thus bridge the public issues of the satires with the more private matter of the lyric and essayistic verse. For if we consider the history of the verse epistle, we find it closely bound up with that of satire. W. A. Laidlaw has said of Horace's *Epistles* that they "are essentially a continuation of the *Satires* in theme, style and metre,"[1] a statement no less true of Pope's verse letters, some of which he called "moral essays." The Horatian epistle, being the discourse of one friend to another, carries its own decorum of style, a style marked by informality and relaxation. At the same time it tries to be a touch more intimate, a touch less acerbic, and touch more dignified than the style required for satire. Michael Grant says of Horace's *Epistles* that they "are the expression of a highly civilized mind—of what the Romans called *urbanitas*. Their taste and their sense are both excellent. They are witty and charming, and they have a new grace of language and metre."[2] Their *urbanitas* and "highly civilized" ethos notwithstanding, Horace's letters do not always concern themselves with high-minded matters—far more often they issue unpretentious dinner invitations or requests for urban gossip that nudge them towards lyric, as indeed some lyric poems can themselves take on a proto-epistolary color (Catullus's "Cenabis, bene, mi Fabulle, apud me,"[3] for instance). That Hunt has clearly modeled his handful of verse letters on Horace's can be gathered from the way in which they parallel situations of the *Epistulae*. However, he has also allowed himself greater lyric largesse than the form ordinarily permits. These purple passages might on the one hand seem to breach epistolary decorum, but on the other they could be viewed as generic enrichments, one of the countless romantic efforts at breeding hybrids from a marriage of kinds. The epistle to Byron is a case in point.

Hunt clearly wrote the poem as a public testament to his solidarity with, and respect for, a poet hounded out of his native land by public opprobrium. It is worth remembering that shortly before the epistle "To the Right Honourable Lord Byron on His Departure for Italy and Greece" appeared in *The Examiner*, Hunt had also published an essay trying to palliate the scandal of Byron's marriage, and urging less judgmental conduct towards the poet:

> What is the case at present? A young Nobleman, to whom the public are indebted for a great deal of poetical enjoyment, is reported to have separated form his Wife; and instantly, without knowing anything of the matter, and as if he had never done anything or possessed any one quality to make reproach hesitate, the story is mixed up with all sorts of inconsistent and villainous accusations, some of them so monstrous that even the first public propagators of the scandal professed the singular delicacy of being able only to hint them.[4]

The same generous impulse carries over into the publication of the epistle a week later (28 April 1816), which in its first version projected a future reconciliation between husband and wife:

> Nor shall that brow, whose haughty lamps of blue
> Turn, almost dimm'd with unaccustomed dew,
> Be long without the light that warm'd its bays,
> Still less for clouds, that poisonous inks would raise,
> And least of all, like Orpheus's of yore,
> For having turned to gaze on her once more.[5]

Byron's marital relations make for troublesome epistolary matter, and it is to Hunt's wish to avoid scandal-laden specifics that we must trace his lyrical tableaux, a feature hardly typical of verse letters. The stylistic decorum of the form tends rather to dictate a prosaic circumspectness and restraint of language. Thus we find Gray (in a letter to Mason) apologizing for a lyrical flight about the Kentish countryside:

[I]n the east the sea breaks in upon you, & mixes its white transient sails & glittering blew expanse with the deeper & brighter greens of the woods & corn. this last sentence is so fine I am quite ashamed but no matter! you must translate it into prose. Palgrave, if he heard it, would cover his face with his pudding sleeve.[6]

If Gray expresses embarrassment over this slight heightening of his diction, what on earth would he have made of the epic periphrasis that turns Byron's eyes into "haughty lamps of blue"?

To measure the full extent of Hunt's deviation from Horatian norms in this poem, we need to consider the *Epistula* addressed to Bullatius (1.11). All letters owe their provenance to a physical separation of the writer from the recipient, but in some the situation is stressed more heavily than in others, especially if the letter is going abroad. Here is how Horace conducts his enquiries, as factually and unglamorously as if he were poring over a gazetteer of the Aegean:

> Quid tibi visa Chios, Bullati, notaque Lesbos,
> quid concinna Samos, quid Croesi regia Sardis,
> Zmyrna quid et Colophon? maiora minorave fama,
> cunctane prae Campo et Tiberino flumine sordent?
> an venit in votum Attalicis ex urbibus una,
> an Lebedum laudas odio maris atque viarum?

> (What did you think of Chios, my Bullatius, and of famous Lesbos? What of charming Samos? What of Sardis, royal home of Croesus? What of Smyrna and Colophon? Whether above or below their fame, do they all seem poor beside the Campus and the Tiber's stream? Or is your heart set upon one of the cities of Attalus? Or do you extol Lebedus, because sick of sea and roads?)[7]

This, as befits a private letter, is unpretentious and unadorned, a simple enquiry by one friend about the topographic responses of the other.

Hunt's letter strikes an altogether different note. It begins conventionally enough as a prompemptikon, offering wishes for a calm sea and a prosperous voyage. Even here, however, he cannot help writing in his idyllic, recreational mode, nor can he help fingerprinting the language with his usual mannerisms. The image we get—we pause to visualize it—is of the ship's perpetually listing, and of Byron's scrabbling to keep his purchase as he lounges on deck:

> May all that hastens, pleases, and secures,
> Fair winds and skies, and a swift ship, be yours,
> Whose sidelong deck affords, as it cuts on,
> An airy slope to lounge and read upon;[8]

It is clear, however, that Hunt's fancy has already taken flight, transforming a commercial ship into a pleasure craft. The realistic context of the voyage has been cut away, leaving Byron as a sort of solitary figurehead, while the "airy slope" of the deck he graces suggests that the vessel is of a piece with the fanciful boat Gautier would later describe in *Les Nuits d'Eté*.

Hunt continues to pile it on. Byron is made to view a dawn couched in the sub-Homeric image of a "happy-blushing" mouth, which is meant to provide a sober foil to the "actual" flight of fancy (a vision, à la Wordsworth in *The World Is Too Much With Us*, of naiads at their toilette):

> And may there be sweet, watching moons at night,
> Or shows, upon the sea, of curious light;
> And morning wake with happy-blushing mouth,
> As though her husband still had "eyes of youth;"
> While fancy, just as you discern from far
> The coast of Virgil and of Sannazar,
> May see the nymphs emerging, here and there,
> To tie up at the light their rolling hair.[9]

If Byron has no pudding sleeve to cover his face at this point, then perhaps we had better imagine his stuffing a cravat into his mouth. But there is more still to come, in Technicolor even more intense, when the epistolary context falls away in the sort of allegorical tableau that Gray presents in *The Bard* ("In gallant trim the gilded vessel goes; / Youth on the prow and Pleasure at the helm"):[10]

> I see you now, half eagerness, half ease,
> Ride o'er the dancing freshness of the seas;
> I see you now (with fancy's eyesight too)
> Find, with a start, that lovely vision true,
> While on a sudden, o'er the horizon's line
> Phoebus looks forth with his long glance divine,
> At which old Ocean's white and shapely Daughters
> Crowd in the golden ferment of the waters,
> And halcyons brood, and there's a glistering show

> Of harps, midst bosoms and long arms of snow;
> And from the breathing sea, in the God's eye,
> A gush of voices breaks up to the sky
> To hail the laurelled Bard, that goes careering by.[11]

In a complex epistemological layering of fancy upon fancy, Hunt subjoins his own vision to the vision he has attributed to Byron—"(with fancy's eyesight too)." The result is a marine idyll, rendered with all the congestion, the unmappability, that marks the full flight of Hunt's fancy. He has remembered Poussin's *Triumph of Amphitrite* and Raphael's *Galatea* (liquidized with the Borghese ceiling of Guido Reni), and the beatific visions of Pozzo and Correggio (for how else do harps enter the picture?) and the bestiary lore from the *Metamorphoses*. The result is miles removed from the letters of Horace or Pope.

Having written in the purplest of inks, Hunt feels a little abashed, and tries to recuperate the whole enterprise by turning a private into a universal response. The *quis est homo* formula he puts to use in this regard is at least as old as the *Stabat Mater*: "And who, thus gifted, but must hear and see / Wonders like these, approaching Italy." Just as Horace uses the first of his second book of epistles, *Ad Augustum*, to ponder the literary relationship of Rome to Greece, so Hunt does the same vis-à-vis England and Italy. Here he versifies some of the precepts that led him to posit Italian rather than French models for the "new school" of romanticism, precepts that in themselves make the poem an interesting document of the period:

> Enchantress Italy,—who born again
> In Gothic fires, woke to a sphery strain,
> And rose and smiled, far lovelier than before,
> Copier of Greece and Amazon no more,
> But altogether a diviner thing,
> Fit for the Queen of Europe's second spring,
> With fancies of her own, and finer powers
> Not to enslave these mere outsides of ours,
> But bend the godlike mind, and crown it with her flowers.[12]

Because the Augustans had taken the *Epistula ad Augustum* as a formulation of their own literary ideals of polish and conformity, Hunt revokes its chief assumptions. Horace celebrates the imperial conquest of Greece, at the same time acknowledging that military victory was balanced by the triumph of Greek culture over Roman: *Graecia capta ferum victorem cepit et artis /*

intulit agresti Latio (Greece, the captive, made her savage victor captive, and brought the arts into rustic Latium).[13] Hunt reinterprets the data to image Rome as habitual militarist ("Amazon") and cultural epigone ("copier"), and therefore an unworthy object of imitation. Having thus rejected the foundation of neoclassicism, he proceeds to instate his own alternative models, models that originate in the Renaissance, a movement Englished by the phrase "born again." Gray and Pope were Augustan enough to shudder at the cultural disruption the barbarian invaders brought with them; Hunt (rather astonishingly) presents them rather as the cleansers of a corrupt civilization, from whose thrice refining fires medieval Italy arises like a phoenix.

Continuing this discourse on Italian art, Hunt implies that the cultural strength of Italy depended on the coequality of its various artists, whether literary, plastic, or musical:

> and right before her throne
> Have sat the intellectual Graces three,
> Music, and Painting, and winged Poetry,
> Of whom were born those great ones, thoughtful-faced,
> That led the hierarchy of modern taste;—[14]

I find it odd that someone writing in 1816 could speak so enthusiastically about the music of Renaissance Italy, for Monteverdi had yet to be rediscovered. Even in *A Fancy Concert* (1845), Hunt goes no further back than Marcello. It would therefore seem that he is advancing a theory of artistic symbiosis at this point, and sacrificing the facts as he perceived them to that theory. His salute to Renaissance painters has an altogether greater ring of truth, and seems to have lodged in Shelley's mind when he came to write *Ozymandias* two years later. Compare "Hands that could catch the very finest airs / Of natural minds, and all that soul express / Of ready concord" with "its sculptor well those passions read / Which yet survive, stamped on these lifeless things, / The hand that mocked them, and the heart that fed."[15]

The next section of the poem covers ground well trodden in the eighteenth century, viz., the influence of climate on national character. Gray abandoned a potentially great poem in *The Alliance of Education and Government* when he realized that Montesquieu had beaten him to its central ideas, but Goldsmith felt no such inhibitions when he wrote *The Traveller*, his own version of the epistolary moral essay. Here he moralizes the climate and topography of Italy:

> But small the bliss that sense alone bestows,
> And sensual bliss is all the nation knows.
> In florid beauty groves and fields appear,
> Man seems the only growth that dwindles here.
> Contrasted faults through all his manners reign:
> Though poor, luxurious; though submissive, vain;
> Though grave, yet trifling; zealous, yet untrue;
> And even in penance planning sins anew.[16]

Without rejecting the Montesquieuvian thought behind such passages, Hunt gives it a rather different color. Another eighteenth-century poem, Gray's *Progress of Poesy*, had claimed that great literature depends on political liberty, a view that Hunt also adopted. Hence he internalizes the warmth of a Mediterranean climate in an idyll of the domestic fireside, reworking the cliché that conceives the home as an English person's castle:

> Not that our English clime, how sharp soe'er,
> Yields in ripe genius to the warmest sphere;
> For what we want in sunshine out of doors,
> And the long leisure of abundant shores,
> By freedom, nay, by sufferance, is supplied,
> And each man's sacred sunshine, his fire-side.[17]

If Hunt has missed an opportunity to relate that boasted "sufferance" to Byron's imminent exile, that is because he has a more exalted issue to pursue at this point.

We can guess from the attack on Boileau in Keats's *Sleep and Poetry* that Hunt perceived the Frenchman as a sort of neoclassical lynchpin, for while he liked and admired *Le Lutrin*, he clearly had reservations about the author's poetics. Boileau was closely associated with an absolute monarch, as Horace himself with Augustus, and thus the neoclassicism he advocated, because it was slavishly bound to ancient models, exemplified a divorce from the liberty upon which Gray and others had predicated true poetry. So for as long England's literary deference to France issued in a deference to Rome, England's poetry suffered a decline. In Hunt's view, the "four great Masters"—Chaucer, Shakespeare, Spenser, and Milton—all predated the Augustan era, and all of them enriched their art with Italian (not Roman) sources:

> But all the four great Masters of our Song,
> Stars that shine out amidst a starry throng,

Have turned to Italy for added light,
As earth is kissed by the sweet moon at night;—
Milton for half his style, Chaucer for his tales,
Spenser for flowers to fill his isles and vales,
And Shakspeare's self for frames already done,
To build his everlasting piles upon.
Her genius is more soft, harmonious, fine;
Ours bolder, deeper, and more masculine;
In short, as woman's sweetness to man's force,
Less grand, but softening by the intercourse,
So the two countries are,—so may they be,—
England the high-souled man, the charmer Italy.[18]

It is ironic that, having implicitly parted company with Horace by rejecting the tenets of neoclassicism, Hunt should unconsciously adapt the *Graecia capta ferum victorem cepit* motto in diagnosing Italy's influence on England, which he projects very much as if it were *agreste Latium*. Significantly, however, the influence does not turn on ideas of correctness, but of "sweetness" and mellifluousness.

Many other writers have coveted the ease of rhyme and phonetic luxury made possible by the terminal vowel in Italian words, as witness this claim by one of England's greatest poetic craftspersons:

in spite of its energy, plenty & crowd of excellent Writers this nation has produced, does yet (I am sorry to say it) retain too much of its barbarous original to adapt itself to musical composition. I should by no means wish myself to have been born any thing but an Englishman; yet I should rejoice to exchange tongues with Italy.[19]

If we set this pronouncement against Pope's version of the *Epistula ad Augustum*—*The First Epistle of the Second Book of Horace Imitated*—we can see a crucial shift away from the ideal of correctness to that of sweetness, making Gray (in this as in so many other instances) an important interface between Augustan and romantic positions on the topic:

We conquer'd France, but felt our captive's charms;
Her Arts victorious triumph'd o'er our Arms:
Britain to soft refinements less a foe,
Wit grew polite, and Numbers learn'd to flow.
Waller was smooth; but Dryden taught to join
The varying verse, the full resounding line,
The long majestic march, and energy divine.

> Tho' still some traces of our rustic vein,
> And splay-foot verse, remain'd, and will remain.
> Late, very late, correctness grew our care,
> When the tir'd nation breath'd from civil war.
> Exact Racine, and Corneille's noble fire
> Show'd us that France had something to admire.[20]

What Gray and Hunt after him imply about the sweetness of Italian is implicit in such phrases as "soft refinements," but the passage centers with much more culminant force on "correctness." All three poets agree on the comparative roughness and energy of the English language, but Gray and Hunt differ from Pope in aspiring to musicality rather than conformation to neoclassical rules. Hunt's idea of romanticism as a rediscovery of the Italian heritage has now been discredited, but in 1816 it seemed as plausible a way as any to distinguish the "new school" from the old. Byron's literal journey to Italy offered an exemplum for literary journeys in the same direction.

At this point, the "banner" statement on romanticism ends, and Hunt lapses into the chattiness and informality more usually associated with the verse letter. He even—and here one sense Byron must have squirmed—he even offers some fatherly advice against the temptations lurking abroad. It is all very well for Italian culture to seduce an English poet with its emollient, "feminine" beauty; it is altogether another for an Italian woman to do the same:

> And pray, my Lord, in Italy take care,
> You that are poet, and have pains to bear,
> Of lovely girls, that step across the sight,
> Like Houris in a heaven of warmth and light,
> With rosy-cushioned mouths and dimples set,
> And ripe dark tresses, and glib eyes of jet.
> The very language, from a woman's tongue,
> Is worth the finest of all others sung.[21]

Epistles like Horace's to Lollius Maximus (*Epistulae* 1.2) demonstrate how firmly the form entrenches ideas of monition and advice, e.g., *Sperne voluptates; nocet empta dolore voluptas* (Scorn pleasures; pleasure bought with pain is harmful).[22] Here Horace is addressing a man considerably younger than himself, and the condescension of experience to youth seems justified. When Hunt addresses a man four years his junior, the effect is rather one of presumption, an effect compounded by the fact that, uttered in the context of a propemptikon, the counsel connects the poem to another tradition, the valediction of father to son. The loci classici are Isocrates' *Ad demonicum* and Cato's *Disticha de moribus ad filium*, but more famous than both is Polonius's farewell speech to Laertes. Speaking so condescendingly to someone only a few years younger than himself (and considerably more worldly-wise), Hunt was asking for trouble from such quarters as *Blackwood's*. In the 1816 version of the poem, the lines on Lady Byron followed at this point, and Hunt seems to have used the "parental" episode as a lead-in, reminding censorious readers that his tolerance ought not to be taken as simple condonation, and in the remaining part of the letter he is careful to point out that he has not been whitewashing Byron's failures. Among the reasons he lists for admiring the poet are his candor and his unhypocritical display of his shortcomings to public inspection. In Hunt's eyes, such candor, by disclosing, paradoxically covers, a multitude of sins:

> For faults unhidden, other's virtues owned;
> Nay, unless Cant's to be at once enthroned,
> For virtues too, with whatsoever blended,
> And e'en were none possessed, for none pretended;—
> . . . .
> For a stretched hand, ever the same to me,—
> And total, glorious want of vile hypocrisy.[23]

The final couplet, because it is typographically detached from the preceding paragraph, creates the expectation of a memorable epigram, a skein-gathering *sententia*. What Hunt offers in this portentous frame is so lame and so flat that one can only hope he intended a joke, like the "bad writing" in Mozart's *Musikalischer Spass*: "Adieu, adieu:—I say no more.—God speed you! / Remember what we all expect who read you."

The couplet structure of the *Epistle to Lord Byron* brings a traditionally aphoristic mode to bear on an informal letter, but when it is filled with inconsequential, doodling verse like that above, bathos is bound to result. If Hunt had written blank verse instead, the discrepancy would have been much less pronounced since, being close to the phatic line of spoken English, it would serve as the *sermo pedestris* of a familiar epistle. That he should have chosen *anapestic* couplets for his other letter poems seems stranger still, for the trisyllabic foot pushes the poetry even further away from spoken prose toward song and incantation. He addresses the issue in the first of the letters, entitled *To Thomas Moore*, and in the process explains why he favors trisyllabic meter in so many of his other poems as well:

> I owe you a letter, and having this time
> A whole series to write you, send them in rhyme;
> For rhyme, with its air, and its step-springing tune,
> Helps me on, as a march does a soldier in June;
> And when chattering to you, I've something about me,
> That makes all my spirits come dancing from out me.[24]

Hunt confesses here to viewing the anapest as a kind of stimulant, for while ostensibly talking about rhyme, he is actually talking about meter. (Rhyme does not provide a tune, nor does it spring the step.) He admits that the emphatic measure induces enough energy to overcome the fatigue of his task, as music makes marching less arduous in hot weather. Hunt's poetry was, by his own admission, recreational. He wrote verse as a sort of therapeutic hobby, with same addictive compulsion that led Father Faber to churn out books on Catholic devotion. For a poetry of self-escape that "makes all [his] spirits come dancing from out [him]," it follows that the writer should choose a measure as far removed from prose as the idyll is from the everyday world. It is almost is if the tune induces the flight of the poem, and enables the poet to glide forward on automatic pilot. In comparison with Keats, say, there is little sense of the inevitable in Hunt's poetry, little sense, when we compare his endless revisions with the original text, that he is driving towards some final, irrevocable wording of some final, immutable perception. The all-of-a-sameness in his alternatives is bound up in the recreational nature of the verse—the precedence it gives to inducing tune over induced substance—and his lyricizing of the letter form should perhaps be viewed in these terms.

Hunt's letter to Thomas Moore would seem superficially to turn on the well-established poles of pastoral—Hampstead as God-made country and London as "man"-made town. But things are not quite what they seem. Even as the poem offers itself as an idyll, it reminds us of the essentially urban nature of the rococo idyll, the temporary and provisional translation of well-bred *mores*, of satin vestments transposed to a country setting. Watteau always seems to remind us that there is an embarkation in the offing, an imminent return.

Hunt introduces the city into his country retreat as an unwanted association (rather as the word "forlorn" will later end the imaginative escape in Keats's *Ode to a Nightingale*). In the course of a Lovelace-like account of how a bee is exploring his manuscript—he is writing "half stretched on the ground"—Hunt recalls a less attractive insect attached to the Tory establishment, and this thought of Gifford cues in thoughts about London:

Here, over my paper another [i.e., a bee] shall go,
Looking just like a traveller lost in the snow,—
Till he reaches the writing,—and then, when he's eyed it,
What nodding, and touching, and coasting beside it!
. . . .
Now he stops at a question, as who should say "Hey?"
Now casts his round eye up the yawn of an A;
Now resolves to be bold, half afraid he shall sink,
And like Gifford before him, can't tell what to think.

Oh the wretched transition to insects like these
From those of the country! To town from the trees!
Ah, Tom,—you who've run the gay circle of life,
And squared it, at last, with your books and a wife,—
Who in Bond street by day, when the press has been thickest,
Have had all the "digito monstror" and "hic est,"
Who've shone at great houses in coach-crowded streets,
Amidst lights, wits, and beauties, and musical treats,
And had the best pleasure a guest could befall,
In being, yourself, the best part of it all,—
Can the town (and I'm fond of it too, when I'm there)
Can the town, after all, with the country compare?[25]

Hunt has effected a seamless transition here. Even though his anapests beat
out the words with an unnatural, bright insistence, he manages plausibly to
reproduce the associative line of a conversation (as Cowper had done before
him in poems such as *Table Talk*), and so to project an intimacy and
unstudiedness well suited to letters of this kind. Something supremely anecdotal—a bee on one's writing paper—has paved the way for a topic of
wider importance and relevance. Such discourse on the comparative merits
of town and country will inevitably bring to mind the satires and letters of
Horace, especially that to Aristius Fuscus (*Epistulae* 1.10):

Urbis amatorem Fuscum salvere iubemus
ruris amatores. hac in re scilicet una
multum dissimiles, at cetera paene gemelli
fraternis animis (quidquid negat alter, et alter)
adnuimus pariter veluti notique columbi.
　　Tu nidum servas; ego laudo ruris amoeni
rivos et muscos circumlita saxa nemusque.
Quid quaeris? vivo et regno, simul ista reliqui
quae vos ad caelum effertis rumore secundo,

utque sacerdotis fugitivus libo recuso;
pane egeo iam mellitis potiore placentis.

(To Fuscus, lover of the city, I, lover of the country, send greetings. In this
one point, to be sure, we differ much, but being in all else much like twins
with the hearts of brothers—if one says "no," the other says "no," too—we
nod a common assent like a couple of old familiar doves.

You keep the nest; I praise the lovely country's brooks, its grove and
moss-grown rocks. In short: I live and reign, as soon as I have left behind
what you townsmen with shouts of applause extol to the skies. Like the
priest's runaway slave, I loathe sweet wafers; 'tis bread I want, and now
prefer to honeyed cakes.)[26]

Just as Horace affirms his general affinity with Fuscus in order to highlight
their differing over this particular preference, so Hunt (as Hazlitt later on)
presents Moore as a kindred spirit who shares his values and priorities
("Dear Tom, who enjoying your brooks and your bowers, / Live just like a
bee, when he's flushest of flowers,— / A maker of sweets, busy, sparkling,
and singing, / Yet armed with an exquisite point too for stinging"[27]. But
whereas Horace rejects the city as a kind of death and enslavement of the
self (or so his living and reigning in the solitude of the country would imply),
Hunt acknowledges that there is enough of himself in Moore to respond to
the glamor and excitement of being lionized in Bond Street or feted in
Belgravia. That means that the battle lines of pastoral can no longer be
clearly drawn. Horace backhandedly acknowledges the cultural glamor of
Rome in the image of the honeyed cakes, but his nausea implies that humankind cannot live by honey alone. Hunt, on the other hand, implies that
the city (as a repository above all of cultural and communal values) also
attracts him. He will develop the idea only in a later poem, choosing mean-
while, in the "Extract from Another Letter to the Same," to take up the
unambivalent stance of pastoral towards the town.

Even here, however, Hunt's imagery half betrays him. He states at the
outset that he is about to offer Moore a lesson in bathos, keeping the worst
wine till last:

Would you change, my dear Tom, your old mode of proceeding,
And make a dull end to a passage worth reading,—
I mean, would you learn how to let your wit down,
You'd walk some fine morning from Hampstead to town.[28]

What follows is a hodoiporikon (or journey poem) in Hunt's most idyllic
mode, its idealism braced by an observation of color and texture that con-

nects the effect of dark mould with causal rain, and pinpoints the exact
gradation of tone in a mown field:

> What think you of going by gardens and bowers,
> Through fields of all colours, refreshed by night-showers,—
> Some spotted with hay-cocks, some dark with ploughed mould,
> Some changed by the mower from green to pale gold,—[29]

Dickens is the great master of hodoiporika in and out of cities, a fact attested
by numerous episodes in *The Old Curiosity Shop*. However, when Little Nell
and her father escape from London, the narrator is careful to document a
transitional zone between urban and rural space:

> brickfields skirting gardens paled with staves of old casks, or timber pil-
> laged from houses burnt down, and blackened and blistered by the flames—
> mounds of dockweed, nettles, coarse grass and oyster shells, heaped in
> rank confusion—small dissenting chapels to teach, with no lack of illus-
> tration, the miseries of Earth, and plenty of new churches, erected with a
> little superfluous wealth, to show the way to Heaven.
>
> At length these streets becoming more straggling yet, dwindled and
> dwindled away, until there were only small garden patches bordering the
> road, with many a summerhouse innocent of paint and built of old timber
> or some fragments of a boat, green as the tough cabbage stalks that grew
> about it. . . .[30]

Hunt, on the other hand, has no intention of softening his pastoral antithesis with intermediate stages of the journey, and plunges straight from the
Hampstead countryside into the heart of London:

> And an air in your face, ever fanning and sweet,
> And the birds in your ears, and a turf for your feet;—
> And then, after all, to encounter a throng of
> Canal-men, and hod-men, unfit to make song of,
> Midst ale-houses, puddles, and backs of street-roads,
> And all sorts of rubbish, and crashing cart-loads,
> And so on, eye-smarting, and ready to choke,
> Till you end in hot narrowness, clatter, and smoke!
> 'Tis Swift after Spenser, or daylight with candles,
> A sea-song succeeding a pastoral of Handel's,
> A step unexpected, that jars one's inside,
> The shout-raising fall at the end of a slide,

> A yawn to a kiss, a flock followed by dust,
> The hoop of a beauty seen after her bust,[31]

Here Hunt is trying on a standard pastoral posture for size, rather as Marvell shifts vantage and allegiance from one poem to another. He tries to voice the stereotyped reservations about the city as a place of noise and congestion; but as he does so, some of his reductive images fail to reduce in the way he intended them to. By opposing Swift to Spenser, he means us to think of such urban poems as *A Description of the Morning* and *A Description of a City Shower*, and so to countervail romance with squalid realism. But too much romance can surfeit, and Swift's energy and focus can come as a welcome aperients after a diet of *The Faerie Queene;* and so too a shanty's salt vigor after the baroque idyll of *Acis and Galatea.* Even such obviously negative similes as the "shout-raising fall" and the "step unexpected" are charged with an incidental excitement. The truth is that even when he attempts pastoral orthodoxy, Hunt's naturally catholic instincts get in the way.

A more honest manifesto of his position with regard to the traditional antitheses of pastoral is set out in an epistle to Hazlitt, written one week later:

> One's life, I conceive, might go prettily down,
> In a due easy mixture of country and town;—
> Not after the fashion of most with two houses,
> Who gossip, and gape, and just follow their spouses,
> And let their abode be wherever it will,
> Are the same vacant, house-keeping animals still;—
> But with due sense of each, and of all that it yields,—
> In the town, of the town,—in the fields, of the fields;
> In the one, for example, we feel as we go on,
> That streets are about us, arts, people, and so on;
> In t'other, to value the stillness, the breeze,
> And love to see farms, and to get among trees.
> Each to his liking, of course,—so that this be the rule—
> For my part, who went in the city to school,
> And whenever I got in a field, felt my soul in it
> *Spring* so, that like a young horse I could roll in it,
> *My* inclinations are much what they were,
> And cannot dispense, in the first place, with air,
> But then I would have the most rural of nooks
> Just near enough town to make use of its books,
> And to walk there, whenever I chose to make calls,
> To look at the ladies, and lounge at the stalls.[32]

Hunt begins by condemning the mindless migrations between country and city that characterizes the fashionable set, implicitly paraphrasing the famous aphorism from Horace: *Caelum non animum mutant qui trans mare currunt.*[33] By contrast, his own oscillations between country and town feed the two different needs of his psyche, freedom (signified as "air") and community. If Horace, rejecting the city in his retirement, nonetheless remains the great purveyor of *urbanitas*, then perhaps we should conceive Hunt as the champion of *suburbanitas*. By rejecting the fashionable migrants, he makes it clear that the traditional values of urbanity have no appeal for him. Polish and conformity in his book would have borne the taint of neoclassicism, the stiff, declamatory manner of Kemble, the derivativeness of Rome. The arts he aligns with streets must not be construed abstractly as an allusion to nurture; they refer rather to the *performing* arts, to the operas and plays that the country cannot stage.

Nor, having rejected the city as the repository of "urbane" values, does Hunt make any claims for the country as a space of moral advancement. It is rather a recreational venue of nooks and walks. We see this even in such jeux d'esprits as the "Extract from Another to the Same [Thomas Moore]," subtitled "The Berkeleian System." Horace uses his leisure to study philosophy and issue sage advice. In his famous epistle to Numicius—*Nil admirari prope res est una*[34]—he presents a sober, intelligent exposition of Stoic apathy. Hunt on the other hand chooses rather to parody the epistemology of Bishop Berkeley in terms as crude as Dr. Johnson's, however spirited and delicate the rococo fancies he has woven from it. Berkeley did not *deny* the existence of matter: he predicated it on the consciousness of God:

> The truth, though it's stale to the present deep age,
> Had once such effect on a good mitred sage,
> That mistrusting those brilliant deceivers the eyes,
> He resolved to put faith in no sort of disguise;
> And (how he contrived, I don't know, with St. Paul)
> Concluded there really was nothing at all.[35]

Philosophy, treated like this, becomes a kind of dilettantish entertainment, a picnic pastime.

Returning to the letter *To William Hazlitt*, we can detect a similarly superficial note in the list of pastoral desiderata—one of many that Hunt delighted in compiling:

> Then turning home gently through field and o'er style,
> Partly reading a purchase, or rhyming the while,

> Take my dinner (to make a long evening) at two,
> With a few droppers-in like my Cousin and you,
> Who can season the talk with the right flavoured attic,
> Too witty, for tattling,—too wise, for dogmatic;—
> Then take down an author, whom one of us mentions,
> And doat, for a while, on his jokes and inventions;
> Then have Mozart touched, on our bottle's completion
> Or one of your fav'rite trim ballads Venetian.[36]

When we read passages like these, it is easy to understand the Keats's passing reaction against Hunt and his circle:

> The night we went to Novello's there was a complete set to of Mozart and punning—I was so completely tired of it that if I were to follow my own inclinations I should never meet any one of that set again, not even Hunt—who is certainly a pleasant fellow when you are with him—but in reallity he is vain, egotistical and disgusting in taste and in morals. . . . Hunt does one harm by making fine things petty and beautiful things hateful—Through him I am indifferent to Mozart, I care not for white Busts—and many a glorious thing when associated with him becames [*for* becomes] a nothing—This distorts one's mind—make[s] one's thoughts bizarre—perplexes one in the standard of Beauty.[37]

As a commentary on the Hunt's verse letter to Hazlitt, this cuts to the heart of the matter. Keats is ready enough to concede the charm of Hunt's personality, but suggests that without the mesmeric presence of the man to compel assent, his discourse can in retrospect seem trivial and even vicious. A sylleptic alignment of Mozart and punning points to the disordered values of the circle that gives them parity. Epideictic puns involve nothing more than a virtuoso play with phonetic surfaces, and, jostling Mozart as they do, seem likewise to trivialize *him* as a composer of brilliant surfaces. Mozart also seems to have been minimized by Hunt's procedure of anthologizing and dipping, so much so that for Keats, he has been reduced to a condition of "pettiness." The judgment is severe but not wholly wide of the mark, for in the epistle to Hazlitt we find just such a butterfly approach. Mozart is "touched," presumably reduced to a handful of harmonic effects and snatches of melody, and his music regarded as condiment for a bottle of wine. Furthermore, the phrasing suggests his coequality, if not with a spate of puns, then certainly with a popular barcarole or two ("one of your fav'rite trim ballads Venetian"). Hunt does not seem to realize how close his fanciful hedonism comes at moments like these to Bentham's philistine assumption that, in terms of the pleasure it supplies, pushpin can level with poetry. Nor is Mozart the only figure to be anthologized—the whole range of literature is also ransacked for moments of beauty, which are detached and admired "for a while." In Catullus's dinner invitation to Fabullus, the word *sal* means "wit," a notion that Hunt takes over and literalizes. The effect is to diminish wit to a seasoning, something that, applied too liberally, will spoil the flavor of table talk, just as dogmatism likewise would threaten its recreational purpose as it steers a course between triviality ("tattling") and conviction. Small doses of greatness, light touches of seriousness—no wonder that Keats should have found great things reduced to small.

Knowing that idyll is a kind of divertissement, Hunt now devotes part of the letter to self-defense and apology. Bentham "theologized" his hedonism by professing to unmask the "hedonism" of theology:

> It may be wondered, perhaps, that in all this while no mention has been made of the *theological* principle; meaning that principle which professes to recur for the standard of right and wrong to the will of God. But the case is, this is not in fact a distinct principle. It was never anything more or less than one or other of the three before-mentioned principles presenting itself under another shape.[38]

The same mischievous intent underlies the epithet "devout" in Hunt's apologia:

> Now this I call passing a few devout hours
> Becoming a world that has friendships and flowers;
> That has lips also, made for still more than to chat to;
> And if it has rain, has a rainbow for that too.[39]

This undercuts the meaning of "devout" so often connected with *contemptus mundi*. Showing scorn for such attitudes, Hunt implies that a slur on the creature and its natural appetites is finally a slur on the Creator, that *contemptus mundi* is nothing more than *contemptus Dei*. If he is to be judged as a trifler and a wastrel, let his judges look to the beams in their own eyes. He seems to have remembered the reckless disregard for the judgment of *senes severiores* in Catullus's celebration of the moment—"Vivamus, mea Lesbia, atque amemus."[40] It is simply a question of what definition of that world has been adduced:

> "Lord bless us!" exclaims some old hunks in a shop,
> "What useless young dogs!"—and falls combing a crop.
> "How idle!" another cries—"really a sin!"

And starting up, takes his first customer in.
"At least," cries another, "it's nothing but pleasure";
Then longs for the Monday, quite sick of his leisure.
"What toys!" cries the sage haggard statesman,—"what stuff!"
Then fillips his ribband, to shake off the snuff.
"How profane!" cries the preacher, proclaiming his message;
Then calls God's creation a vile dirty passage.
"Lips too!" cries a vixen,—and fidgets, and stirs,
And concludes (which is true) that I didn't mean hers.[41]

There is some logical and some moral sleight of hand here. Hunt appears to give an exhaustive catalog of "worldly" response and so to present the appearance of a watertight case for his life of pleasure. Yet even while he pretends to have addressed the issue, he has simply discredited the source of the argument rather than the argument per se. It might be that some shopkeepers are cheats, but is it fair to make one's symbolic spokesperson dishonest, and so brand an entire trade? Does the preacher who inveighs against the world inveigh against the beauties of Hampstead or the squalor of the marketplace? All these spokespersons pose the question of responsibility, that of the labor that makes an idyll possible. It is a question Hunt chooses to evade, vanishing like a squid behind an ink screen of caricature.

Even though his is a world far removed from Wordsworth's, I am reminded of a comparable poem on the naming of places. In *Point Rash Judgement* the speaker and his friends have taken a leisurely walk in the countryside, and judge a laborer for not taking part in the harvest. They feel penitent when they realize that the man is ill, but never wrestle with the issue of privilege. It is a fact that Wordsworth's inheritance exempted him from having to work. Hunt shows a similar complacency in the letter to Hazlitt, so much so that one suspects Dickens might have used it in his characterization of Skimpole. Both Skimpole and Hunt project commerce as a necessary evil, mocking the dreariness of the occupation and at the same time claiming entitlement to its fruits:

I blame (you'll bear witness) these tricksters and hiders
No more than I quarrel with bats or with spiders:—
All, all have their uses, though never so hideous;—
But bats shouldn't fancy their eyesight prodigious.[42]

Unlike Skimpole, who is wholly a drone, Hunt claims that he sings for his supper; but this claim to industry is weakened when we realize that his idea of verse is something that pours out currente calamo—it is a lark, after all, that peers uncomprehendingly into the dark places of commerce before taking wing and "mounting his steps of wild music to heaven." While the argument exerts its charm, it also masks a certain deviousness and complacency. It is sobering to recall that charm, deviousness and complacency are also the ingredients from which Dickens whisked up the portrait of Skimpole. For Hunt, the issue of privileged leisure becomes an occasion for whimsical epigrams, so extravagant and frail that they disarm the impulse to examine their "logic," since few of us share Pope's ruthless urge to attack the Lord Herveys of this world. To mask irresponsibility with charm, Hunt even resurrects the *adunantia* of Metaphysical poetry—impossibility catalogs so decorative and so *inarguably* silly that what at first seems to be airy trellis-work actually becomes as impregnable as a battlement:

> They only would have us dig on like themselves,
> Yet be all observation to furnish their shelves;
> Would only expect us (inordinate crew!)
> To be just what they are, and delight them all too!
> As well might they ask the explorers of oceans
> To make their discoveries, as doctors do lotions;
> Or shut up some bees in the till with their money,
> And look, on the Sabbath, to breakfast on honey.[43]

Yes, but honey has still to be bought (or borrowed from friends).

The letter *To Barron Field* directs its pastoral thrust in a different direction, defining the city in terms of unhealthy surfeit, the country by healthful abstemiousness. Hunt has obviously sought inspiration in Horace, *Sermones* 2.2. Although he avoids supplying his own bill of fare in this particular poem, he no doubt means us to carry over the supper menu from the letter to Hazlitt—the vividly rendered pale yellow, pale green and white of a vegetarian supper—"Then an egg for your supper, with lettuces white." (This seems even more abstemious than Pope's boast of being able to "piddle here / On Broccoli and mutton round the year.")[44] What better way than by egg and lettuce salad to realize the Horatian dictum *non in caro nidore voluptas / summa sed in te ipso est?*[45] It supplies Hunt with a norm by which to describe the excess of city banquets:

> *Dinner's* the place for the hottest of services;
> *There's* the array, and the ardour to win,
> The clashing, the splashing, and crashing, and din;

> With fierce intercepting of convoys of butter,
> And phrases and outcries tremendous to utter,—
> Blood, devils, and drum-sticks,—now cut it—the jowl there—
> Brains, bones, head and shoulders, and into the sole there!
> The veterans too, round you—how obviously brave!
> Some red as a fever, some pallid as death,
> Some ballustrade-legged, others panting for breath,
> Some jaundiced, some jaded, some almost a jelly,
> And numbers with horrid contusion of belly.[46]

Whereas a supper in Hampstead confirms social bonds by offering a sacrament of friendship, a London feast is a species of warfare—disorderly, incoherent, congested, and trenching on cannibalism. (Since, to my knowledge, the *jowls* of animals are not eaten, we have a momentary sense of human cheeks.) In the melee, it is hard to distinguish profanity from food-stuff, and hard to separate nourishment from poison.

After cataloging some of the more barbarous and bizarrely presented meat dishes to be found at such banquets, he moves, as though he were writing a familiar essay, to his controlling generalization—"This made, t'other day, a physician declare, / That disease, bona fide, was part of part of our fare."[47] In this he finds a cue to exploit the comedy of the enthymeme, and makes it the basis for a banquet in which the pathological effect is served up instead of its causal food:

> As, "Pray, Sir, allow me,—a slice of this gout;
> I could get no St. Anthony's fire—it's quite out.
> Mr. P. there,—more nightmare? my hand's quite at leisure?
> A glass of slow fever? I'm sure with great pleasure.
> My dear Mrs. H., why your plate's always empty!
> Now can't a small piece of this agony tempt ye?"[48]

When in *The Feast of the Poets* Hayley enquired after Apollo with all the silken clichés of polite speech, they jarred against the godhead he was blandishing; here similar clichés jar against infernal substantives—it is as though we were witnessing a well-conducted dinner party in Hell.

The last of the letters, *To Charles Lamb*, also derives its comic moments from unexpected substitutions, in this case the certainty that bad weather will prompt the Lambs to visit Hampstead. While the intent of supplying a manifesto of the idyllic life imparts a certain coherence and progressive shape to the letter addressed to Hazlitt, the Charles Lamb affair is a real gallimaufry. Ostensibly a *cletic* (or invitatory) letter like Catullus's to Fabullus, it begins by saluting the friend in terms so heartfelt and honorific as to recall Horace's salutes to Maecenas—"Home-lover, thought-feeder, abundant-joke-giving; / Whose charity springs from deep-knowledge."[49] Then follows the joke about bad weather visits, which pretends that storms are a necessary condition for Lamb's coming, rather than a measure of his faithfulness. Hunt inverts the jest by apologizing for the "repulsive" pleasantness of his situation in Hampstead, and the piece tails off in a Mendelssohnian fancy about travelers' lanterns and fairies, and the quite unexpected tableau of the sleeping Galatea. Like Byron's allegorical voyage through droves of sea-nymphs in the first of the letters, the Polyphemus passage is a carryover from the odes of sensibility, not a "legitimate" component of the verse letter. But then Hunt outstripped almost all his romantic contemporaries in his eagerness to mix genres, prompted no doubt by a desire to proclaim his contempt for neoclassical decorum and the rule-bound poetics of the Augustan writers.

Sonnets

The same impatience with inherited tradition, and the desire to modify and amend as the spirit dictated, can be seen in Hunt's handling of the sonnet. Some of these poems are highly orthodox and conventional, written perhaps as a Cubist might on occasion produce an academically "correct" drawing, as it were to prove that the liberties taken elsewhere have sprung from the aesthetic play with données, not from ignorance or incompetence. Other sonnets again are only nominally so, funneling contingent or chatty material through the stanza, but ignoring the demands for sonnet doubleness, for protasis and apodosis, for debate and resolution. Stuart Curran has provided an eloquent assessment of Hunt's achievement in this regard, pointing to avant-garde adaptations that, overtaken by later experiments in turn, seem to have lost their bite:

> The village is celebrated not for its romantic qualities but for its very lack of them. Its balance between London to the south and open nature to the north represents an equilibrium between poles. Life in Hampstead is easy, pleasant, by no means uncommitted politically or culturally, yet calm, eschewing austerity or intensity. The first pre-Raphaelite, devoted to the early Italian Renaissance, Hunt transports Petrarch (as he did Dante and Tasso) to his suburban village, where he also relocates the by now conventional subjects of the Romantic sonnet. To peruse this sequence of sonnets

is to be impressed by their modernity, that must appear quaint to a later time.[50]

The first of the sonnets, entitled *Quiet Evenings* and dedicated to Thomas Barnes, is an epistolary sonnet, recapitulating some of the components of the Hazlitt and Lamb poems:

> Dear Barnes, whose native taste, solid and clear,
>   The throng of life has strengthened without harm,
>   You know the rural feeling, and the charm
> That stillness has for a world-fretted ear:—
> 'Tis now deep whispering all about me here
>   With thousand tiny hushings, like a swarm
> Of atom bees, or fairies in alarm,
> Or noise of numerous bliss from distant sphere.
>
> This charm our evening hours duly restore,—
>   Nought heard through our little, lulled abode,
> Save the crisp fire, or leaf of book turned o'er,
>   Or watch-dog, or the ring of frosty road.
> Wants there no other sound then?—Yes, one more,—
>   The voice of friendly visiting, long owed.[51]

For a sonnet, this is uncharacteristically casual. Hunt has jettisoned solemnity and high-mindedness along with most other aspects of sonnet decorum. Whereas the sestet (in the hands of more orthodox sonneteers) would move from the specifics of the octave to impersonal reflection, here it simply extends the content of the opening quatrains, and keeps their domestic tenor. As a result, the "charge" of *volta* is reduced to a mere change of rhyme. Hunt's epistolary salute also unkeys the sonnet, and so too does his fairy lore, a signature of fancy—as witness his remarks on *The Rape of the Lock*—rather than imagination. Thus a near-Wordsworthian moment ("You know the rural feeling, and the charm / That stillness has for a world-fretted ear") is minimized when Hunt paraphrases that stillness in the rococo of Regency pantomime: "With thousand tiny hushings, like . . . fairies in alarm." He has sought inspiration not in the tradition of the sonnet, but rather in the fanciful odes of sensibility.

Although there are no exact verbal parallels to demonstrate the influence, there is little doubt that Hunt is writing with Collins in mind. In the *Ode to Evening* we find a comparably poised attentiveness to the sounds of evening. Compare Hunt's "'Tis now deep whispering all about me here" and "Nought heard through our little, lulled abode / Save the crisp fire" with Collins's "Now air is hushed, save where the weak-eyed bat / With short shrill shriek flits by on leathern wing."[52] Both poems likewise celebrate evening as part of a restorative cycle: in Hunt, "This charm our evening hours duly restore"; in Collins, "As musing slow, I hail / Thy genial loved return!"

The genius of Collins also presides over the first of the three Hampstead sonnets that Hunt composed in prison (1813–14). A specially poignant nostalgia pervades these poems, which deserve a place in the tradition of exilic verse stretching from Ovid's poems in Pontus to Rupert Brooke's *Grant-chester* and beyond. The romantics were fond of dramatizing city life as a species of imprisonment—Keats's sonnet *To one who has been long in city pent*[53] is a case in point, and so is Coleridge's *This Lime-Tree Bower My Prison* ("for thou hast pined / And hunger'd after Nature, many a year, / In the great City pent")[54]—and yet here an actual prisoner says nothing about his plight. That stoic reticence gives an almost heroic tone to the simple descriptive gestures of the sonnets. The first is in effect a miniature ode in which Hunt has substituted a genius loci for the usual eighteenth-century abstraction. He invokes Hampstead as Collins invokes evening, as mentor and guide, and (again like Collins) stresses the recurrent nature of his homage:

> Sweet upland, to whose walks with fond repair
>   Out of thy western slope I took my rise
>   Day after day, and on these feverish eyes
> Met the moist fingers of the bathing air,—
> If health, unearned of thee, I may not share,
>   Keep it, I pray thee, where my memory lies,
>   In thy green lanes, brown dells, and breezy skies,
> Till I return, and find thee doubly fair.
>
> Wait then my coming, on that lightsome land,
>   Health, and the Joy that out of nature springs,
>   And Freedom's air-blown locks;—but stay with me,
> Friendship, frank entering with cordial hand,
>   And Honour, and the Muse with growing wings,
>   And Love Domestic, smiling equably.[55]

It is almost as if Collins's *Ode to Evening* had been boiled down and reset in a sonnet mold, so frequently do parallels arise. The very upland recalls the "upland fallows grey," while there can be no doubt that the vaporous prosopopoeia of "moist fingers" has been adapted from Evening's "dewy fingers." In similar vein, the topographic ascriptions of "thy green lanes, brown dells, and breezy skies" recall similar possessives in the Collins poem ("Like thy own solemn springs, / Thy springs and dying gales")[56] while the tableau of the sestet—one of the few occasions when Hunt attempts to generalize outward from his local material—surely has its roots in the grouped personifications at the end of the earlier ode:

> So long, sure-found beneath the sylvan shed,
> Shall Fancy, Friendship, Science, rose-lipped Health,
>   Thy gentlest influence own,
>   And hymn thy favourite name![57]

Yet even despite this effort at generality, "Sweet upland, to whose walks" owes nothing to the shifts from external to internal landscape we find in typical romantic sonnets. Hunt does not present his landscape as a psychological correlative but as a psychological succor. Those moral abstractions are presented as having emanated from the soil of Hampstead, not from the mind of the poet.

Because they are poems of enforced exile, the first three Hampstead sonnets have a strong regionalist charge. Like, say, Rupert Brooke's *Grantchester*, they recall a beloved place in all the minutiae of its being. Indeed in most regionalist poetry the attachment to place is so strong and so obsessive that the writer often celebrates materials that other eyes might find unglamorous. Hunt takes up the challenge in the second of the sonnets, "They tell me, when my tongue grows warm on thee," addressing the fact that Hampstead's beauty is impaired by the absence of any impressive body of water (an element intimately connected with the topographic sonnets of Bowles and Wordsworth). Even though he cannot do more than affirm his love in the face of the deficiency, it is significant that he affirms the humdrum reality of Hampstead *above* the rococo decor of the idyll—one of the few instances in his poetry where such an alternative is embraced:

> It may be so,—casual though pond or brook:—
>   Yet not to me so full of all that's fair,
>   Though fruit-embowered, with fingering sun between,
> Were the divinest fount in Fancy's nook,
>   In which the Nymphs sit tying up their hair,
>   Their white backs glistening through the myrtles green.[58]

The same sort of regionalism informs the next of the sonnets, where, rather like Tennyson tracking the journey of Hallam's corpse throughout the earlier parts of *In Memoriam*, he projects Hampstead as it must appear five months after his going to jail. Though the poem can lay only tenuous claim to being a sonnet, it is an exceptionally fine lyric, austere and minimalist in a way that Hunt, caught up in his surfeit of idyllic luxuries, would never again manage. We can appreciate Stuart Curran's point about the modernity of such a poem if we place its winter landscape beside that in Robert Wells's *Winter's Task*.[59] The diction sets the poems apart, but they otherwise show a striking continuity of sensibility and vision. Here is Hunt's sonnet:

> Winter has reached thee once again at last;
>   And now the rambler, whom thy groves yet please,
>   Feels on his house-warm lips the thin air freeze;
> While on his shrugging neck the resolute blast
> Comes edging; and the leaves, in heaps down cast,
>   He shuffles with his hastening foot, and sees
>   The cold sky whitening through the wiry trees,
> And sighs to think the loitering noons have passed.
>
> And do I love thee less to paint thee so?
>   No: this the season is of beauty still
>   Doubled at heart,—of smoke with whirling glee
> Uptumbling ever from the blaze below,
>   And home remembered most,—and oh, loved hill,
>   The second, and the last, away from thee.[60]

To respond to a "cold sky whitening through the wiry trees" is to reveal an aesthetic austerity to which the indolent, comfortable side of Hunt's nature will otherwise seldom rise. A key to the intense yearning of this poem is perhaps to be sought in the word "rambler," with its implication of untrammeled, undirected freedom. In the following sonnet, written shortly after Hunt left jail, he presents himself as a figure from romance recently released from an immobilizing spell. The poem sustains the idea of Hampstead as a gentle female presence, paralleling topographical features with the human physique. We have seen how in *Hero and Leander* Hunt deplored sexual prudishness; he also had the temerity to salute Queen Victoria's breasts in "To the Infant Princess Royal"—"Nor dost thou know thy very mother's / Balmy bosom from another's / Though thy small blind lips pursue it"[61]— and here he eroticizes Hampstead Hill with a frankness astonishing for his time:

> When I beheld, in momentary sun,
>> One of thy hills gleam bright and bosomy,
> Just like that orb of orbs, a human one,
>> Let forth by chance upon a lover's eye.[62]

Goldsmith had personified Auburn as a country beauty in *The Deserted Village* ("Sweet smiling village, loveliest of the lawn, / Thy sports are fled, and all they charms withdrawn")[63] but without so much as a whiff of Hunt's eroticism.

The preceding sonnet ("The baffled spell, that bound me, is undone") and the one that follows it ("As one who after long and far-spent years") attempt to give a biographical color to the two-tier structure of the form. Instead of opposing statement and resolution, or other purely formal modes of antithesis, Hunt sets the years of his confinement against the moment of reunion, and so simulates a sense of arrival and completion. The "as/so" structure helps to reinforce the effect. In the *Description of Hampstead,* however, there is not even this factitious kind of development. Whereas the other Hampstead sonnets borrowed elements from the ode of sensibility, amongst them its apparatus of personified abstractions, the poem in hand is simply a chorographic exercise, Hampstead's southern zone detailed in the octave, its northern in the sestet. Although it is hard to know whether such insouciant floutings of form should be hailed as innovations or deplored as betrayals, the sonnet nonetheless works as lyric vignette, and it is as a lyric vignette, with an accretion of sonnetary rhyme, that it is best regarded:

> A steeple issuing from a leafy rise,
>> With farmy fields in front, and sloping green,
>> Dear Hampstead, is thy southern face serene,
> Silently smiling on approaching eyes.
> Within, thine ever-shifting looks surprise,—
>> Streets, hills, and dells, trees overhead are seen,
>> Now down below, with smoking roofs between,—
>
> A village revelling in varieties.
> Then northward what a range,—with heath and pond,
>> Nature's own ground; woods that let mansions through,
> And cottaged vales with pillowy fields beyond,
>> And clump of darkening pines, and prospects blue,
> And that clear path through all, where daily meet,
> Cool cheeks, and brilliant eyes, and morn-elastic feet.[64]

A more eloquent testament to Hunt's *suburbanitas* would be hard to come by. He conceives the entire prospect as an intertexture of nature and nurture. It is easy to imagine the unseemly mirth in Edinburgh when the claim of "Nature's own ground" was quickly followed with references to "mansions," "cottaged vales," "pillowy fields" and the convenience of a "clear path through all." For all his vigorous campaigning on behalf of the new school, Hunt has not progressed beyond the visual habits and preoccupations that define the landscape of sensibility. The "steeple issuing from a leafy rise" is a cousin of the "dim-discovered spires" of the *Ode to Evening*, and Cowper's country rambles are likewise dotted with "smoking roofs." Even the coulisses of the "darkening pines" and the blue vanishing point of the prospect argue the organizing frame of a Claude glass.

The Hampstead sonnets, odd and slight though they seem, show a level of originality to which Hunt would seldom rise in his subsequent efforts with the form. Most of these are album verses, memoranda of friendship or accompanying notes for pictures and keepsakes. A *lusus naturae* like the *Iterating Sonnet, Written During the Talk of a War between England and the United States*[65] looks forward to the "computer" poems of Edwin Morgan in our century, but poems like the address to Hunt's wife (*To Mrs. L. H. on Her Modelling a Bust of the Author*)[66] and sister-in-law (*To Miss K. Written on a Piece of Paper Which Happened to be Headed with a Long List of Trees*)[67] are so dated, so fixed in the amber of their domestic origins, that they can be enjoyed only with the condescension we bring to bear on the enjoyment of any other "period piece" that has failed to break from its matrix of history. One might nonetheless wish to make an exception of the sonnet suite entitled *The Fish, the Man, and the Spirit*. The first two poems are charming riddle efforts, rather in the manner of Symphosius. By elemental crossviews, they hold the adaptations of a species up to ridicule, and recall the *contentiones* of medieval tradition, those ultimately pointless claims for supremacy between nightingales and owls. It is the third sonnet in which the fish, Tiresias-fashion, turns into a person and then into a spirit, that Hunt strikes a chord of modernity. For instead of offering a meaningless anthropocentric adjudication, he anticipates the animal rights movement of the twentieth century. Fish do not have to serve the ends of humankind— their very being is their raison d'être. Hunt manages an almost Keatsian empathy as he evokes that being: "The fish is swift, small-needing, vague yet clear, / A cold, sweet, silver life, wrapped in round waves, / Quickened with touches of transporting fear."[68]

Good though the fish and some of the Hampstead sonnets are, they are eclipsed by two more that are worthy of a place in any anthology. Taking

them in rising of order of importance, let us begin with the sonnet addressed
To the Grasshopper and the Cricket:

> Green little vaulter in the sunny grass,
>   Catching your heart up at the feel of June,
>   Sole voice that's heard amidst the lazy noon,
> When ev'n the bees lag at the summoning brass;—
> And you, warm little housekeeper, who class
>   With those who think the candles come too soon,
>   Loving the fire, and with your tricksome tune
> Nick the glad moments as they pass;—
>
> Oh sweet and tiny cousins, that belong,
>   One to the fields, the other to the hearth,
> Both have your sunshine; both, though small, are strong
>   At your clear hearts; and both were sent on earth
> To sing in thoughtful ears this natural song,—
>   In doors and out,—summer and winter,—Mirth.[69]

Unlike most Hunt sonnets, this offers a covert philosophical proposition—
his philosophy of cheer. On the surface the poem appears to offer a rococo
dalliance, since insects, like fairies, are closely associated in his mind with
the exercise of fancy (one of the Hampstead sonnets construes silence si-
multaneously as the "hushings" of "atom bees or fairies in alarm").[70] However, the poem's rich heritage of echoes and parallels amplifies what might
at first glance seem to be a trifle. Hunt no doubt knew Nicias's epitaph on
a cicada in *The Greek Anthology*:

> No longer curled under the leafy branch shall I delight in sending forth a
> voice from my tender wings. For I fell into the hand . . . of a boy, who
> caught me stealthily as I was seated on the green leaves.[71]

And he had certainly read *Upon Appleton House*:

> And now into the Abbyss I pass
> Of that unfathomable Grass,
> Where Men like Grashoppers appear,
> But Grashoppers are Gyants there:
> They, in there squeking Laugh, contemn
> Us as we walk more low then them:

> And from the Precipices tall
> Of the green spir's, to us do call.[72]

An essay on Anacreon in *The Seer*, even though it was written many years after the poem, suggests furthermore that he was familiar both with that poet's celebration of the grasshopper (though he points out that the poem is actually addressed to a cicada)[73] and its translation by Cowley. Add to these Lovelace's *Grasse-hopper* ("Oh thou that swing'st upon the waving haire / Of some well-filled Oaten Beard")[74] and we have a handful of antecedents for Hunt's fanciful empathy with the insect, sharing with them all that crucial readjustment of scale that takes us down to inhabit its world. When he speaks of a "Green little vaulter," for example, he places us at eye level with the creature, since vaults are viewed from a lateral rather than a vertical point of vantage. And thus cohabiting with his grasshopper "in the sunny grass," he embraces the festive Anacreontic readings of its emblem, and rejects what Don Cameron Allen has called the "prudent variant of the Aesopica,"[75] which had more recently been taken over by La Fontaine. This is a creature of energy not of indolence, of energy expended in pleasure. Its vaultings replicate the leapings of its heart as it celebrates the beneficence of summer, and seem to place it in the throng of animals that praise the Creator in the *Benedicite*. From this, Hunt moves to a sense of Divine Providence that has placed it on earth (along with the more diligent and domestic cricket) as an emissary of God—"both were sent on earth / To sing this natural song." Simply by responding to natural beauty, the grasshopper justifies its being. It resembles the lark in the letter to Hazlitt, the bird that peers uncomprehendingly at the world of urban business before soaring into the heavens, and challenges the doctrine of utility that has always subordinated grasshoppers to ants.

While the sonnet *To the Grasshopper and the Cricket* is a charming miniature, that entitled *The Nile* is a truly magisterial piece, eclipsing the efforts of Keats and Shelley in the same contest. I agree with Ernest Pereira in finding it "the most Keatsian [poem Hunt] ever wrote."[76] It is also the most Shelleyan:

> It flows through old hushed Egypt and its sands,
> > Like some grave mighty thought threading a dream,
> > And times and things, as in a vision, seem
> Keeping along it their eternal stands.—
> Caves, pillars, pyramids, the shepherd bands

> That roamed through the young world, the glory extreme
> Of high Sesostris, and that southern beam,
> The laughing queen that caught the world's great hands.
>
> Then comes a mightier silence, stern and strong,
> As of a world left empty of its throng,
>   And the void weighs on us; and then we wake,
> And hear the fruitful stream lapsing along
>   Twixt villages, and think how we shall take
>   Our own calm journey on for human sake.

As in many poems by Shelley, the subject has been clothed in several epistemological veils. These occasion a miragelike wavering that, by disorienting the reader, creates a sense of visionary experience. When, for example, the first line refers to "old hushed Egypt," we are uncertain whether the epithet evokes the Egypt of 1818, old by virtue of its present antiquity, or the Egypt of the pharaohs, to which we have been transported in a dream. Similarly the participial adjective "hushed"—is this Egypt as it is now, hushed and marginalized by the course of its subsequent history, or are we meant to penetrate behind the epithet to an Egypt potent before its hushing? The reference to "sands" imparts a further instability, since sands are associated with the lapse of time, with insecure foundations, and with sublime innumerability.

The flowing Nile in the midst of flowing sands anticipates the insubstantial simile that follows, a simile that, like so many of Shelley's, vaporizes the ideas that other poets would want to solidify, and substitutes phantasm for tactile image. Thoughts are abstract; dreams are abstract; the Nile and the desert take on their abstraction. A sylleptic coupling of times and things sustains the dreamy loss of focus. "Time" in the plural is more concrete than time in the abstract singular—for it suggests the shape and the content of specific historical eras—but "times" still remain abstract enough to infect the things that flank them with their own insubstantiality. But since the world is transient, and its glory with it, the majesty of Egypt has become a semblance, to be recovered imaginatively only in dream-states. What is ordinarily reserved for nature—the immutable eternity of cycle—has for a moment been ascribed to human achievement: "Keeping along it their eternal stands." Keats might have remembered this line when he wrote his sonnet *On the Sea*—"It keeps eternal whisperings around / Desolate shores."[77]

Because "stands" carry with them so marked a sense of immobility, it is odd that they should provide the answer rhyme for the shifting sands in line one, and equally odd that they should also encompass the "the shepherd bands / That *roamed*." Such oddities contribute, however, to the dreamlike drift and blur of the sonnet. The catalog is itself confusing. We think we are mounting a climax of evolution in the progressive shift from caves through pillars to pyramids, but the shepherds seem to revoke the line of development, and follow the permanence of settlement (pyramids) with the waywardness of nomadry. Moreover, since Egyptian caves are more closely associated in the popular imagination with Christian ascetics like St. Anthony than they are with pharaonic culture, even the time scale warps and buckles in this visionary mirage, just as, in the space of a mere two lines, "world" shifts meaning from objective environment to metonymic personification in "the world's great hands," where Caesar no longer represents a young, but rather a mature, a civilized, world.

Since Hunt has doubled back on the line of history, the consecutive "then" at the start of the sestet poses a new problem of construal. We have been uncertain of where we are or when we are in the reverie of the opening quatrains, but the *volta* reorients us. Having as it were turned off the sound track in the first line ("old hushed Egypt"), and allowed only Cleopatra's laughter to sound across the centuries, Hunt proceeds to map a new gradation of quiet in "a mightier silence," as, coming out of our trance, we experience the silence of death and loss. But again Hunt's simile (which is meant to help focus our senses) brings in ontological problems of its own. How in a prenuclear age could a reader even begin to imagine a "world left empty of its throng"—the mind would have collapsed in its effort to conceptualize the inconceivable. It is inconceivable, however, because it is offered within the framework of a dream. We have still to wake up from a nightmare of loss and vacuity, into the pastoral reality of Egypt in 1818, where the Nile is not a vague and vaporous symbol but an irrigating medium and a sustainer of "villages," those humble, anonymous successors to the dynastic splendors of "old hushed Egypt." (That Hunt was fascinated by displacements of this sort can be gathered from his poem *The Trumpets of Doolkarnein*, in which birds nest in, and demystify, grandiose structures.)

Because the Nile has been reconceived as a nurturer of life rather than a memorial to past glories (Hunt never cared for Rome, and knew that Sesostris was the figment of an historiographical muddle), the final line becomes a sort of meliorist "Excelsior." The confused, cumbrous, dictatorial past is leading as our senses re-sort themselves (we hear the Nile for the first time) to a better, democratic future. Elgar is supposed to have said of the trio of the first *Pomp and Circumstance* march ("Land of Hope and

Glory") that it was a tune that came once in a lifetime. Hunt could have made much the same boast about the Nile sonnet, for it is the most memorable and magisterial poem he ever wrote, and one that many greater poets would be proud to have conceived.

BLANK VERSE

Hunt's often cavalier disregard for the full range of sonnetary effects, evident above all in the way he preferred description to argument, suggests that, unlike Wordsworth's nuns, he sometimes fretted his convent's narrow room. And, given this resistance to exacting forms (his "rewriting" of the heroic couplet also comes to mind), one might expect that blank verse, carrying no real constraints of structure, would bring out the best in him. On examining the specimens he has left behind, however, we find that he lacked the discipline to make an incontrovertible success of the measure. Failing, as so often, to take the long view and to plan towards the completion of his statement, he either produced fragments—most of the blank verse poems are the leavings of an abandoned project, a sort of suburban *Excursion*, which was to have been called *A Day with the Reader*[78]—or, in the case of *An "Indicator" in Verse*,[79] he used some of his essay strategies to give a loose shape to the enterprise. Hunt was well aware that some French essayists moved at will between the media of prose and verse:

> The French have a lazy way, in some of their compositions, of writing prose and verse alternately. The author, whenever, it is convenient for him to be inspired, begins dancing away in rhyme. The fit over, he goes on as before, as if nothing had happened. We have essays in prose and verse by Cowley (a delightful book) in which the same piece contains both; but with one exception, they are rather poems with long prefaces.
> If ever this practice is allowable, it is to a periodical writer in love with poetry. He is obliged to write in prose; he is tormented with the desire to vent himself in rhyme; he rhymes, and has not the leisure to go on. Behold us, as a Frenchman would say, with our rhyme and our reason![80]

To which one is tempted to reply, *De te fabula*. For Hunt, prose and verse enterprises can be interchanged at the drop of a hat (or wishing cap). For example, he will write a "letter" to Thomas Moore in indecorous anapests, admitting that their mesmeric tune has served to get him underway, and he will write an essay in blank verse in order to exorcise the desire to "rhyme."

I find it significant that he should talk of "venting himself in rhyme," an expression that points to the therapeutic impulse behind much of his poetry, and also perhaps to an unconsciously superficial sense of that poetry as a manipulation of end-words rather than an embodiment of vision. That being so, we might expect his blank verse would take the form of his ordinary prose, but enhanced by a more definite rhythm.

Unfortunately, however, that is not always the case. Hunt will sometimes use his verse measure to license other, more obtrusive, kinds of decoration. The following extract from *A Thought on Music Suggested by a Private Concert, May 13, 1815* provides a case in point:

> To sit with downward listening, and crossed knee,
> Half conscious, half unconscious, of the throng
> Of fellow-ears, and hear the well-met skill
> Of fine musicians,—the glib ivory
> Twinkling with a numerous prevalence,—the snatch
> Of brief and birdy flute, that leaps apart,—
> Giddy violins, that do whate'er they please,—
> And sobering all with circling manliness,
> The bass, uprolling deep and voluble;—
> Well may the sickliest thought, that keeps its home
> In a sad heart, give gentle way for once,
> And quitting its pain-anchored hold, put forth
> On that sweet sea of many-billowed sound,
> Floating and floating in a summer boat,
> Till heaven seems near, and angels travelling by.[81]

If this reads like a cruel *Blackwood's* parody, it is because Hunt has packed sixteen lines with as many of his mannerisms as he could, presumably with an aim of flighting the prose discourse. In a poem like *Rimini*, the repeated jingle of the rhyme helps accommodate many fanciful extravagances of diction; in other poems again, the unreality of the anapestic waltz rhythm camouflages unrealities of language. But here, where there is insufficient "background noise" to hide their oddity, the extravagances cannot be recuperated. Couched in a medium that should diverge little as possible from the norms of spoken language, they seem merely grotesque. How, for example, is one to parse a line like this: "To sit with downward listening, and crossed knee"? If Hunt has crossed his legs and is staring at the floor, why the Cubist scramble of sentence parts? Presumably because, for all the world like an Augustan poetaster, Hunt is frightened that straightforward spade-naming might compromise the decorum of his form. And if he seems to have been reconstituted as a sort of syntactic Demoiselle d'Avignon, sitting alongside a half-personified gerund, then in the next two lines he appears as prematurely to have entered the world of Dali. What an extraordinary thing to be conscious of—"a throng / Of fellow-ears"—as though these alone were occupying the chairs of the concert room. The sounds that assail these sedentary ears are no less alarming. Hunt seems to have had an especial fascination for the word "glib," applying it even to Italian eyeballs in one of his poems.

Here he seems to disregard its negative charge of specious facility, and, more disastrously, its implication of slipperiness: "the glib ivory / Twinkling with numerous prevalence." Glib ivory, I would have thought, would be a sure recipe for wrong notes—but the reader's mind is not allowed to dwell on this upsetting thought. It is too busy trying to make sense of "numerous prevalence." Hunt seems to have written the phrase with a vague recollection of the "many-twinkling feet" in Gray's *Progress of Poesy*. But in Gray, *pace* Dr. Johnson, the syntactic blur evokes the indecipherable speed of a dance, whereas in Hunt it disembodies the pianist and has the instrument surrealistically play itself. *What* it plays virtually defies interpretation. Possibly Hunt intends "numerous" as a Latinism for "harmonious," but this little pedantry fails to hold out against the sense of numbers conjured up by "prevalence." The antics of the flute somehow match the antics of the syntax. This "leaps apart," not because, as Hunt intends, it is soaring in a rarefied realm, but because the center cannot hold. The piano concerto (Heaven help the soloist) has a highly erratic accompaniment. What can Hunt have meant by celebrating *giddy* violins, intractable to musical command? And then—after all this pretentious straining that falls only a few decibels short of "raging rocks and shivering shocks"—*nascetur ridiculus mus*. The idea of music as an anodyne for care and pain is all too commonplace. It had been rendered much more prettily and much more succinctly in *Henry VIII*: "In sweet music is such art, / Killing care and grief of heart."[82]

Things get better, however. The second part of the poem tries to render into words the programmatic responses of a sensitive but unacademic listener. Where formerly the verse texture was tricksy and overwritten, now it takes on a noble quietude and certainty that might well owe something to Wordsworth. A footnote to a later blank verse fragment ("Apollo and the Sunbeams")[83] suggests that Hunt had studied and profited by the example of Wordsworthian blank verse. As at a comparable moment of *Tintern Abbey*, the measure here acts as an instrument of thought, and evokes the slow wresting forth and formulation of ideas that otherwise resist formulation.:

>   For not the notes alone, or new-found air
>   Or structure of elaborate harmonies,
>   With steps that to the waiting treble climb,
>   Suffice a true-touched ear. To that will come
>   Out of the very vagueness of the joy,
>   A shaping and a sense of things beyond us,
>   Great things and voices great: nor will it reckon
>   Sounds, that so wake up the fond-hearted air,
>   To be the unmeaning raptures they are held,
>   Or mere suggestions of our human feeling,
>   Sorrow, or mirth, or triumph. Infinite things
>   There are, both small and great, whose worth were lost
>   On us alone,—the flies with lavish plumes,—
>   The starry-showering snow,—the tints and shapes
>   That hide about the flowers,—gigantic trees,
>   That crowd for miles up mountain solitudes,
>   As on the steps of some great natural temple,
>   To view the godlike sun:— . . .[84]

Compare:

>   And I have felt
>   A presence that disturbs me with the joy
>   Of elevated thoughts; a sense sublime
>   Of something far more deeply interfused,
>   Whose dwelling is the light of setting suns,
>   And the round ocean and the living air,
>   And the blue sky, and in the mind of man:
>   A motion and a spirit, that impels
>   All thinking things, all objects of all thought,
>   And rolls through all things. . . . [85]

Although Hunt cannot match Wordsworth for the strength and cogency of an enjambment that drives towards its resolution, both passages manage to fill the abstraction of "things" with a content all the more powerful for being vague, and both impart a sense of ineluctable process—Hunt's serene future verbs and the plastic force of the "shaping" seem to recall the rolling and impulsion of Wordsworth's spirit.

Skillful though this section of *A Thought on Music* is, and momentarily impressive though the versification becomes, the poem is, after all, a fragmentary thought, whereas Wordsworth's offers a declaration of a worldview.

Trying to fit an alternative reading to those anthropocentric views of nature that Regency England inherited from the eighteenth century, Hunt does not have the energy or the staying power to do more than make a provisional note. His subjunctive and adverbs of possibility point to the tentative nature of the enterprise, as does his omission of a strong gnomic line ("Music's the voice of Heaven without the words") that, had it been retained, might have closed the poem more forcefully. He is altogether more candid about the incomplete state of his poem on Paganini, which he subtitled *A Fragment.* Like *A Thought on Music* it attempts to relay musical experience in words— a form which we might call "melophrasis"—and like that poem, it has moments of linguistic forcing that try to break the evenness of blank verse. Also like the preceding poem, however, it manages to shake off initial mannerisms such as "sphery hand" (that hand, thus horribly encumbered, has somehow to wield a bow!) and move on to better things. Like many poems by Hunt, *Paganini* goes back to eighteenth-century models and, beyond those, to Dryden's great odes for music. It tries to register the variety of Paganini's musical effects not, as in the case of Dryden, by virtuoso metrics, but by shifts of imagery and verse deportment.

For example, the antithetic tug of heaven and earth, sacred and profane, in the image of the desert father is rendered programmatically by contrary motion in the syntax of the lines, while the grotesquerie of those that follow try to enact the hobble and jump of a witches' sabbath:

> or he turned
> To heaven instead of earth, and raised a prayer
> Mighty with want and all poor human tears,
> That never saint, wrestling with earthly love,
> And in mid-age unable to get free,
> Tore down from heav'n such pity. Or behold,
> In his despair, (for such, from what he spoke
> Of grief before it, or of love, 'twould seem,)
> Jump would he into some strange wail uncouth
> Of witches' dance, ghastly with whinings thin
> And palsied nods—mirth wicked, sad, and weak.[86]

As musical criticism goes, this running commentary of images is disappointingly subjective, though preferable to the pseudotechnicalities of glib ivory and birdy flutes. But if we remember its date of composition, and bear in mind that Berlioz had not yet written his *Symphonie Fantastique* (with its motif of impossible love and its Walpurgisnacht), we can nonetheless appreciate the way in which Hunt has managed to speak here for a whole generation of romantic music lovers.

Easily one of the best of Hunt's blank verse poems, *Thoughts in Bed upon Waking and Rising* not only maintains a consistent level of dignity, but also boasts a beginning, a middle, and an end by virtue of its "borrowed" essay form. (Hunt subtitled it *An "Indicator" in Verse.*) While it is true that essay decorum has prevented Hunt from lapsing into the tumidities that disfigure *A Thought on Music*, the even register might also owe something to a different model. No longer does he flail unsuccessfully in an effort to match the "sublime" blank verse of Milton; instead he chooses to fly at the more comfortable and homely altitude of Cowper. One seems to hear echoes of *The Task* in a passage such as this:

> No thought, ye powers of habit and sweet sleep
> And sweet remorse, for bed! catholic bed!
> The universal, wilful, sweet, stretched bed!
> Bed that lays prostrate half the world in turn,
> And hugs us in the heaven of our own arms?[87]

This mock-panegyric might well owe something to the playful way in which Cowper salutes the sofa as an epitome of comfort:

> But neither sleep
> Of lazy nurse, who snores the sick man dead,
> Nor his who quits the box at midnight hour
> To slumber in the carriage more secure,
> Nor sleep enjoy'd by curate in his desk,
> Nor yet the dozings of the clerk, are sweet,
> Compar'd with the repose the SOFA yields.[88]

However, although the blank verse has not led to excess of any kind, we might well ask what advantage it has conferred on the material. None, really—the essay offers no occasion for plangency or solemn incantation or thematic foregrounding. At most it provides a slight "lift" in diction from which the poet can bump gently into bathos, as when he hails the bed. But that, I am sure, was not Hunt's motive in choosing the form. He simply wanted to indulge an impulse to write poetry and meet the call of the printer's devil at the same time.

Our Cottage is titled in such a way as to suggest the topographic reality of a piece by Mary Mitford, and Hunt sustains the deception long enough to give his sleight of hand time to work. He begins with the formula of privileged access, familiar from such famous set pieces as Oberon's "I know a bank," and proceeds to pen a characteristic idyll. His utopian intention betrays itself, however, in that catalog of exemptions and abolitions so central the genre—think, for example, of the old hymn, "Jerusalem, my happy home," where "no sorrow may be found, / No grief, no care, no toil."[89] Hunt would not, in more "straight-faced" celebrations of escape, have banished the stress and flurry of the nineteenth century in quite such absolute terms:

> No news comes here; no scandal; no routine
> Of morning visit; not a postman's knock,—
> That double thrust of the long staff of care.
> We are as distant from the world, in spirit
> If not in place, as though in Crusoe's isle,
> And please ourselves with being ignorant
> Ev'n of the country some five miles beyond.[90]

The break comes with an eager interjection from a reader-*adversarius*, who, in a lively stichomythic passage of which Pope might been proud, begs admission to this paradise:

> "And where (cries some one) is this blessed spot?
> May I behold it? May I gain admittance?"
>   Yes, *with a thought;—as we do.*
>   "Woe is me!
> Then no such place exists!"
>   None such to us,
> Except in thought; but *that*—
>   "Is true as fiction?"[91]

The irony of *Our Cottage* lies partly in the fact that although it is touched here and there with wish fulfillment and blurred by a haze of nostalgia, it is based closely on the facts of Hunt's Hampstead experience. The idyll is modest enough to be grasped as a reality, and only partly belongs to the realm of romance. Hunt himself admits in *Bodryddan* that "Our fairest dreams are made of truths, / Nymphs are sweet women, angels youths, / And Eden was an earthly bower,"[92] and at the end of *Our Cottage* one of the clauses in the hymn to fancy celebrates its interconnection with fact:

> Fancy's the wealth of wealth, the toiler's hope,
> The poor man's piecer-out; the art of Nature,

> Painting her landscapes twice; the spirit of fact,
> As matter is the body; the pure gift
> Of heav'n to poet and to child; which he
> In all things fitted else, is most a man;[93]

If this codetta has a familiar ring, it is because Hunt seems to have modeled it on Herbert's *Prayer (I)*, which reveals the same apositive structure, and also pushes the utterance in the direction of litany. Fancy occupies a position in Hunt's life comparable to that occupied by prayer in Herbert's—it offers enablement, bridging, and compensation.

Bridging spirit and matter is the primary task to which Hunt puts the fancy in *Reflections of a Dead Body*. The tradition of addressing the transition between mortality and timelessness goes back to Hadrian's famous address to his soul ("Animula vagula blandula, / hospes comesque corporis, / quae nunc abibis in loca, / pallidula, rigida, nudula, / nec ut soles dabis iocos")[94] but Hunt goes beyond Hadrian's reliance on future verbs, and tries to imagine the condition of the spirit *post mortem*. The idea had been exploited before—one thinks of Haydn's "Spirit's Song" ("All pensive and alone, / I sit and see thee weep / Thy head upon the stone / Where my cold ashes sleep")[95] and Hunt's own poem on the death of Princess Charlotte ("His Departed Love to Prince Leopold"), where a ghost addresses a living person by a kind of tactual telepathy: "Thou canst not touch or come to me, / But all this power is mine; / And I can touch thy bosom still; / And now I do so by that thrill."[96]

However, while the situation itself might not be new to poetry, Hunt is one of the first to have amplified and sustained it, anticipating Cardinal Newman's *Dream of Gerontius* by decades and Thornton Wilder's *Our Town* by a century:

> I feel warm drops falling upon my face:
> They reach me through the rapture of this cold.—
> My wife! My love!—'tis for the best thou canst not
> Know how I know thee weeping, and how fond
> A kiss meets thine in these unowning lips.[97]

This is moving in the way that Wilder is moving, since it juxtaposes a beatific happiness with a sorrow it cannot assuage, as when Emily addresses her mother in the graveyard.[98] Altogether less successful is the imaginative effort Hunt put into the soul's dissolution—as in *A Thought on Music* there seems to be a proportional relation between mannerism and attempted "sublimity." While Hunt is fussy and even grotesque, Goethe's *Ganymed* presents the same event as a simple yet rapturous confluence of rising soul and descending Deity:

> Up, up, lies my course.
> While downward the clouds
> Are hovering, the clouds
> Are bending to meet yearning love.
> For me,
> Within thine arms
> Upwards!
> Embraced and embracing!
> Upwards into thy bosom,
> Oh Father all-loving![99]

It is quite as unfair of me to invoke Goethe in this instance as it is of other critics to set *The Story of Rimini* in the shadow of Dante, but we need to be reminded how the rococo exuberance to which Hunt's poetry habitually tends can often spoil its effects with floridity:

> I thy life,
> Life of thy life, bird of the bird, ah ha!
> Turn my face forth to heav'n—ah ha! ah ha!
> Oh the infinitude and the eternity!
> The dimpled air! the measureless conscious heaven!
> The endless possession! the sweet, mad, fawning planets
>   [*It speaks with a hurried vehemence of rapture.*
> Sleeking, like necks, round the beatitudes of the ubiquitous sun-
>   / god
> With bee-music of innumerable organ-thunders.
> And the travelling crowds this way, like a life-tempest,
> With rapid angelical faces, two in one,
> Ah ha! ah ha! and the stillness beyond the stars—
> My Friend! my Mother!—I mingle through the roar.
>   [*Spirit*
> *vanishes.*[100]

Cardinal Newman was rebuked for the vulgar mirth of the demons in *The Dream of Gerontius*, but Meriol Trevor has at least been able to find a thematic function for that vulgarity: "Some felt devils yelling 'ha ha' and jeering at chastity were perhaps a little vulgar; Newman had a realistic view of devilry and did not go in for Satanic grandeur."[101] But how on earth are

we to account for Hunt's "ah ha-ing" the spirit towards its apotheosis, as
though it had just managed to solve a long division sum? Nor is the as-
tronomy very sound that tries to mix globular planets and serpentine necks
in a queasy metaphoric cocktail.

A Rustic Walk and Dinner, trying much less, succeeds where *Reflections
of a Dead Body* lost itself in bombast. Indeed, it is a fine summation of
Hunt's ability with blank verse, and a worthy successor to Cowper's versified rambles through the countryside of Olney. Since, like the second epistle
to Thomas Moore, *A Rustic Walk* is a hodoiporikon, Hunt's prefatory note
about his measure deserves quoting: "The style of the blank verse, except
here and there, is intentionally unelevated, in accordance with the familiar
and colloquial nature of the subject;—it is literally *sermo pedestris*,—poetry
on foot."[102] With poet and poetry both on foot, moreover, there are no
disfigurements in the diction, and Hunt rises to the level where his talent
best displays itself. We recognize the informing model of the familiar essay
once again: the abstractly posed *quaestio* ("How fine to walk to dinner, not
too far, / Through a green country"), and its casual development and its
resolution. Since the idyll requires an idyllic idiom, Hunt reserves the right
to rococo license, but, having made the token claim, never again construes
a holiday spirit as an invitation to extravagance:

> The grass *lie-down-upónable.*—Avaunt,
> Critics, or come with us, and learn the right
> Of coining words in the quick mint of joy.[103]

The *capriccio* has a close relationship with rococo art, not only in the freedom it claims in selecting its materials, but also the freedom in developing
them. That is why Hunt takes the walk as a structural metaphor for this, one
of his most typical and most successful poems. The route of the walker is
conditioned entirely by impulse, not by the external constraints of roadway
or river:

> But walking's freest. Riding, you must keep
> To roads; coaching, still more so; and your boat
> Must be got home. In walking, you command
> Time, place, caprice; may go on, or return,
> Lie down, expatiate, wander; laugh at gates,
> That poze the loftiest-minded fox-hunter;
> Hills animate, brooks lull, woods welcome you,
> Like lovers' whispers; you may go within,

> Into the secret'st shade, and there climb banks
> And bowers of rooty and weedy luxury,
> Knee-deep in flowers, upborne by nutty boughs,
> Into a paradise of sunny shade,
> And sit, and read your book, beside the birds[104]

In "expatiate" we have a nice intersection of physical and verbal roaming. *Our Cottage* laid its pastoralism on thick, and then confessed that it was largely an exercise of fancy; *A Rustic Walk* reverses this transition, first offering itself as manual for walkers, and then drifting from plausible topography to fanciful conceits, which develop through a thicket of *y* suffixes.

Telltale congestions in the imagery show that Hunt has lapsed into luxurious reverie, suspended between flowers and boughs: "Knee-deep in flowers, up-borne by nutty boughs." Later on, a parenthetic aside shows a more conscious decision to weave fancy into factual observation. Whenever Hunt invokes fairies, we know where his poetry is tending:

> Blest heavens! what heaps of loveliness for ever
> Work under ground, and are for ever thrusting
> There sweet heads forth, or stealing up their way
> Through trunks of trees, touching (as we may fancy)
> The hearts of those rough gravities with some sense
> Of pure and sweet; and thence at nicest tips
> Of twig, and draping every numerous bough,
> Unfold green elegance, as of fairy shops,
> And hang their glimmering tents 'twixt us and heaven![105]

Here the Chapmanly combination of concrete adjective with abstract noun ("rough gravities"; "green elegance") parallels the other blends of fact and fancy upon which the poem is erected. We see this especially in a later exchange with a nonce "Reader" (Hunt is a social being, and unable, like Wordsworth, to contemplate in grave, majestic solitude). The companion, springing from wish fulfillment, does not have that educable gap of attitude and knowledge that characterizes the *adversarius* of satire, so perhaps we ought to christen him or her the *socius iucundus*:

> *Reader.*   Sinbad's stories
> Are *true*, they say! at least, "founded in truth";
> I hope, not too entirely. 'Twere a pity
> To stint the wondrous to the known, and leave
> The imagination not a world to conquer.[106]

To which "Author" replies "No fear of that, e'en could we walk the stars, / As long as known itself remains unknown / In its first cause, and every leaf a wonder." The "Reader," with a slight excess of eager assent responds in turn:

> *Reader.* Ay; and thus may we welcome fresh true wonders,
> Most Sinbad-like, nor give up dear astonishment.

Small wonder that Hunt should later exclaim, "We suit each other as if made to do so!" But, as so often in Hunt, idealism is not pitched so high as to betray itself by its impossibility. This ideal reader has a basis in his own friendship with Shelley, as a poignant modulation from fancy to biographical fact makes clear:

> (O Shelley! 'twas a bond 'twixt thee and me,
> That power to eat the sweet crust out of doors!
> You laughed with loving eyes, wrinkled with mirth,
> And cried, high breathing, "What! can you do *that?*"[)][107]

Because it is such a relaxed and commodious poem, *A Rustic Walk and Dinner* has a little bit of everything, including a number of lyric vignettes and idylls that have been ingested by its essayistic structure. More often than not, however, Hunt allowed such vignettes and idylls to stand on their own, and this is the material I shall survey in the last division of the chapter.

MISCELLANEOUS POEMS

Of all poetic forms, the lyric is the least demanding as a test of structural rigor, and one might thus expect it to suit Hunt best of all. However, Hunt proves as unpredictable here as in the sphere of blank verse. Even the most transparent and un-Metaphysical lyric depends on processes of distillation and excision, and although he wrote with the improvisatory ease and facility that makes for good beginnings, he lacked the patience and the craft to carry his first drafts toward perfection. The lax charm of his writing holds the promise of memorable lyrics but not the reality. Perhaps we ought to blame the freedom that Hunt claimed from the "oppressiveness" of neoclassicism. Because he adopted a policy of "anything goes," he replaced the hidebound formulas of poetic diction with his own peculiar fidgetiness, that often anarchic quest for neologism and that habitual violation of English idiom.

Whereas once a Grub Street hack would have taken down his *Gradus*, Hunt chooses rather to plunder his idiolect. So, combining speed with verbal disregard, he tossed of pieces like the *Ode for the Spring of 1814:*

> The vision then is past
> That held the eyes of nations,
>   Swept in his own careering blast,
> That shook the earth's foundations!
>   No more throughout the air
>   Settles the burning glare,
> That far and wide, metallic twilight, shone;
>   No more the bolts from south to north.
>   Leap in their fiery passion forth:
> We looked and saw the Wonder on his throne;
> We raised our eyes again, and lo, his place was gone.[108]

Given the apocalyptic tenor of his ode, Hunt has rightly chosen to model his stanza on that of Milton's *Hymn on the Morning of Christ's Nativity*, adding an extra three lines, but retaining the terminal alexandrine and the trimeter couplet, which, like the *chiave* of an Italian *canzone*, gives the design an additional nudge of momentum. Because his natural facility enabled him to take this complex pattern in his stride, his haste betrays itself not so much in slovenly metrics as in violations of idiom and in imprecise imagery.

One of the categories in Empson's *Seven Types of Ambiguity* centers on those moments "when the author is discovering his idea in the act of writing, or not holding it all in his mind at once, so that, for instance, there is a simile which applies to nothing exactly, but lies half-way between two things when the author is moving from one to the other."[109] While he acknowledges the power that can spring from this sort of blurriness, Empson also admits that meanings can seem "not so much untied as hurried on top of each other,"[110] a reservation that would certainly apply to the way Hunt shifts from the stasis of a vision that can "hold" the eyes of Europe to a self-demolishing "blast." Less obvious, but ultimately as disturbing, is the tension between the comprehensiveness of "throughout the air" (implying permeation) and "settles" (which implies the specific locality of a resting body), and the way "glare," a side effect of "burning," is problematically assimilated to its cause in "burning glare." This glare Hunt in turn describes as having "shone," a verb with an entirely different semantic charge. Sometimes the jars and shocks of mismarried idioms register more visibly on the Richter scale, as in "With frank eyes listening to the glassy spheres," where, having failed to separate the vision of the spheres from their music, Hunt

has scrambled sense registers. This is not synaesthesia, it is carelessness—
the same sort of carelessness that in the *National Song* invests England, the
"Queen of the West," with "*princely* white feet."[111]

So eager is Hunt to create the impression of an effortless outpouring of
poetry that he is prepared to waste several lines of a poem on improvisatory
expletives. These have achieved notoriety, along with the rural spots and
marrying scores of *Rimini*, as a sample of Hunt at his worst:

> Hallo!—what?—where?—what can it be
> That strikes up so deliciously?
> I never in my life—what? no!
> That little tin-box playing so?[112]

While this ostentatious informality might suggest a poem of little worth,
the rest of it is full of Huntian charm. In one particularly successful passage,
he mimics the repetitive nature of his subject by "rotating" parallel similes:

> Now we call thee heavenly rain,
> For thy fresh, continued strain,
> Now a hail, that on the ground,
> Splits into light leaps of sound;
> Now a concert, neat and nice,
> Of a pigmy paradise;
> Sprinkles then from singing fountains,
> Fairies heard on tops of mountains;
> Nightingales endued with art,
> Caught in listening to Mozart:
> Stars that make a distant twinkling;
> Sound for scattered rills to flow to;
> Music, for the flowers to grow to.[113]

The poem for his son John develops this incantatory technique still further.
Disclosing its origin by a frank subtitle—*A Nursery Song*—Hunt shows how
well he understood children. They love to be mesmerized by repeating
patterns and paratactic chains:

> Or whistling like the thrushes,
> With voice in silver gushes,
> Or twisting random posies,
> With daisies, weeds, and roses;
> And strutting in and out so,

> Or dancing all about so,
> With cock-up nose so lightsome,
> And sidelong cheeks so brightsome,
> And cheeks as bright as apples,
> And head as rough as Dapple's,
> And arms as sunny shining
> As if their veins had wine in.[114]

Good though this is as children's verse, it is to an adult, not a child, that Hunt directs his simile about wine in the veins, and even the "silver gushes" seem too mannered for the nursery. As a result, the poem falls between two stools: grown-ups will wince at some lines, children puzzle over others. That Hunt seems to have had only a vague sense of the difference between these audiences can be gathered from the way he employs the insistent trimetric patter and the unrelenting quiver of trisyllabic rhymes in "adult" poems like that *To the Lares*.[115] So, too, the octosyllabic bounce of *Christmas*,[116] with its tried-on suite of metaphors and its flurried *acervatio*, even though its subtitle (*A Song for the Young and the Wise*) tries to cajole us into accepting them like children.

Along with the poems *To May, To June,* and *A Hymn to Bishop St. Valentine,* these octosyllabic effusions form a distinct type among Hunt's lyrics. Distantly related to Milton's *L'Allegro,* they have that patter-inducing lilt which once underway gives him effortless momentum. The relentless way in which they turn to feminine rhyme also suggests that (either consciously or unconsciously) Hunt was attempting to italianize the native grain of English. Menotti, who has written and composed in both languages, and is therefore in a position to adjudicate between the musicality of each, has pointed out that the vocalic ends of Italian words have been overpraised, and that in their efforts to get a stronger effects, Verdi and Puccini frequently contracted *amore* to *amor'*, and *dolore* to *dolor'*. It is ironic therefore that Hunt should do the very opposite in his improvisatory list poems, and create a structural weakness in his quest for musicality.

Another distinctive type that we find in the lyric poems is the amplified conceit, something so seldom essayed by other romantic poets that one is tempted to trace it back to Hunt's antiquarian sorties into the poetry of the seventeenth century. They resemble the tri- and octosyllabic list poems to the extent that they heap up parallel instances and developments of the central extravagance, but they are distinguished from them by the oddity of that germinal thought. Hunt seems half to acknowledge the seventeenth-century source for this vein in the pastiche poem *Verses on a Full-Flowing Peruke by Richard Honeycomb, Esq., 1673*,[117] but *Alter et Idem, A Chemico-Poetical Thought*[118] is written *in propria persona*, and claims that unlikely metaphors are ultimately "true" because everything can be reduced to a common denominator of elements. *Love Letters Made of Flowers, On a Print of One of Them in a Book*[119] turns on the comedy of enthymeme, short-circuiting the division between letter and flower, and the more sentimental *Angel in the House*[120] claims that children are a proleptic version of the same—an idea that Byron, plagued by the Hunt brood in Italy, would have rejected with a vehement snort.

Related to these conceit poems, but different yet again, are the brief moralizing lyrics of Hunt's final years. Their paradoxical nature derives not from a display of wit but from his practice of "Christianism." Into this group fall such aperçu poems as *A Dream within a Dream, or, A Dream in Heaven; or, Evil Minimized*[121] and *Death*, which, by "hushing" the arguments contra, cannot be said to offer a cogent defense of universalism:

> But has guilt passed it [the road of Death]? Men not fit to die
> Oh hush,—for He that made us all, is by.
> Human were all; all men; all born of mothers;
> All our own selves, in the worn shape of others;
> Our *used*, and oh! be sure, not to be *ill*-used brothers.[122]

Hunt disingenuously tries to cover these unorthodox beliefs in his "Royal Family" poems, servile hints about a laureateship that fell on deaf ears. They rank amongst his worst verse, trivial and time-serving flatteries. *To the Queen, An Offering of Gratitude on Her Majesty's Birthday* makes ridiculous use of Virgil's Fourth Eclogue in its millenarian *coda*:

> And when the sword hath bowed beneath the pen,
> May her own line a patriarch scene unfold,
> As far surpassing what these days behold
> E'en in the thunderous gods, iron and steam,
> As they the sceptic's doubt, or wild man's dream!
> And to this end—oh! to this Christian end,
> And the sure coming of its next great friend,
> May her own soul, this instant, while I sing,
> Be smiling, as beneath some angel's wing,
> O'er the dear life in life, the small, sweet, new,
> Unselfish self, the filial self of two[123]

Like Virgil's Fourth Eclogue this envisages a new world order, but, with an eye on the queen's piety, Hunt pretends to Christianize that vision, speaking in terms of Christian teleology and the Parousia, both of which doctrines he rejected. He deserves to be arraigned here for "mince-piety," a word of his own invention.

The same messianic vision, relayed with the bounce of a list poem *(To the Infant Princess Royal),* becomes unbearably facile: "Hail, matured humanity! / Earth has outgrown want and war; / Earth is now no childish star."[124] What compels our assent and moves us in Shelley's *Hellas* cannot be forced onto the occasion of a royal birth without a sense of expediency, on the one hand, and bathos, on the other. Not content with sly manipulations of Virgil, Hunt also borrows an effect or two from Gray's *Bard* in *Three Visions on the Birth of the Prince of Wales,* speaking in a prophetic present tense with all the standard decor of parting clouds and swift dissolutions of radiance. Here, however, he tries to salve conscience by pretending that Victoria will address the lot of the poor.

Much more substantial are *The Nymphs* and *The "Choice,"* too substantial indeed to count as lyric poems, but banished by the shifting criteria of the other groupings—the subject matter of "Political and Critical Poems" and the formal differentia of "Blank Verse"—to a place among the "Miscellaneous Poems." We have already touched on *The Nymphs* in the opening chapter, but we can glance at it once again (alongside *The "Choice"*) to measure the distance that Hunt tried to place between himself and the eighteenth century. For while *The Nymphs* seems at first sight to be unprecedented, the sort of rococo idyll sui generis that Hunt added to the heritage of English verse, it does have an eighteenth-century precursor in Akenside's *Hymn to the Naiads.* Reading the poems in sequence, we are in a position to see how they differ. After a scenic prolusion that owes a great deal to the odes of Collins, especially the *Ode to Evening,* Akenside gets down to his task:

> Where shall my song begin, ye Nymphs, or end?
> Wide is your praise and copious—first of things,
> First of the lonely powers, ere Time arose,
> Were Love and Chaos. Love, the sire of Fate;
> Elder than Chaos. Born of Fate was Time,
> Who many sons and many comely births
> Devour'd, relentless father; till the child
> Of Rhea drove him from the upper sky,
> And quell'd his deadly might. Then social reign'd
> The kindred powers, Tethys and reverent Ops,[125]

Hunt has all too frequently suffered by comparison with first-class talents, so it is only just that we fix some fairer gradations of excellence, and use the journeyman verse of Akenside to measure the lyric achievement of *The Nymphs*. The extract above is a pedestrian summary of Hesiod, adding nothing to the prosaic genealogy of the original except the honorable plod of competence and scholarship. Indeed the whole of the *Hymn to the Naiads* proves to be a cento of classical sources. For example, the section beginning "those powerful strings / That charm the mind of gods"[126] translates Pindar's First Pythian Ode, but whereas Gray *refracts* and adapts the same source material in *The Progress of Poesy* and renders it into verse of transcendent beauty, Akenside's version would not seem out of place in a Loeb crib. Turning from this drab to the shot silk of Hunt's poem, all ripple and iridescence, we find free-flowing fancy where Akenside could offer only a text-hugging caution. Hunt, like Keats and Shelley after him, is able to forge his own mythology, which he slyly passes off as a sort of archaeological discovery:

> And O ye sweet and coy Ephydriads,
> Why are you names so new
> To islands which your liquid lips serene
> Keep ever green?[127]

On another occasion in the poem, he similarly turns fancy into fact by implying that some of his observations are firsthand, and others supplemented by imaginative projection:

> Too far for me to see, the Limniad takes
> Her pleasure in the lakes;
> She, that with hills about her, loves to be
> At once at home and at her liberty.
> Far off I fancy, 'twixt their bowery isles,
> Her and her sisters playing their sweet wiles
> About a boat, . . .[128]

While the sleight of hand requires Hunt to remain, like the Limniads, "at once at home and at liberty," at other points of the poem he travels effortlessly from venue to venue. This fanciful transcendence of space is something of a leitmotif in his verse—it figures in *Politics and Poetics*; it is the raison d'être of the fragmentary *Fancy's Party*; and it is also given memorable treatment in the *Thoughts in Bed upon Waking and Rising*.

> I hear the windows thick with wateriness,
> Which ever and anon the gusty hand
> Of the dark wind flings full, I make my morn
> Still beauteous if I please, with sunny help
> Of books or my own thoughts, sending them up
> Like nymphs above the sea of atmosphere,
> To warm their winking cheeks against the sun,
> And laugh 'twixt islands of the mountain tops.[129]

Coming from someone unfamiliar with airplanes, this strikes me as being a remarkable effort of fancy. Few people, even today, remain conscious of the discontinuity of weather above and beneath a cloud cover. The spatial elision at the start of *The Nymphs* belongs to the same order of vision, and looks forward directly to the *Ode to a Nightingale*:

> For a new smiling sense has shot down through me,
> And from the clouds, like stars, bright eyes are beckoning to me.
>
> Arrived! Arrived! O shady spots of ground,
> What calmness ye strike round,
> Hushing the soul as if with hand on lips![130]

How grateful that easy swing from hexameter to a five- and then to a three-foot line.

Since we are matching Huntian ease against starchy, formal verse by eighteenth-century poetasters, we had better pause here to consider what it entails. I cannot agree with Richard Hengist Horne when he projects the demeanor as a sort of *curiosa felicitas*:

> His excessive consciousness of grace in the turning of a line, and of richness in the perfecting of an image, is what some people have called "coxcombry"; and the manner of it approaches to that conscious, sidelong, swimming gait, balancing between the beautiful and the witty. . . .[131]

Huntian grace is much nearer the grace of serendipity, of something snatched beyond the reach of art, as in this more plausible claim by C. H. Herford: "[Hunt's] chief function in literature was to further . . . ease, vivacity and grace."[132] Witness the proem to his adaptation of Pomfret's *Choice*:

> I have been reading Pomfret's *Choice* this spring,
> A pretty kind of—sort of—kind of thing,

> Not much a verse and poem none at all,
> Yet, as they say, extremely natural.[133]

This is not the self-conscious grace of *maniera*, but rather a self-conscious negligence. Hunt's declared intention is to write a similar manifesto poem but with a rather different attitude to his task: "*I'll* write a *Choice*, said I: and it shall be / Something 'twixt labour and *extempore*; / Not long, yet not too quick on the conclusion, / And for its ease I'll call it an effusion."[134] The *capriccios* of Guardi are remarkable for the freedom of their brushwork, and in Watteau, too, there is no trace of the solemn academic finish of his baroque predecessors—rococo artists to a person seek out effects of "extemporariness." Many Hunt poems try to seem effortless by cultivating the rough surface of the workshop.

One such effort is *Doggrel on Double Columns and Large Type*, which contains an outrageous brace of couplets: "The *Dublin University* / Might also spell his name with *g*,— / With *o* and *g*, and call himself / The *Doubling*,—therefore fit for the shelf."[135] As a man who, in a matter of hours, could compose a fine sonnet like that on the Nile, Hunt was justifiably proud of his facility, but it could also issue in a wearying insouciance. In stature and achievement he resembles his contemporary Gaetano Donizetti, who also prided himself on his speed of composition (the last act of *La Favorite* is supposed to have been written in an evening). But, like Donizetti, a potentially first-rate lyric talent, Hunt compromised the quality of his verse by rejecting *labor limae* as something incompatible with rapidity and ease.

Of course, no such facility can be detected in the portly verse of Pomfret, as worthy and as dull as an alderman's speech. There can be no doubting the fact that Hunt's unpremeditated looseness finally has greater appeal than the careful husbanding of platitudes and safe effects, just as Donizetti's music, flawed though it may be, outshines the cautious idiom of Mayr, his teacher. This is how Pomfret's *Choice* gets underway:

> If Heaven the grateful Liberty would give,
> That I might chuse my Method how to live;
> And all those Hours propitious Fate should lend,
> In blissful Ease, and Satisfaction spend.
>
> Near some fair Town, I'd have a private Seat,
> Not Uniform, not little, nor too great:
> Better if on a rising Ground it stood;

On this side Fields, on that a neighb'ring Wood:
It should within, no other Things contain,
But what were Useful, Necessary, Plain:
Methinks 'tis Nauseous, and I'd ne'er endure
The needless Pomp of Gaudy Furniture.[136]

When we examined *The Nymphs*, Akenside provided the foil of his pedestrian talent to offset the delicacy of that poem. In this instance Hunt even more brilliantly outshines the negligible gift of Pomfret. Where Pomfret gives us a bare architectural diagram, Hunt supplies a quick impressionistic sketch:

First, on a green I'd have a low, broad house,
Just seen by travellers through the garden boughs;
And that my luck might not seem ill bestowed,
A bench and spring should greet them on the road.
My grounds should not be large; I like to go
To Nature for a range, and prospect too,
And cannot fancy she'll comprise for me,
Even in a park, her all-sufficiency.
Besides, my thoughts fly far; and when at rest,
Love, not a watch-tower, but a lulling nest.[137]

Pomfret's choice is that of Horace on his Sabine farm; for Hunt that sufficiency needs the amplification of the fancy. His recurrent obsession with mental flight once again declares itself in the desire to escape the enclosure of property but, even as it roams, his fancy sets equally characteristic limits and barriers. Hunt's rejection of the sea supplies a predictable corollary to his endless harping on nests and bowers:

But sure I am I'd not live near the sea,
To view its great flat face, and have my sleeps
Filled full of shrieking dreams and foundering ships;
Or hear the drunkard, when his slaughter's o'er,
Like Sinbad's monster scratching on the shore.[138]

These reductive images from "low life" and fairy tale are quite at home in a self-declared caprice like this, a caprice in which one line ("I love you, e'en in vales / Of cups and saucers, and such Delfic dales") runs painted china—Delft—into sublime landscape—Delphi. As so often in other poems by Hunt in which he recoils from sublimity, there is imaginative energy in the very recoil. In "great flat face" he has managed a vividness and linguistic tang in spite of himself. Again and again as we leaf through the "Miscellaneous Poems", we find that while his sympathetic landscapes—the "Pearly Shore," say, in *Thoughts of the Avon*[139]—tend to issue in a smothering excess of decor, alien ones are rendered with unexpected power. *Power and Gentleness* shows this fine austerity in a "ghastly castle, that eternally / Holds its blind visage out to the lone sea"[140]—almost certain to have lodged in the mind of Keats—and in the presentment of the pyramids "whose small doors / Look like low dens under precipitous shores."[141] And again in *Ronald of the Perfect Hand* the infertility of salt water seems to frustrate the sowing metaphor, and so to redouble its effort:

> 'Tis evening quick;—'tis night:—the rain
> Is sowing wide the fruitless main,
> Thick, thick;—no sight remains the while
> From the farthest Orkney isle.[142]

If we make allowance for the melodramatic stop and start of the phrasing, those lines seem worthy of Gray's translations of Nordic verse.

Returning, however, to the cozy outlook of *The "Choice,"* we cannot but sense how self-indulgence in Hunt's subject matter issues in a comparable self-indulgence of language. There is that tone of nattering intimacy, and an inconsequential play of images, rising extempore, half-summoned by the rhyme:

> One of the rooms should face a spot of spots,
> Such as would please a squirrel with his nuts;
> I mean a slope, looking upon a slope,
> Wood-crowned and delled with turf, a sylvan cup
> Here, when our moods were quietest, we'd praise
> The scenic shades, and watch the doves and jays,[143]

Again the Beckmessers in us resist the participial "delled" not because it is a neologism, but because it relates to shape while "turf" relates to color and texture. Nor is "cup" a happy metaphor for a vessel with sloping sides.

David Smith has asked apropos of Hunt, "How does one write about a man of considerable talent, who, it is asserted, never wrote anything absolutely of the first rank but whose work you nevertheless wish to commend?"[144] My own answer, in this chapter, as in this book, would be this: sift through verse of a poet who wrote too much and edited too little, and then, taking the corpus of poems that benefit from such free compositional methods, read them in ways appropriate to their style and content, and read the humble claims the poet himself made for them. Read them, above all, with criteria that foreground decorative effect and background substantial ideas, that privilege momentary inspiration above teleological plan, and that accept without undue regret the fragmentary results of a fancy finally unable to weld and fix its materials in memorable form. Treat them, in a word, as the utterances of a rococo artist.

Epilogue

In the "Prefatory Essay" to *A Jar of Honey from Mount Hybla*, Hunt made the following announcement:

> One of the especial parts of our vocation is to draw sweet out of bitter; . . . when this our Honey first made its appearance at the periodical table of Mr. Ainsworth, and was thence diffused over the country, [judges] exclaimed from all quarters, after the most benignant meditation, "With this sauce a man might swallow some of the bitterest morsels of life." "This is the condiment to sweeten every man's daily bread." "There is the right Christian aroma in the sacrificial part of the offering of these dulcitudes."
>
> We blush, of course, with the requisite modesty in repeating these approvals; and, indeed, should blush a great deal more if we thought that the contents of our Jar (as far as they originate with ourselves) had any merit beyond such as might easily be competed with by thousands throughout the land, upon the strength of their own thoughts and good-will, assisted by a little reading and cheerfulness; . . .[1]

We can commandeer the claims and the demurrals of this extract for our final assessment of Hunt's achievement as a poet.

While it is true that his verse fails to sustain the level of excellence he managed in his essays, it has nonetheless suffered far too long from injudicious and intemperate dismissals. Recalling the fierceness of the *Blackwood's* attack, and of others written in our own century that seem hardly less vehement, we need first of all to note the humility of the claims Hunt makes for his writing—"We . . . should blush a great deal more if we thought that the contents of our Jar . . . had any merit beyond such as might easily be competed with by thousands throughout the land. . . ." By his own admission on this and on other platforms, he was not a prophet-poet like Shelley, nor a craftsperson as searching and self-critical as Keats. Nor, despite having claimed a part in the "new school," was he an avante-garde writer of Wordsworth's stature, pushing poetry over new frontiers of expression. His verse was so nourished by the fancies of the Age of Sensibility—a legacy that, as we have seen, extends far behind the echo-chamber effort of the *Juvenilia*—that he was disqualified from seeing far enough into the future of romanticism. Literary history has been written in terms very different from those that Hunt proposed for his own generation, and his notion that romantic poets were rediscovering the Italian heritage of English poetry no longer seems tenable. Indeed, the fact that he should have conceived romanticism in these terms might well account for the comparatively marginal status his poetry now enjoys in surveys of the period. It was Gray, after all, arch poet of sensibility, who began to look toward Italy again after the long dalliance with France; Coleridge found romantic inspiration on German rather than Italian soil (we know that Petrarch left him cold). Furthermore, conditioned as it was by his early devotion to Gray and Collins, Hunt's sensibility differed again from Byron's. Byron also had roots in the eighteenth century, but in its earlier decades, whence that strange and potent confluence of Augustan common sense and romantic extravagance that makes his poetry—especially his satire—so much more distinctive than the comparable effort, say, of *The Dogs*.

In the preface to *A Jar of Honey* Hunt suggested that his talents as an essayist were not unique, and he would have been quite as ready to say the same of his verse. The fact that he should make no great claims for himself as writer redounds to his credit, for we know that his self-effacement was sincere. However, it is all too easy to regard such modesty as an invitation to neglect the modest accomplishment it acknowledges. Like Jane Austen, painting miniatures on pieces of ivory, Hunt knew his limitations, and generally worked within them. The sense of limitation failed, however, to bring with it the kind of perfection that characterizes the novels of his contemporary. That is because, humbly aware that his poetry was not poetry of the first order, he never tried to work it into any state of polish. Keats knew that the faults of *Endymion* were largely incorrigible, and therefore did not misspend energy trying to make it greater than it was; Hunt knew that his poetry fell short of greatness and never wrestled it into excellence. The *apparatus criticus* of the Milford edition of his poems might call this judgment into question, but the moment we study the endless textual variants, we realize that he was prepared only to tinker with the surface of the completed poem, never to reconceive it thoroughly. The variant readings are themselves extremely variable; sometimes they improve, as often as not they offer an alternative of comparable quality, and sometimes they fall short of the first inspiration.

But once we have made all these concessions and fixed these limits, we can recur to the prefatory remarks set out above and express our gratitude for the honey that Hunt poured so unstintingly from his jar. One could not ask for a more apposite metaphor. While honey might be void of protein, and while it might lack the necessary complement of vitamins, we would be guilty of error—let us be New Critical, and call it the generic fallacy—if we asked it to supply the sort of nourishment it never professed to offer. Its function is not to build but to sweeten; it has a "decorative" rather than a central use in the kitchen. It is also true that, taken by itself, honey can cloy. There are undoubtedly moments when the poetry flaunts its "sweetness" and the reader feels the same surge of irritation that drove Dickens to the injustices of the Harold Skimpole portrait. There are other moments when, with the stock decor of the idyll and recycling of rococo surface effects, the poetry seems to take on the desperate sameness of a draught of honey, and one yearns for more shade to offset the glare of golden light. Hunt's recipe of "cheerfulness" can in some moods seem one of a piece with the good-natured prescriptions of the *beatus ille* tradition; in others it seems more akin to the shallow professions of a Pollyanna. Since by his own admission "Dull admonition provokes opposition,"[2] one occasionally wishes that instead of the endless sketches of picnic spots, he had essayed a poem on the Austra-lian hinterland or the shores of Antarctica.

But if our worse, our Blackwoody, selves do feel these contra-suggest-ible and mean-spirited impulses, a solution is easily found. Unlike Winnie-the-Pooh, who swallowed jars of honey at a sitting, we take can take ours in sensible doses. Read in moderation, Hunt reveals his charm. No longer do we seem to drown in a viscous, formless surge of indigestible sweetness, but rather feel replenished and energized by an optimism seldom offered in the darkness of our century. Nor ought we to forget the biographical matrix of Hunt's endless idylls. His right to recreative escape was in many respects earned; he probably did more for the cause of liberty than all his detractors put together. Ian Jack dichotomizes man and poet in an otherwise just and balanced assessment: "Yet if there was an element of cheapness in his sub-urban epicureanism, there was an element of unmistakeable nobility in the man himself."[3] If, however, we allow that nobility to carry over into the verse, and balance the bitter herbs of Hunt's imprisonment with the honey of his rococo poems, we can banish the specter of Harold Skimpole that seems to haunt it when it is read *in vacuo*. For, approached with the right tact, and with due acknowledgment of the minority of his minor talent, Hunt often seems to reenact the famous riddle in *Judges*, bringing forth sweetness out of *strength*.

Notes

Preface and Acknowledgments

1. Jerome McGann, *The Beauty of Inflections* (Oxford: Clarendon Press, 1985), 61–62.
2. *The Complete Works of William Hazlitt*, edited by P. P. Howe, 21 vols. (London: J. M. Dent, 1934), 19:55; "Mr. Crabbe."
3. Ibid., 11:105–6; "Mr. Malthus."
4. Ibid., 19:56; "Mr. Crabbe."
5. Quoted on the acknowledgments page of Anne Blainey, *Immortal Boy: A Portrait of Leigh Hunt* (London: Croom Helm, 1985).
6. *Leigh Hunt: A Reference Guide*, edited by Timothy K. Lulofs and Hans Ostrom (Boston: G. K. Hall, 1985), 83.
7. Charles Dickens, *Bleak House* (London: Oxford University Press, 1948), 69.
8. Edmund Blunden, *Leigh Hunt: A Biography* (London: Cobden-Sanderson, 1930), 362.
9. *The Poetical Works of Leigh Hunt*, edited by H. S. Milford (London: Oxford University Press, 1923).
10. My decision to omit Hunt's translations from this book has obviously entailed skipping such additional catchall categories as the "Narrative Modernizations."
11. Leigh Hunt, *Autobiography* (London: Cresset, 1949), 384.
12. *The Life and Times of Leigh Hunt: Papers Delivered at a Symposium at the University of Iowa, April 13, 1984* (Iowa City: Friends of the University of Iowa Libraries, 1985.
13. James R. Thompson, *Leigh Hunt* (Boston: Twayne, 1977).
14. John O. Hayden, "Leigh Hunt's *Story of Rimini*: Reloading the Romantic Canon," *Durham University Journal* 79 (1987): 279–87.

Chapter 1. Fancy and Its Effects

1. Samuel Taylor Coleridge, *Biographia Literaria*, 2 vols. (Oxford: Clarendon Press, 1907), 1:202.
2. Ibid., 86.
3. Catherine Miles Wallace, *The Design of Biographia Literaria* (London: George Allen & Unwin, 1983), 49.
4. *The Prose Works of William Wordsworth*, edited by W. J. B. Owen and Jane Worthington Smyser, 3 vols. (Oxford: Clarendon Press, 1974) 3:36; "Preface of 1815."

5. Ibid.

6. M. H. Abrams, *The Mirror and the Lamp* (1953; rpt., New York: W. W. Norton, 1958), 182.

7. James Scoggins, *Imagination and Fancy* (Lincoln: University of Nebraska Press, 1966), 5.

8. Leigh Hunt, *Imagination and Fancy* (London: Smith, Elder, & Company, 1891), 2.

9. Ibid., 27.

10. David Masson, *Wordsworth, Shelley, Keats, and Other Essays* (London: Macmillan, 1875), 202; "Theories of Poetry."

11. Hunt (above, note 8), 1.

12. Stephen Fogle, *Some British Romantics* (Columbus: Ohio State University Press, 1966), 125; "Leigh Hunt and the End of Romantic Criticism."

13. Ibid.,137.

14. Hunt (above, note 8), 27–28.

15. Owen and Smyser (above, note 4); "Preface of 1815."

16. Hunt (above, note 8), 2.

17. Leigh Hunt, *Autobiography* (London: Cresset, 1949), 27.

18. *The Complete Works of William Hazlitt*, edited by P. P. Howe, 21 vols. (London: J. M. Dent, 1934), 11:170; "The Spirit of the Age."

19. Ibid., 171–72.

20. The contradiction has been noted by Ian Jack, *Keats and the Mirror of Art* (Oxford: Clarendon Press, 1967), 13ff. We know, furthermore, that the Cowden Clarkes had an engraving of the Reni fresco in their "snuggery"—cf. Richard Altick, *The Cowden Clarkes* (London: Oxford University Press, 1948), 85.

21. Greg Kucich, "Leigh Hunt and Romantic Spenserianism," *Keats-Shelley Journal* 30 (1981): 125.

22. Ibid., 114.

23. Donald Posner, *Antoine Watteau* (London: Weidenfeld and Nicolson, 1984), 267.

24. *Leigh Hunt's Literary Criticism*, edited by Lawrence Huston Houtchens and Caroline Washburn Houtchens (New York: Columbia University Press, 1956), 179; "On the Latin Poems of Milton."

25. Jerome McGann, *The Beauty of Inflections* (Oxford: Clarendon Press, 1985), 9.

26. Howe (above, note 18), 10:22–23; "The Dulwich Gallery."

27. Ibid., 6:70; "Lectures on Comic Writers."

28. Ibid., 10:23; "The Dulwich Gallery."

29. A. C. Sewter, *Baroque and Rococo* (New York: Harcourt Brace Jovanovich, 1972), 163.

30. Posner (above, note 23), 15.

31. Masson (above, note 10), 185.

32. *Keats: The Critical Heritage*, edited by G. M. Matthews (London: Routledge and Kegan Paul, 1971), 101; John Gibson Lockhart, "Lockhart's Attack in *Blackwood's*."

33. Marlon Ross, *The Contours of Masculine Desire* (New York: Oxford University Press, 1989), 170.

34. R. B. Johnson, *Leigh Hunt* (London: Swan Sonnenschein & Co., 1896), 115.

35. Germain Bazin, *Baroque and Rococo* (London: Thames and Hudson, 1964), 177–78.

36. Ibid., 231.

37. Sewter (above, note 29), 195–96.

38. Jacques Thuillier and Albert Châtelet, *French Painting from Le Nain to Fragonard*

(Geneva: Albert Skira, 1964), 181.

39. Posner (above, note 23), 208.

40. Bazin (above, note 35), 197–98.

41. Jerome J. McGann, *The Romantic Ideology* (Chicago: Chicago University Press, 1983), 117.

42. Posner (above, note 23), 181.

43. Thuillier and Châtelet (above, note 38), 180.

44. Houtchens and Houtchens (above, note 24), 133; "Preface to *Foliage*."

45. Ibid., 173; "Sketches of the Living Poets: Coleridge."

46. Ibid., 198; "On the Latin Poems of Milton."

47. Ibid., 180.

48. Kucich (above, note 21), 114.

49. Houtchens and Houtchens (above, note 24), 623; "The Late Mr. Ollier."

50. Owen and Smyser (above, note 4),3:36; "Preface of 1815."

51. William Wordsworth, *The Prelude: A Parallel Text*, edited by J. C. Maxwell (Harmondsworth: Penguin, 1971), 239.

52. Ross (above, note 33), 47–48.

53. Ibid., 44.

54. Maxwell (above, note 51), 523.

55. Alan Richardson, "Romanticism and the Colonization of the Feminine," in *Romanticism and Feminism*, edited by Anne K. Mellor (Bloomington: Indiana University Press, 1988).

56. Stuart Curran, "The Altered I," in ibid., 190.

57. *William Wordsworth*, edited by Stephen Gill (Oxford: Clarendon Press, 1984), 175; *Home at Grasmere*.

58. John Keble, *The Christian Year* (London: Oxford University Press, n.d.), 3.

59. Quoted in Curran (above, note 56), 185.

60. Quoted in Ross (above, note 33), 15–16.

61. *The Poetical Works of John Keats*, edited by H. W. Garrod (London: Oxford University Press, 1970), 48.

62. Ross (above, note 33), 17.

63. Sewter (above, note 29), 195–96.

64. *Tennyson: The Critical Heritage*, edited by John Jump (London: Routledge and Kegan Paul, 1967), 81; "J. W. Croker on Poems [1833]."

65. Maria Edgeworth, *Castle Rackrent and The Absentee* (London: Macmillan, 1895), 102.

66. Hunt (above, note 17), 243.

67. Ross (above, note 33), 156.

68. Mrs. Henry Tighe, *Psyche, with Other Poems* (London: Longman, Hurst, Rees, Orme, and Brown, 1816), 5.

69. Ibid., 231.

70. Nancy Armstrong, *Desire and Domestic Fiction* (New York: Oxford University Press, 1987), 60.

71. *The Poetical Works of Leigh Hunt*, edited by H. S. Milford (London: Oxford University Press, 1923), 188.

72. Mary Poovey, *The Proper Lady and the Woman Writer* (Chicago: Chicago University Press, 1984), 6.

73. Adam Smith, *The Theory of Moral Sentiments*, 2 vols. (London: T. Cadel and W. Davies, 1804), 2:400.

74. Poovey (above, note 72), 56–57.

75. Mary Wollstonecraft, *A Vindication of the Rights of Woman*, edited by Carol H. Poston (New York: Norton, 1975), 59.

76. McGann (above, note 41), 131.

77. Ibid., 132.

78. McGann (above, note 25), 61n.

79. Hunt (above, note 17), 275.

80. McGann (above, note 25), 80.

81. McGann (above, note 41), 34.

82. Ibid., 53.

83. Lisa Vargo, "Unmasking Shelley's *Mask of Anarchy*," *English Studies in Canada* 13 (1987): 50.

84. Milford (above, note 71), 293.

85. *Selected Poems of Percy Bysshe Shelley*, edited by Timothy Webb (London: J. M. Dent, 1977), 200–201.

86. Matthews (above, note 32), 42; H. J. L. Hunt, "Leigh Hunt Introduces a New Poet."

87. William Keach, "Cockney Couplets: Keats and the Politics of Style," *Studies in Romanticism* 25 (1986): 184.

88. Houtchens and Houtchens (above, note 24), 368; review of Alfred and Charles Tennyson

89. Milford (above, note 71), 321.

90. Houtchens and Houtchens (above, note 24), 471; "Old Books and Bookshops—Randolph's 'Orchard Robbing of the Fairies.'"

91. Ibid., 472.

92. Milford (above, note 71), 326.

93. Houtchens and Houtchens (above, note 24), 140; "Preface to *Foliage*."

94. Ibid., 130.

95. Milford (above, note 71), 188.

96. Ross (above, note 33), 164.

97. Milford (above, note 71), 320.

98. Houtchens and Houtchens (above, note 24), 107; "The Late Mr. Sheridan."

99. Ibid., 161; "Sketches of the Living Poets: Mr. Campbell."

100. Nicholas Joukovsky, in *Notes and Queries* 220 (1975): 112–13, has pointed out that the author was in fact H. B. Peacock, not Thomas Love Peacock.

101. Houtchens and Houtchens (above, note 24), 532; "An Effusion upon Cream."

102. Ibid., 533.

103. Ibid., 535.

104. Ibid., 537.

105. Ibid., 108; "The Late Mr. Sheridan."

106. Graham Hough, *The Romantic Poets* (London: Hutchinson, 1957), 160–61.

107. Houtchens and Houtchens (above, note 24), 78; "On Periodical Essays."

108. Ibid., 631n; "The Late Mr. Sheridan."

109. Ibid., 139; "Preface to *Foliage*."

110. Milford (above, 71), 325.

111. Ibid., 327.

112. Cosmo Monkhouse, *Life of Leigh Hunt* (London: Walter Scott, 1893), 47.

113. Houtchens and Houtchens (above, note 24), 250; "Remarks Suggested by *The Plain Speaker.*"

114. Ibid., 490; *Words for Composers.*

115. Matthews (above, note 32), 56; H. J. L. Hunt, "Leigh Hunt Announces a New School of Poetry."

116. Ibid., 55.

117. Milford (above, note 71), 329.

118. Ibid., 356.

Chapter 2. Narrative Poems: I

1. *The Poems and Fables of John Dryden*, edited by James Kinsley (London: Oxford University Press, 1970), 524–25.

2. Edmund Blunden, *Leigh Hunt: A Biography* (London: Cobden-Sanderson, 1930), 326.

3. Leigh Hunt, *Juvenilia* (London: John Whiting, 1803), 120ff.

4. John O. Hayden, "Leigh Hunt's *Story of Rimini*: Reloading the Romantic Canon," *Durham University Journal* 79 (1987): 281.

5. *The Works of Geoffrey Chaucer*, edited by F. N. Robinson (London: Oxford University Press, 1966), 38.

6. Blunden (above, note 2), 67.

7. *The Poetical Works of Leigh Hunt*, edited by H. S. Milford (London: Oxford University Press, 1923), 5.

8. Karl Kroeber, *Romantic Narrative Art* (Madison: University of Wisconsin Press, 1966), 122.

9. Leigh Hunt, *Autobiography* (London: Cresset, 1949), 257.

10. Louis Landré, "Leigh Hunt: His Contribution to English Romanticism," *Keats-Shelley Journal* 8 (1959): 142.

11. Hayden (above, note 4), 280.

12. Milford (above, note 7), 1.

13. Blunden (above, note 2), 101.

14. Kinsley (above, note 1), 715.

15. Milford (above, note 7), 1.

16. Georg Lukács, *The Historical Novel* (London: Merlin Press, 1962), 60.

17. Ibid., 42.

18. Peter and Linda Murray, *A Dictionary of Art and Artists* (Harmondsworth: Penguin, 1959), 314.

19. Milford (above, note 7), 127ff.

20. Ibid., 130ff.

21. Kroeber (above, note 8), 124.

22. *Leigh Hunt: A Reference Guide*, edited by Timothy K. Lulofs and Hans Ostrom (Boston: G. K. Hall, 1985), 21.

23. Ibid., 20.

24. Barnette Miller, *Leigh Hunt's Relationship with Byron, Shelley and Keats* (New York: Columbia University Press, 1910), 24.

25. *The Complete Works of Percy Bysshe Shelley*, edited by Thomas Hutchinson (Oxford: Clarendon Press, 1904), 300.

26. Ibid., 299.

27. Lulofs and Ostrom (above, note 22), 29.

28. Milford (above, note 7), 1.

29. Ibid., 2.

30. Ibid., 3.

31. Ibid., 6.

32. Ibid., 8.

33. Ibid., 3.

34. Ibid., 3–4.

35. Quoted in Blunden (above, note 2), 306.

36. Donald Reiman, "Leigh Hunt in Literary History," in *The Life and Times of Leigh Hunt*, edited by Robert A. MacCowan (Iowa City: Friends of the University of Iowa Libraries, 1985), 89.

37. Ibid., 90.

38. *The Poetical Works of John Keats*, edited by H. W. Garrod (London: Oxford University Press, 1970), 10.

39. Milford (above, note 7), 7.

40. Ibid., 5.

41. Ibid., 7.

42. E. M. W. Tillyard, *The English Epic and Its Background* (London: Chatto and Windus, 1954), 10.

43. Milford (above, note 7), 8.

44. *The Poetical Works of George Crabbe*, edited by Norma Dalrymple-Champneys and Arthur Pollard, 3 vols. (Oxford: Clarendon Press, 1988), 2:88–89.

45. Milford (above, note 7), 9.

46. Ibid., 8.

47. Ibid., 9.

48. Quoted in Blunden (above, note 2), 277.

49. Milford (above, note 7), 9.

50. Ibid., 11.

51. Anne Radcliffe, *The Mysteries of Udolpho* (New York: Oxford University Press, 1966), 17.

52. Milford (above, note 7), 11.

53. Ibid.

54. *The Poems of Alexander Pope*, edited by John Butt (London: Methuen, 1963), 135.

55. Dalrymple-Champneys and Pollard (above, note 44), 2:76.

56. Kinsley (above, note 1), 704.

57. Milford (above, note 7), 670.

58. Ibid., 11–12.

59. Hunt recalls in his *Autobiography* (above, note 9) how a clergyman of his school-days was fixated on two phrases, "the dispensation of Moses," and "the Mosaic dispensation" (p. 63).

60. L. R. M. Srachan, "'Fry' in Dryden and Leigh Hunt," *Notes and Queries* 11 (1910): 321.

61. Milford (above, note 7), 12.

62. Ibid.

63. Ibid., 13.

64. Ibid.

65. *The Complete Poems and Major Prose of John Milton*, edited by Merritt Y. Hughes (New York: Odyssey Press, 1957), 258.

66. John Hadfield, *The Book of Delights* (London: Hulton Press, 1955), vii.

67. Milford (above, note 7), 14.

68. Ibid., 13.

69. Ibid., 14.

70. William Shakespeare, *Hamlet* (London: Methuen, 1982), 284.

71. Milford (above, note 7) 14.

72. Ibid., 14–15.

73. Ibid., 15.

74. Ibid., 21.

75. Ibid., 15.

76. Ibid., 19.

77. John Holloway, *Widening Horizons in English Verse* (London: Routledge and Kegan Paul, 1966), 46–47.

78. Milford (above, note 7), 16.

79. Ibid., 17–18.

80. Ibid., 16.

81. Ibid., 17.

82. Miller (above, note 24), 136.

83. Milford (above, note 7), 16.

84. *The Poems of Samuel Taylor Coleridge*, edited by Ernest Hartley Coleridge (London: Oxford University Press, 1907), 297.

85. Milford (above, note 7), 22.

86. Ibid.

87. Ibid.

88. Ibid.

89. Dante, *The Divine Comedy*, 3 vols. (Harmondsworth: Penguin, 1946–62), 1:101.

90. Charles Williams, *The Figure of Beatrice* (London: Faber, 1943), 119.

91. Quoted in John O. Hayden, *The Romantic Reviewers* (London: Routledge and Kegan Paul, 1969), 181.

92. Milford (above, note 7), 20.

93. Ibid., 19.

94. Ibid., 20.

95. Hayden, "Hunt's *Story of Rimini*" (above, note 4), 181.

96. Cecil Day-Lewis, *The Poetic Image* (London: Jonathan Cape, 1947), 126–27.

97. Milford (above, note 7), 21.

98. Clarice Short, "The Composition of Hunt's *The Story of Rimini*," *Keats-Shelley Journal* 21 (1972): 212.

99. Milford (above, note 7), 22.

100. Ibid.

101. Ibid., 23.

102. Ibid.

103. Ibid., 24.

104. Ibid., 26.
105. Ibid.
106. Ibid., 26–27.
107. Garrod (above, note 38), 220.
108. Milford (above, note 7), 27.
109. Ibid.
110. *The Poems of Gray, Collins and Goldsmith*, edited by Roger Lonsdale (London: Longman, 1963), 123; *Elegy Written in a Country Churchyard*.
111. Milford (above, note 7), 27.
112. Ibid., 27–28.
113. Ibid., 28.
114. Ibid.
115. Ibid., 29.
116. Lulofs and Ostrom (above, note 22), 118.
117. Milford (above, note 7), 30.
118. James R. Thompson, *Leigh Hunt* (Boston: Twayne, 1977), 31.
119. Milford (above, note 7), 30.
120. Ibid., 36.
121. *The Complete English Poems of John Donne*, edited by A. J. Smith (Harmondsworth: Penguin, 1971), 48.
122. Milford (above, note 7), 37.
123. Lonsdale (above, note 110), 123; *Song from Shakespeare's "Cymbeline."*
124. Milford (above, note 7), 34.
125. Ibid., 34–35.
126. Lukács (above, note 16), 26.
127. Milford (above, note 7), 662.
128. Short (above, note 98), 211.
129. Milford (above, note 7), 663.
130. Ibid., 663.
131. Ibid., 667.
132. Ibid., 669.
133. Lulofs and Ostrom (above, note 22), 69.
134. Milford (above, note 7), 672.
135. Leigh Hunt, *Poetical Works* (London: Warne and Routledge, 1860), 33.
136. Edmund Blunden, *Shelley: A Life Story* (London: Collins, 1946), 205.

Chapter 3: The Narrative Poems: II

1. *Leigh Hunt: A Reference Guide*, edited by Timothy K. Lulofs and Hans Ostrom (Boston: G. K. Hall, 1985), 61.
2. Barnette Miller, *Leigh Hunt's Relationship with Byron, Shelley and Keats* (New York: Columbia University Press, 1910), 23.
3. Ibid., 95.
4. Charles Dickens, *Bleak House* (London: Oxford University Press, 1948), 70.
5. Donald H. Eriksen, "Harold Skimpole and the 'Art for Art's Sake' Movement," *Journal of English and Germanic Philology* 72 (1973): 55.

6. Leigh Hunt, *The Religion of the Heart* (London: John Chapman, 1853), 199–200.

7. *The Poetical Works of Leigh Hunt*, edited by H. S. Milford (London: Oxford University Press, 1923), 37.

8. Leigh Hunt, *The Indicator*, part 1 (London: Edward Moxon, 1845), 48.

9. Matthew Arnold, *Literature and Dogma* (London: Smith, Elder and Co., 1891), 58.

10. Hunt, *Religion of the Heart* (above, note 6), 3.

11. Hunt, *The Indicator*, part 2 (above, note 8), 48.

12. Douglas Bush, *Mythology and the Romantic Tradition in English Poetry* (Cambridge: Harvard University Press, 1937), 179.

13. Leigh Hunt, *Autobiography* (London: Cresset Press, 1949), 330.

14. Hunt, *The Indicator*, part 2 (above, note 8), 7.

15. One might want to note in passing that Robert Browning has adduced the essay as a possible influence on *Sketches by Boz*: "I think that Dickens learned from Hunt this technique of a congery of simple sentences (often in the passive)"—*Dickens and the Twentieth Century*, edited by John Gross and Gabriel Pearson (London: Routledge and Kegan Paul, 1962), 23; Browning, "Sketches by Boz."

16. Milford (above, note 7), 37.

17. William Shakespeare, *Macbeth*, edited by Kenneth Muir (London: Methuen, 1964), 48–49.

18. William Shakespeare, *The Merchant of Venice*, edited by John Russell Brown (London: Methuen, 1964), 125.

19. William Shakespeare, *Measure for Measure*, edited by J. W. Lever (London: Methuen, 1967), 89.

20. Milford (above, note 7), 37.

21. Ibid., 38.

22. Anne Blainey, *Immortal Boy: A Portrait of Leigh Hunt* (London: Croom Helm, 1985), 99.

23. Milford (above, note 7), 39.

24. Ibid., 40.

25. George Chapman, *Homer's Batrachomyomachia, etc.* (London: John Russell Smith, 1888), 229; Musaeus, *Hero and Leander*.

26. Milford (above, note 7), 41.

27. Musaeus, in Chapman (above, note 25), 224.

28. Ovid, *Heroides and Amores* (London: William Heinemann, 1914), 262–63.

29. Milford (above, note 7), 41.

30. Ibid., 41.

31. Hunt, *The Indicator*, part 1 (above, note 8), 48.

32. Milford (above, note 7), 41–42.

33. Ibid., 42.

34. Ibid.

35. Ibid., 43

36. Ibid.

37. *The Poems of Tennyson*, edited by Christopher Ricks (London: Longman, 1969), 871.

38. Ibid., 785.

39. Milford (above, note 7), 43.

40. Musaeus, in Chapman (above, note 25), 323.

41. Milford (above, note 7), 44.

42. *The Poems of Gray, Collins and Goldsmith*, edited by Roger Lonsdale (London: Longman, 1969), 200; *The Bard*.

43. Hunt, *Autobiography* (above, note 13), 77.

44. Ovid (above, note 28), 120–23.

45. Milford (above, note 7), 44.

46. Ovid (above, note 28), 122–23.

47. *The Poems of Alexander Pope*, edited by John Butt (London: Methuen, 1963), 134.

48. Milford (above, note 7), 44.

49. Ibid., 45.

50. Robert Graves, *The Greek Myths*, 2 vols. (Harmondsworth: Penguin, 1955), 1:339–40.

51. Milford (above, note 7), 45.

52. E. M. Forster, *Two Cheers for Democracy* (1951; rpt., Harmondsworth: Penguin, 1965), 76; "What I Believe."

53. Hunt (above, note 6), 30.

54. Ibid., 32.

55. *The Poetical Works of John Keats*, edited by H. W. Garrod (London: Oxford University Press, 1970), 50.

56. Ibid., 51.

57. Milford (above, note 7), 45.

58. Hunt (above, note 6), 13.

59. Milford (above, note 7), 46.

60. Ibid., 46.

61. Ibid., 47.

62. Ibid., 51.

63. Leigh Hunt, *The Companion* (London: Edward Moxon, 1845), 70.

64. Milford (above, note 7), 683.

65. Ibid., 51.

66. Garrod (above, note 55), 212.

67. Milford (above, note 7), 52.

68. Ibid., 111.

69. Ibid., 110.

70. Leigh Hunt, *Juvenilia* (London: J. Whiting, 1803), 107.

71. Philostratus, *The Life of Apollonius of Tyana*, 2 vols. (London: William Heinemann, 1912), 1:121.

72. Milford (above, note 7), 53.

73. Hunt (above, note 6), 141.

74. Ibid., 68–69.

75. Milford (above, note 7), 93.

76. Ernest F. Leisy, "Hunt's *Abou Ben Adhem*," *Explicator* 5 (1946): 9.

77. Joseph Wolfe and Linda Wolfe, "An Earlier Version of 'Abou'," *Notes and Queries* 105 (1960): 113.

78. Milford (above, note 7), 94.

79. Ibid., 100.

80. Ibid., 95.

81. James Atterbury Davies, "Leigh Hunt and John Forster," *Review of English Studies* 19 (1968): 38.

82. Milford (above, note 7), 102.

83. Ibid., 103.

84. Hunt, *Poetical Works* (London: Warne and Routledge, 1860), 54–55.

85. Milford (above, note 7), 55.

86. Ibid., 56.

87. Ibid., 58.

88. Ibid., 59.

89. Ibid., 61.

90. Ibid., 684.

91. Ibid., 65.

92. Ibid., 62.

93. Stephen F. Fogle, "Leigh Hunt and the Laureateship," *Studies in Philology* 55 (1958): 612.

94. Milford (above, note 7), 62.

95. Ibid., 65.

96. Hunt (above, note 13), 101.

97. Milford (above, note 7), 65.

98. Ibid., 66.

99. Ibid., 67.

100. Ibid., 68.

101. Ibid., 74

102. Ibid., 74–75.

103. Ibid., 77.

104. *The Poems and Ballads of Schiller*, translated by Bulwer-Lytton (London: Frederick Warne, 1887), 109.

105. Milford (above, note 7), 78.

106. Ibid., 79.

107. Ibid.

108. Hunt, *The Religion of the Heart* (above, note 6), 212.

109. Milford (above, note 7), 80

110. John Gay, *The Beggars' Opera and Polly* (London: Chapman and Dodd, 1923), 30.

111. Milford (above, note 7), 81.

112. Ibid., 80.

113. Chapman (above, note 25), 107.

114. Milford (above, note 7), 81.

115. Hunt (above, note 6), 124.

116. Milford (above, note 7), 81.

117. Ibid.

118. Charles Dickens, *A Christmas Carol and Other Christmas Books* (London: J. M. Dent, 1907), 251; "The Battle of Life."

119. Milford (above, note 7), 82.

120. Ibid.

121. Ibid.

122. Ibid., 85–86.

123. *The Works of George Herbert*, ed. F. E. Hutchinson (Oxford: Clarendon Press, 1941), 115.

124. William Shakespeare, *Hamlet*, ed. Harold Jenkins (London: Methuen, 1982), 324.

125. William Makepeace Thackeray, *Vanity Fair* (London: Oxford University Press, 1983), 361.

126. [John Keble], *The Christian Year* (London: Oxford University Press, n.d.), 48.

127. Milford (above, note 7), 82.

128. Ibid., 83.

129. T. S. Eliot, *On Poetry and Poets* (London: Faber and Faber, 1957), 156; "Milton II."

130. Milford (above, note 7), 83.

131. Ibid., 84.

132. Ibid., 86.

133. Ibid., 87.

134. Garrod (above, note 55), 366.

135. George Gilfillan, "Leigh Hunt," *Tait's Edinburgh Magazine* 13 (1844): 659.

136. *The Poems of Robert Southey*, edited by Maurice H. Fitzgerald (London: Oxfrod University Press, 1909), 365.

137. Milford (above, note 7), 86.

138. James Thompson, *Leigh Hunt* (Boston: Twayne, 1977), 47.

139. Milford (above, note 7), 698.

140. Ibid., 88.

141. Ibid., 90.

142. Hunt (above, note 6), 113.

143. Milford (above, note 7), 91.

144. Ibid., 93.

145. Hunt (above, note 6), 217.

146. Cecil Frances Alexander, "Once in Royal David's City," in *The English Hymnal* (London: Oxford University Press, 1933), 781

147. *Langland's Piers the Plowman and Richard the Redeless*, edited by Walter Skeat, 2 vols. (London: Oxford University Press, 1886), 1:166.

148. Blainey (above, note 22), 130.

149. Milford (above, note 7), 103.

150. Ibid., 104.

151. *English Verse*, edited by T. Peacock, 5 vols. (London: Oxford University Press, 1952), 2:435.

152. Milford (above, note 7), 105.

153. Ibid.

154. Ibid.

155. Ibid., 106.

156. Ibid., 109.

157. Ibid., 97.

158. Ibid., 103.

Chapter 4: Political and Critical Poems

1. Leigh Hunt, *Wit and Humour* (London: Smith, Elder, & Co., 1890), 6–7.

2. Stuart Tave, *The Amiable Humorist* (Chicago: University of Chicago Press, 1960), 21.

3. *The Poems of Alexander Pope*, edited by John Butt (London: Methuen, 1963), 597.

4. *The Poetical Works of Leigh Hunt*, edited by H. S. Milford (London: Oxford University Press, 1923), 141.

5. Butt (above, note 3), 602.

6. Milford (above, note 4), 141.

7. Ibid.

8. Hunt (above, note 1), 14–15.

9. *The Poetical Works of George Crabbe*, edited by Norma Dalrymple-Champneys and Arthur Pollard, 3 vols. (Oxford: Clarendon Press, 1988), 1:142.

10. Milford (above, note 4), 140.

11. Butt (above, note 3), 233–34.

12. Milford (above, note 4), 141.

13. Ibid., 142.

14. W. S. Gilbert, *The Savoy Operas* (London: Macmillan, 1962), 526; *Ruddigore*.

15. Charles Dickens, *The Pickwick Papers* (London: Oxford University Press, 1948), 183–84.

16. William Shakespeare, *King Lear*, edited by Kenneth Muir (London: Methuen, 1963), 116.

17. Milford (above, note 4), 142.

18. Ibid., 708.

19. Charles Dickens, *A Christmas Carol and Other Christmas Books* (London: J. M. Dent, 1907), 42.

20. Milford (above, note 4), 142.

21. *The Poems of Gray, Collins and Goldsmith*, edited by Roger Lonsdale (London: Longman, 1969), 168; *The Progress of Poesy*.

22. Milford (above, note 4), 143.

23. *Leigh Hunt's Literary Criticism*, edited by Lawrence Huston Houtchens and Carolyn Washburn Houtchens (New York: Columbia University Press, 1958), 195; "On the Latin Poems of Milton."

24. *The Poems and Letters of Andrew Marvell*, edited by H. M. Margoliouth, Pierre Legouis, and E. Duncan-Jones, 2 vols. (Oxford: Clarendon Press, 1971), 1:52.

25. Lonsdale (above, note 21), 50–51; *Ode to the Spring*.

26. Ibid., 176–77; *The Progress of Poesy*.

27. Leigh Hunt, *Juvenilia* (London: John Whiting, 1803), 123.

28. *The Poetical Works of John Keats*, edited by H. W. Garrod (London: Oxford University Press, 1970), 45.

29. Butt (above, note 3), 131.

30. Lonsdale (above, note 21), 20; *[Lines on Beech Trees]*.

31. *The Poems of Tennyson*, edited by Christopher Ricks (London: Longman, 1969), 784.

32. Milford (above, note 4), 144.

33. Garrod (above, note 28), 46.

34. Cf. Donald H. Eriksen, "Harold Skimpole and the 'Art for Art's Sake' Movement," *Journal of English and Germanic Philology* 72 (1973): 48–49.

35. Milford (above, note 4), 144.

36. Ibid.

37. Edmund Blunden, *Leigh Hunt: A Biography* (London: Cobden-Sanderson, 1934), 64.

38. *The Non-Dramatic Works of Sir John Suckling*, edited by Thomas Clayton (Oxford: Clarendon Press, 1971), 72.

39. Lucian, *Works*, 8 vols. (London: William Heinemann, 1961), 7:321–23.

40. Milford (above, note 4), 144–45.

41. Lonsdale (above, note 21), 147; *A Long Story*.

42. Milford (above, note 4), 145–46.

43. William Shakespeare, *The Sonnets*, edited by John Dover Wilson (Cambridge: Cambridge University Press, 1969), 11.

44. Lonsdale (above, note 21), 248; *The Candidate*.

45. Milford (above, note 4), 147.

46. Leigh Hunt, *The Seer* (London: William Tegg, 1850), 46.

47. *Leigh Hunt's Literary Criticism*, edited by Lawrence Huston Houtchens and Carolyn Washburn Houtchens (New York: University of Columbia Press, 1958), 122; "The Extraordinary Case of the Late Mr. Southey."

48. Clayton (above, note 38), 73.

49. Milford (above, note 8), 147.

50. Ibid., 147–48.

51. Ibid., 148.

52. Ibid., 149.

53. Ibid., 150.

54. Ibid.

55. Ibid., 152.

56. Paul Dawson, "Byron, Shelley and the 'New School'," in *Shelley Revalued*, edited by Kelvin Everest(Leicester: Leicester University Press, 1983), 98.

57. Milford (above, note 4), 153.

58. Ibid., 154–55.

59. *The Poems of Robert Herrick*, edited by L. C. Martin (London: Oxford University Press, 1965), 119.

60. Milford (above, note 4), 156.

61. Ibid., 158.

62. Ibid., 181.

63. Ibid., 177.

64. Ibid., 178.

65. Lonsdale (above, note 21), 463; *Ode to Evening*.

66. Garrod (above, note 28), 205.

67. Milford (above, note 4), 178.

68. Ibid., 186.

69. Leigh Hunt, *Men, Women and Books* (London: T. Werner Laurie, 1943), 319.

70. Ibid.

71. Leigh Hunt, *Autobiography* (London: Cresset Press, 1949), 217.

72. Milford (above, note 4), 160.

73. Ibid., 711.

74. Ibid., 159.

75. Ibid., 338.

76. Ibid., 161.

77. Ibid.

78. Ibid., 165.

79. William Shakespeare, *A Midsummer Night's Dream*, edited by Harold F. Brooks (London: Methuen, 1979), 58.

80. Milford (above, note 4), 166.

81. Barbara Herrnstein Smith, *Poetic Closure* (Chicago: University of Chicago Press, 1968).

82. Milford (above, note 4), 167.

83. Ibid., 170.

84. Ibid.

85. Ibid., 176.

86. Edmund Blunden, *Hunt's "Examiner" Examined* (London: Cobden-Sanderson, 1928), 21.

87. Lonsdale (above, note 21); *An Elegy on the Death of a Mad Dog.*

88. Milford (above, note 4), 192.

89. Hunt (above, note 1), 34.

90. Milford (above, note 4), 194.

91. Leigh Hunt, *The Town* (London: Hutchinson, 1906), 64.

92. Milford (above, note 4), 195–96.

93. F. W. Cornish, trans., *Catullus, Tibullus and Pervigilium Veneris* (London: William Heinemann, 1968), 4.

94. Milford (above, note 4), 198.

95. Cf. R. A. Soloway, *Prelates and People* (London: Routledge and Kegan Paul, 1969).

96. Milford (above, note 4), 200.

97. Lorenzo da Ponte, *Don Giovanni*, libretto for the EMI recording of Mozart's opera (London, 1966), SAN 172–75.

98. Cesare Sterbini, *Il Barbiere di Siviglia*, libretto for the RCA recording of Rossini's opera (New York, n.d.): C30.212.

99. Charles Dickens, *American Notes and Pictures from Italy* (London: Oxford University Press, 1957), 190.

100. Milford (above, note 4), 204.

101. Hunt (above, note 1), 8.

102. J. A. R. Marriott, *England Since Waterloo* (London: Methuen, 1913), 41.

103. Milford (above, note 4), 208.

104. Hunt (above, note 1), 25.

105. Milford (above, note 4), 216.

106. Ibid., 215.

107. Ibid., 213.

108. *The Book of Common Prayer* (London: Oxford University Press, 1954), 504.

109. Milford (above, note 4), 210.

110. James Thompson, *Leigh Hunt* (Boston: Twayne, 1977), 45.

111. Quoted in Paul Mowbray Wheeler, "The Great Quarterlies of the Early Nineteenth Century and Leigh Hunt," *South Atlantic Review* 29 (1930): 289.

Chapter 5: Miscellaneous Verse

1. W. A. Laidlaw, *Latin Literature* (London: Methuen, 1951), 154.

2. Michael Grant, *Roman Literature* (Harmondsworth: Penguin, 1964), 206.

3. F. W. Cornish, trans., *Catullus, Tibullus and Pervigilium Veneris* (London: William Heinemann, 1968), 18.

4. *Leigh Hunt's Literary Criticism*, edited by Lawrence Huston Houtchens and Carolyn Washburn Houtchens (New York: Columbia University Press, 1958), 95; "Distressing Circumstance in High Life."

5. *Leigh Hunt's Poetical Works*, edited by H. S. Milford (London: Oxford University Press, 1923), 223.

6. *Correspondence of Thomas Gray*, edited by Paget Toynbee and Leonard Whibley, 3 vols. (London: Oxford University Press, 1935), 3:927.

7. Horace, *Satires, Epistles and Ars Poetica* (London: William Heinemann, 1970), 322.

8. Milford (above, note 5), 221.

9. Ibid.

10. *The Poems of Gray, Collins and Goldsmith*, edited by Roger Lonsdale (London: Longman, 1969), 192; *The Bard.*

11. Milford (above, note 5), 221.

12. Ibid., 221–22.

13. Horace (above, note 7), 408–9.

14. Milford (above, note 5), 222.

15. *The Complete Poetical Works of Shelley*, edited by Thomas Hutchinson (Oxford: Clarendon Press, 1904), 605.

16. Lonsdale (above, note 10), 638; *The Traveller.*

17. Milford (above, note 5), 222.

18. Ibid.

19. Toynbee and Whibley (above, note 6), 2:812.

20. *The Poems of Alexander Pope*, edited by John Butt (London: Methuen, 1963), 644–45.

21. Milford (above, note 5), 223.

22. Horace (above, note 7), 26–27.

23. Milford (above, note 5), 223.

24. Ibid., 224.

25. Ibid., 225.

26. Horace (above, note 7), 314–15.

27. Milford (above, note 5), 224.

28. Ibid., 226.

29. Ibid.

30. Charles Dickens, *The Old Curiosity Shop* (London: Oxford University Press, 1951), 115.

31. Milford (above, note 5), 226.

32. Ibid., 228.

33. Horace (above, note 7), 324.

34. Ibid., 286.

35. Milford (above, note 5), 227.

36. Ibid., 228–29.

37. *The Letters of John Keats: A New Selection*, edited by Robert Gittings (London: Oxford University Press, 1970), 180–81.

38. Jeremy Bentham, "An Introduction to the Principles of Morals and Legislation," in *Value and Obligation*, edited by Richard B. Brandt (New York: Harcourt, Brace & World, 1961), 185.

39. Milford (above, note 5), 229.

40. Catullus, in Cornish (above, note 3), 6.

41. Milford (above, note 5), 229.

42. Ibid., 230.

43. Ibid., 229.

44. Butt (above, note 20), 623.

45. Horace (above, note 7), 136–38.

46. Milford (above, note 5), 231.

47. Ibid., 231.

48. Ibid.

49. Ibid., 233.

50. Stuart Curran, *Poetic Form and British Romanticism* (New York: Oxford University Press, 1986), 50.

51. Milford (above, note 5), 235.

52. Lonsdale (above, note 10), 464; *Ode to Evening*.

53. *The Poetical Works of John Keats*, edited by H. W. Garrod (London: Oxford University Press, 1970), 37.

54. *The Poetical Works of Samuel Taylor Coleridge*, edited by Ernest Hartley Coleridge (London: Oxford University Press, 1912), 179.

55. Milford (above, note 5), 235.

56. Lonsdale (above, note 10), 463; *Ode to Evening*.

57. Ibid., 467; *Ode to Evening*.

58. Milford (above, note 5), 236.

59. Robert Wells, *The Winter's Task* (Manchester: Carcanet, 1977).

60. Milford (above, note 5), 236.

61. Ibid., 371.

62. Ibid., 237.

63. Lonsdale (above, note 10), 677; *The Deserted Village*.

64. Milford (above, note 5), 238.

65. Ibid., 253.

66. Ibid., 241.

67. Ibid.

68. Ibid., 251.

69. Ibid., 240.

70. Ibid., 235.

71. *The Greek Anthology*, translated by W. R. Paton, 5 vols. (London: William Heinemann, 1914–16), 2:113.

72. *The Poems and Letters of Andrew Marvell*, edited by H. M. Margoliouth, Pierre Legouis, and E. E. Duncan-Jones, 2 vols. (Oxford: Clarendon Press, 1971), 1:74.

73. Leigh Hunt, *The Seer; or, Common-places Refreshed* (London: William Tegg, 1850), 32.

74. *The Poems of Richard Lovelace*, edited by C. H. Wilkinson (Oxford: Clarendon Press, 1930), 38.

75. Don Cameron Allen, "Richard Lovelace: 'The Grasse-hopper,'" in *Seventeenth-Century English Poetry*, edited by William R. Keast (New York: Oxford University Press, 1962), 285.

76. E. Pereira, "Sonnet Contests and Verse Compliments in the Keats-Hunt Circle," *Unisa English Studies* 1 (1987): 19.

77. Keats (above, note 53), 365.

78. Leigh Hunt, *Autobiography* (London: Cresset Press, 1949), 433.

79. Milford (above, note 5), 257.

80. Leigh Hunt, *Men, Women and Books* (London: T. Werner Laurie, 1943), 140; *On Seeing a Pigeon Make Love*.

81. Milford (above, note 5), 254.

82. William Shakespeare, *King Henry VIII*, edited by R. A. Foakes (London: Methuen, 1957), 91.

83. Milford (above, note 5), 262.

84. Ibid., 256.

85. *The Poems of William Wordsworth*, edited by John O. Hayden, 2 vols. (Harmondsworth: Penguin, 1977), 1:360.

86. Milford (above, note 5), 256.

87. Ibid., 259.

88. *The Poetical Works of William Cowper*, edited by H. S. Milford and Norma Russell (London: Oxford University Press, 1967), 131.

89. *Hymns Ancient and Modern* (London: William Clowes and Sons, n.d.), 860.

90. Milford (above, note 5), 263.

91. Ibid., 265.

92. Ibid., 364.

93. Ibid., 267.

94. *Minor Latin Poets* (London: William Heinemann, 1954), 444.

95. *Contralto Songs*, 2 vols. (London: Boosey & Co, n.d.), 1:52–53.

96. Milford (above, note 5), 319.

97. Ibid., 267.

98. Thornton Wilder, *Our Town, The Skin of Our Teeth, The Matchmaker* (Harmondsworth: Penguin, 1962), 88.

99. Goethe, *Poems* (London: George Bell and Sons, 1885), 183.

100. Milford (above, note 5), 269.

101. Meriol Trevor, *Newman: Light in Winter* (London: Macmillan, 1962), 365.

102. Milford (above, note 5), 269.

103. Ibid., 270.

104. Ibid.

105. Ibid., 271.

106. Ibid., 273.

107. Ibid., 271.

108. Ibid., 282.

109. William Empson, *Seven Types of Ambiguity* (1930; rpt., Harmondsworth: Penguin, 1961), 184.

110. Ibid., 189.

111. Milford (above, note 5), 314.

112. Ibid., 313.

113. Ibid., 315.

114. Ibid., 316–17.

115. Ibid., 333.

116. Ibid., 360.

117. Ibid., 349.

118. Ibid., 350.

119. Ibid., 355.

120. Ibid., 354.

121. Ibid., 377.

122. Ibid., 379.

123. Ibid., 369–70.

124. Ibid., 370.

125. *The Poetical Works of Mark Akenside* (Edinburgh: James Nichol, 1957), 238.

126. Ibid., 245.

127. Milford (above, note 5), 323.

128. Ibid., 322.

129. Ibid., 258.

130. Ibid., 320.

131. Richard Hengist Horne, *A New Spirit of the Age* (London: Oxford University Press, 1907), 229.

132. C. H. Herford, *The Age of Wordsworth* (London: George Bell and Sons, 1897), 84.

133. Milford (above, note 5), 339.

134. Ibid., 340.

135. Ibid., 362.

136. John Pomfret, *Poems upon Several Occasions* (London: Ed. Cooke, 1736), 1–2.

137. Milford (above, note 5), 341.

138. Ibid.

139. Ibid., 331.

140. Ibid., 333.

141. Ibid., 334.

142. Ibid., 335.

143. Ibid., 348.

144. David Q. Smith, "Genius and Common Sense: The Romantics and Leigh Hunt," *Books at Iowa* 40 (1984): 41.

Epilogue

1. Leigh Hunt, *A Jar of Honey from Mount Hybla* (London: John Murray, 1897), 2–3.

2. *The Poetical Works of Leigh Hunt*, edited by H. S. Milford (London: Oxford University Press, 1923), 260.

3. Ian Jack, *English Literature: 1815–1832* (Oxford: Clarendon Press, 19630), 148.

Select Bibliography

Primary Texts

Hunt, James Henry Leigh. *The Autobiography of Leigh Hunt*, edited by J. E. Morpurgo. London: Cresset Press, 1949.

———. *Imagination and Fancy; or, Selections from the English Poets, Illustrative of Those First Requisites of Their Art; with Markings of the Best Passages, Critical Notices of the Writers, And an Essay in Answer to the Question "What is Poetry?"* London: Smith, Elder, & Co, 1891.

———. *The Indicator, and The Companion: A Miscellany for the Fields and the Fire-Side*. London: Edward Moxon, 1845.

———. *A Jar of Honey from Mount Hybla*. London: John Murray, 1897.

———. *Juvenilia; or, A Collection of Poems. Written between the Ages of Twelve and Sixteen by J. H. L. Hunt, Late of the Grammar School of Christ's Hospital*. London: J. Whiting, 1803.

———. *Leigh Hunt's Dramatic Criticism*. Edited by Lawrence Huston Houtchens and Carolyn Washburn Houtchens. 1949. Reprint, New York: Octagon Books, 1977.

———. *Leigh Hunt's Literary Criticism*. Edited by Lawrence Huston Houtchens and Carolyn Washburn Houtchens, with an Essay in Evaluation by Clarence Dewitt Thorpe. New York: Columbia University Press, 1958.

———. *Men, Women and Books: A Selection of Sketches, Essays, and Critical Memoirs from the Uncollected Prose Writings of Leigh Hunt*. London: T. Werner Laurie, 1943.

———. *The Poetical Works of Leigh Hunt Now Finally Collected, Revised by Himself and Edited by his Son, Thornton Hunt*. London: Routledge, Warne, and Routledge, 1860.

———. *The Poetical Works of Leigh Hunt*. Edited by H. S. Milford. London: Oxford University Press, 1923.

———. *The Religion of the Heart: A Manual of Faith and Duty*. London: John Chapman, 1853.

———. *The Seer; or, Common-places Refreshed*. London: William Tegg, 1850.

———. *The Town: Its Memorable Characters and Events, St. Paul's to St. James*. London: Hutchinson, 1906.

———. *Wit and Humour Selected from the English Poets with an Illustrative Essay and Critical Comments*. London: Smith, Elder, & Co., 1890.

Secondary Texts

Aaron, Jane. "'On Needle-Work': Protest and Contradiction in Mary Lamb's Essay." In *Romanticism and Feminism*, edited by Anne K. Mellor, 167–84. Bloomington and Indianapolis: Indiana University Press, 1988.

Abraham, Gerald. "Operas and Incidental Music." In *Tchaikovsky: A Symposium*, edited by Gerald Abraham. London: Lindsay Drummond, 1945.

Abrams, M. H. *The Mirror and the Lamp: Romantic Theory and the Critical Tradition.* 1953. Reprint, New York: W. W. Norton, 1958.

Akenside, Mark. *The Poetical Works, With Memoir and Critical Dissertation by the Rev. George Gilfillan.* Edinburgh: James Nichol, 1857.

Alexander, J. H. "*Blackwood's*: Magazine as Romantic Form," *The Wordsworth Circle* 15 (1984): 57–68.

Allen, Don Cameron. "Richard Lovelace: 'The Grasse-hopper.'" In *Seventeenth-Century Poetry: Modern Essays in Criticism.* Edited by William R. Keast. New York: Oxford University Press, 1962.

Allentuck, Marcia. "Leigh Hunt and Shelley: A New Letter." *Keats-Shelley Journal* 33 (1984): 50.

Altick, Richard D. *The Cowden Clarkes.* London: Oxford University Press, 1948.

———. "Harold Skimpole Revisited." In *The Life & Times of Leigh Hunt: Papers Delivered at a Symposium at the University of Iowa, April 13, 1984, Commemorating the 200th Anniversary of Leigh Hunt's Birth*, edited by Robert A. McCown. Iowa City: Friends of the University of Iowa Libraries, 1985.

Amis, Kingsley. "The Curious Elf: A Note on Rhyme in Keats." *Essays in Criticism* 1 (1951): 189–92.

Armstrong, Nancy. *Desire and Domestic Fiction: A Political History of the Novel.* New York: Oxford University Press, 1987.

Arnold, Matthew. *Literature and Dogma: An Essay Towards a Better Apprehension of the Bible.* London: Smith, Elder and Co., 1891.

Bate, Walter Jackson. *From Classic to Romantic: Premises of Taste in Eighteenth-Century England.* 1946. Reprint, New York: Harper and Row, 1961.

Bazin, Germain. *Baroque and Rococo.* Translated by Jonathan Griffin. London: Thames and Hudson, 1964.

Blainey, Ann. "A Portrait of Leigh Hunt." *Books at Iowa* 40 (1984): 10–20.

———. *Immortal Boy: A Portrait of Leigh Hunt.* London: Croom Helm, 1985.

———. "The Wit in the Dungeon: Leigh Hunt in Surrey Gaol." *Books at Iowa* 34 (1981): 9–14.

Blunden, Edmund. *Leigh Hunt: A Biography.* London: Cobden-Sanderson, 1934.

———. *Leigh Hunt's "Examiner" Examined, Comprising Some Account of that Celebrated Newspaper's Contents &c. 1808–25 and Selections, by or Concerning Leigh Hunt, Lamb, Keats, Shelley, and Byron, Illustrating the Literary History of That Time, for the Most Part Previously Unreprinted.* London: Cobden-Sanderson, 1928.

————. "Marianne Hunt: A Letter and Fragment of a Diary." *Keats-Shelley Memorial Bulletin* 10 (1959): 30–32.

————. "Most Sincerely Yours." *Medical Bulletin* 2 (1954): 86–90.

————. *Shelley: A Life Story.* London: Collins, 1946.

Boas, Guy. "Great Englishmen at School." *Essays and Studies* 7 (1954): 1–41.

The Book of Common Prayer and Administration of the Sacraments and Other Rites of the Church Together with the Form and Manner of Making, Ordaining and Consecrating of Bishops, Priests and Deacons. London: Oxford University Press, 1954.

Brandt, Richard B., ed. *Value and Obligation: Systematic Readings in Ethics.* New York: Harcourt, Brace & World, 1961.

Brawner, J. P. "Leigh Hunt and His Wife Marianne." *West Virginia University Bulletin* 37 (1937): 25–31.

Browning, Robert. "Sketches by Boz." In *Dickens and the Twentieth Century*, edited by John Gross and Gabriel Pearson. London: Routledge and Kegan Paul, 1962.

Bush, Douglas. *Mythology and the Romantic Tradition in English Poetry.* Cambridge: Harvard University Press, 1937.

Butler, Marilyn. "Myth and Mythmaking in the Shelley Circle." In *Shelley Revalued: Essays from the Gregynog Conference*, edited by Kelvin Everest. Leicester: Leicester University Press, 1983.

Cameron, Kenneth Neill. "Leigh Hunt." In *Romantic Rebels: Essays on Shelley and His Circle*, edited by Kenneth Neill Cameron. Cambridge: Harvard University Press, 1973.

Carpenter, Mary Wilson. "The Hair of the Medusa: Leigh Hunt, *Tait's Edinburgh Magazine* and the Criticism of Female Beauty." In *The Life & Times of Leigh Hunt: Papers Delivered at a Symposium at the University of Iowa, April 13, 1984, Commemorating the 200th Anniversary of Leigh Hunt's Birth.*, edited by Robert A. McCown. Iowa City: Friends of the University of Iowa Libraries, 1985.

Chapman, George. *Chapman's Homer: The Iliad, The Odyssey and the Lesser Homerica.* Edited by Allardyce Nicoll. 2 vols. London: Routledge and Kegan Paul, 1957.

————, trans. *Homer's Batrachomyomachia, Hymns and Epigrams, Hesiod's Works and Days, Musaeus' Hero and Leander, Juvenal's Fifth Satire.* London: John Russell Smith, 1888.

Chaucer, Geoffrey. *The Works.* Edited by F. N. Robinson. London: Oxford University Press, 1966.

Cheney, David R. "Leigh Hunt and the Dashwood Annuity." *Books at Iowa* 45 (1986): 50–61.

————. "Leigh Hunt, Essayist." *Books at Iowa* 40 (1980): 31–40.

————. "The Leigh Hunt Letters." *Keats-Shelley Memorial Bulletin* 35 (1984): 40–53.

————. "Leigh Hunt's Efforts to Encourage an Appreciation of Classical Music." *Keats-Shelley Journal* 17 (1968): 89–96.

————. "The Original of a Leigh Hunt Translation Identified." *Notes and Queries* 107 (1962): 182.

————. "Source Wanted." *Notes and Queries* 104 (1961): 308.

Cohen, B. Bernard. "Haydon, Hunt, and Scott and Six Sonnets (1816) by Wordsworth." *Philological Quarterly* 29 (1950): 434–37.

Coleridge, Samuel Taylor. *Biographia Literaria*. Edited by J. Shawcross. 2 vols. Oxford: Clarendon Press, 1907.

———. *The Poems, Including Poems and Versions of Poems Herein Published for the First Time*. Edited by Ernest Hartley Coleridge. London: Oxford University Press, 1912.

Contralto Songs. 2 vols. London: Boosey & Co., n.d.

Cornish, F. W., trans. *Catullus, Tibullus and Pervigilium Veneris*. London: William Heinemann, 1968.

Counihan, Daniel. "Leigh Hunt and Dickens." *Times Literary Supplement*, 5 October 1951, 629.

Cowper, William. *Poetical Works*. Edited by H. S. Milford. Revised by Norma Russell. London: Oxford University Press, 1967.

Croker, John Wilson. "Croker's Attack in the *Quarterly*." In *Keats: The Critical Heritage*, edited by G. M. Matthews. London: Routledge & Kegan Paul, 1971.

———. "Poems [1833]." In *Tennyson: The Critical Heritage*, edited by John G. Jump. London: Routledge & Kegan Paul, 1967.

Crabbe, George. *The Complete Poetical Works*. Edited by Norma Dalrymple-Champneys and Arthur Pollard. 3 vols. Oxford: Clarendon Press, 1988.

Crompton, Louis. "Satire and Symbolism in *Bleak House*." *Nineteenth-Century Fiction* 12 (1958): 284–303.

Curran, Stuart. "The I Altered." In *Romanticism and Feminism*, edited by Anne K. Mellor, 185–207. Bloomington and Indianapolis: Indiana University Press, 1988.

———. *Poetic Form and British Romanticism*. London: Oxford University Press, 1986.

Dante. *The Comedy of Dante Alighieri the Florentine*. Translated by Dorothy Sayers and Barbara Reynolds. 3 vols. Harmondsworth: Penguin, 1949–62.

da Ponte, Lorenzo. *Don Giovanni*. Libretto for the EMI recording of Mozart's opera. London, 1966. SAN 172–75.

Davies, James Atterbury. "Leigh Hunt and John Forster." *Review of English Studies* 19 (1968): 25–40.

Dawson, P. M. S. "Byron, Shelley, and the 'New School'." In *Shelley Revalued: Essays from the Gregynog Conference*, edited by Kelvin Everest. Leicester: Leicester University Press, 1983.

Day-Lewis, Cecil. *The Poetic Image: The Clark Lectures Given at Cambridge in 1946*. London: Jonathan Cape, 1947.

Dickens, Charles. *American Notes and Pictures from Italy*. Introduced by Sacheverell Sitwell. London: Oxford University Press, 1957.

———. *Bleak House*. Introduced by Osbert Sitwell. London: Oxford University Press, 1948.

———. *A Christmas Carol and Other Christmas Books*. Introduced by G. K. Chesterton. London: J. M. Dent, 1907.

———. *Great Expectations*. Introduced by Frederick Page. London: Oxford University Press, 1953.

———. *The Old Curiosity Shop*. Introduced by the Earl of Wicklow. London: Oxford University Press, 1951.

————. *The Pickwick Papers.* Introduced by Bernard Darwin. London: Oxford University Press, 1948.

Donne, John. *The Complete English Poems.* Edited by A. J. Smith. Harmondsworth: Penguin, 1971.

Dryden, John. *The Poems and Fables.* Edited by James Kinsley. London: Oxford University Press, 1970.

Duff, J. Wight, and Arnold M. Duff, trans. *Minor Latin Poets.* London: William Heinemann, 1954.

Edgecombe, Rodney Stenning. "Leigh Hunt and the Rococo." *Keats-Shelley Journal* 41 (1992): 164–77.

Edgeworth, Maria. *Castle Rackrent and The Absentee.* Introduced by Anne Thackeray Ritchie. London: Macmillan, 1895.

Eliot, T. S. *On Poetry and Poets.* London: Faber and Faber, 1957.

Emerson, Francis Willard. "The Spenser-Followers in Leigh Hunt's Chaucer." *Notes and Queries* 103 (1958): 284–86.

Empson, William. *Seven Types of Ambiguity.* 1930. Reprint, Harmondsworth: Penguin, 1961.

The English Hymnal. London: Oxford University Press, 1933.

Ericksen, Donald H. "Harold Skimpole and the 'Art for Art's Sake' Movement." *Journal of English and Germanic Philology* 72 (1973): 48–59.

Everest, Kelvin, ed. *Shelley Revalued: Essays from the Gregynog Conference.* Leicester: Leicester University Press, 1983.

Fenner, Theodore. "Ballet in Early Nineteenth-Century London as Seen by Leigh Hunt and Henry Robertson." *Dance Chronicle* 1 (1977–78): 75–93.

————. "The Making of an Opera Critic: Leigh Hunt." *Musical Quarterly* 55 (1969): 439–63.

Fielding, K. J. "Leigh Hunt and Skimpole: Another Remonstrance." *The Dickensian* 64 (1968): 5–9.

Fielding, K. J. "Skimpole and Leigh Hunt Again." *Notes and Queries* 100 (1955): 174–75.

FitzGerald, Murroe. "Leigh Hunt, Landor and Dickens." *Times Literary Supplement,* 26 October 1951, 677.

Fogle, Stephen F. "Leigh Hunt and the End of Romantic Criticism." In *Some British Romantics: A Collection of Essays,* edited by James V. Logan, John E. Jordan, and Northrop Frye. Columbus: Ohio State University Press, 1966.

————. "Leigh Hunt and the Laureateship." *Studies in Philology* 55 (1958): 603–15.

————. "Leigh Hunt, Thomas Powell, and the *Florentine Tales.*" *Keats-Shelley Journal* 14 (1965): 79–87.

————. "Leigh Hunt's Lost Brother and the American Legacy." *Keats-Shelley Journal* 8 (1959): 95–101.

————. "Skimpole Once More." *Nineteenth-Century Fiction* 7 (1952): 1–18.

Forster, Edward Morgan. *Two Cheers for Democracy.* 1951. Reprint, Harmondsworth: Penguin, 1965.

Forster, John. *The Life of Charles Dickens*. London: Chapman and Hall, n. d.

Gates, Eleanor M. "Leigh Hunt, Lord Byron, and Mary Shelley: The Long Goodbye." *Keats-Shelley Journal* 35 (1986): 149–67.

Gates, Payson G. "Leigh Hunt's Review of Shelley's *Posthumous Poems*." In *The Papers of the American Bibliographical Society* 42 (1948): 1–40.

Gay, John. *The Beggars' Opera and Polly together with the Airs of the Music from the Original Editions of 1728 and 1729*. London: Chapman and Dodd, 1923.

"George Peabody and Others." *Times Literary Supplement,* 11 December 1959, 732.

Gilbert, W. S. *The Savoy Operas: Being the Complete Text of the Gilbert and Sullivan Operas as Originally Produced in the Years 1875–1896*. London: Macmillan, 1962.

Gilfillan, George. "Leigh Hunt." *Tait's Edinburgh Magazine* 13 (1844): 655–60.

Gill, Stephen, ed. *William Wordsworth*. 1984. Reprint, Oxford: Oxford University Press, 1987.

Goethe, Wolfgang. *Poems*. Edited by Edgar Alfred Bowring. London: George Bell and Sons, 1885.

Grant, Michael. *Roman Literature*. Harmondsworth: Penguin, 1964.

Gray, Thomas. *Correspondence*. Edited by Paget Toynbee and Leonard Whibley. 3 vols. London: Oxford University Press, 1935.

Graves, Robert. *The Greek Myths*. 2 vols. Harmondsworth: Penguin, 1955.

Green, David Bonnell. "The First Publication of Leigh Hunt's 'Love Letters Made of Flowers'." *The Papers of the Bibliographical Society of America* 52 (1958): 52–55.

———. "Leigh Hunt an Honorary Citizen of Philadelphia." *Keats-Shelley Journal* 9 (1960): 6.

———. "Leigh Hunt's Hand in Samuel Carter Hall's *Book of Gems*." *Keats-Shelley Journal* 8 (1959): 103–17.

———. "The Publication of Leigh Hunt's *Imagination and Fancy*." *Studies in Bibliography* 12 (1959): 227–30.

Grigely, Joseph C. "Leigh Hunt and the *Examiner* Review of Keat's [*sic*] *Poems*." *Keats-Shelley Journal* 33 (1984): 30–37.

Hadfield, John. *A Book of Delights: An Anthology of Words and Pictures*. London: Hulton Press, 1955.

Hanlin, Frank S. "The Brewer-Leigh Hunt Collection at the State University of Iowa." *Keats-Shelley Journal* 8 (1959): 91–94

Hayden, John O. "Leigh Hunt's *Story of Rimini*: Reloading the Romantic Canon." *Durham University Journal* 79 (1987): 279–87.

———. *The Romantic Reviewers: 1802–1824*. London: Routledge and Kegan Paul, 1969.

Hazlitt, William. *The Complete Works*. Edited by P. P. Howe after the edition by A. R. Waller and Arnold Glover. 21 vols. London: J. M. Dent and Sons, 1934.

Herbert, George. *The Works of George Herbert*. Edited by F. E. Hutchinson. Oxford: Clarendon Press, 1941.

Herford, C. H. *The Age of Wordsworth*. London: George Bell, 1897.

Herrick, Robert. *Poems*. Edited by L. C. Martin. London: Oxford University Press, 1965.

Hill, T. W. "Hunt-Skimpole." *The Dickensian* 41 (1945): 114–20, 180–84.

Holloway, John. *Widening Horizons in English Verse*. London: Routledge & Kegan Paul, 1966.

Hood, Thomas. *The Complete Poetical Works*. Edited by Walter Jerrold. London: Henry Frowde, 1906.

Horace. *Satires, Epistles and Ars Poetica*. Translated by H. Rushton Fairclough. London: Heinemann, 1970.

Horne, Richard Hengist. *A New Spirit of the Age*. Introduced by Walter Jerrold. London: Oxford University Press, 1907.

Hough, Graham. *The Romantic Poets*. London: Hutchinson, 1957.

Hunt, Henry James Leigh. "Leigh Hunt Announces a New School of Poetry, 1817." In *Keats: The Critical Heritage*, edited by G. M. Matthews. London: Routledge & Kegan Paul, 1971.

———. "Leigh Hunt Introduces a New Poet." In *Keats: The Critical Heritage*, edited by G. M. Matthews. London: Routledge & Kegan Paul, 1971.

Hymns Ancient & Modern Revised. London: William Clowes and Sons, n.d.

Jack, Ian. *English Literature 1815–1832*. Oxford: Clarendon, 1963.

———. *Keats and the Mirror of Art*. Oxford: Clarendon, 1967.

Johnson, Richard Brimley. *Leigh Hunt*. London: Swan Sonnenschein & Co., 1896.

Jones, David L. "Hazlitt and Leigh Hunt at the Opera House." *Symposium* 16 (1962): 5–16.

Joukovsky, Nicholas A. "A Mistaken Peacock Attribution: 'A Can of Cream from Devon.'" *Notes and Queries* 220 (1975): 112–13.

Kaier, Anne. "John Hamilton Reynolds: Four New Letters." *Keats-Shelley Journal* 30 (1981): 182–90.

Keach, William. "Cockney Couplets: Keats and the Politics of Style." *Studies in Romanticism* 25 (1986): 182–96.

Keats, John. *Letters: A New Selection*. Edited by Robert Gittings. London: Oxford University Press, 1970.

———. *Poetical Works*. Edited by H. W. Garrod. London: Oxford University Press, 1970.

[Keble, John.] *The Christian Year*. London: Oxford University Press, n.d.

Kirkland, Richard I., Jr. "Byron's Reading of Montaigne: A Leigh Hunt Letter." *Keats-Shelley Journal* 30 (1981): 47–51.

Kroeber, Karl. *Romantic Narrative Art*. Madison: University of Wisconsin Press, 1966.

Kucich, Greg. "Leigh Hunt and Romantic Spenserianism." *Keats-Shelley Journal* 37 (1988): 110–35

Laidlaw, W. A. *Latin Literature*. London: Methuen, 1951.

Landré, Louis. "Leigh Hunt: A Few Remarks about the Man." *Keats-Shelley Memorial Bulletin* 10 (1959): 1–6.

———. "Leigh Hunt: His Contribution to English Romanticism." *Keats-Shelley Journal* 8 (1959): 133–44.

Langland, William. *The Vision of William Concerning Piers the Plowman in Three Parallel Texts together with Richard the Redeless*. Edited by William Skeat. 2 vols. London: Oxford University Press, 1886.

Legouis, Émile, Louis Cazamian, and Raymond Las Vergnas. *A History of English Literature*. London: J. M. Dent, 1967.

Leigh-Hunt, Desmond. "Leigh Hunt's New World Forebears." *Books at Iowa* 40 (1984): 2–9.

Leisy, Ernest E. "Hunt's *Abou Ben Adhem*." *The Explicator* 5 (1946), item 9.

Lockhart, John Gibson. "Lockhart's Attack in *Blackwood's*." In *Keats: The Critical Heritage*, edited by G. M. Matthews. London: Routledge & Kegan Paul, 1971.

Lonsdale, Roger, ed. *The Poems of Thomas Gray, William Collins and Oliver Goldsmith*. London: Longman, 1969.

Lucian. *Works*. Translated by M. D. Macleod. 8 vols. London: William Heinemann, 1961.

Lukács, Georg. *The Historical Novel*. Translated by Hannah Mitchell and Stanley Mitchell. London: Merlin Press, 1962.

Lulofs, Timothy J., and Hans Ostrom. *Leigh Hunt: A Reference Guide*. Boston: G. K. Hall, 1985.

McGann, Jerome. *The Beauty of Inflections: Literary Investigations in Historical Method and Theory*. Oxford: Clarendon Press, 1985.

———. *The Romantic Ideology: A Critical Investigation*. Chicago: University of Chicago Press, 1983.

———. *Social Values and Poetic Acts: The Historical Judgment of Literary Work*. Cambridge: Harvard University Press, 1988.

Mackerness, E. D. "Leigh Hunt's Musical Journalism." *Monthly Musical Review* 86 (1956): 212–22.

Marlowe, Christopher, and George Chapman. *Hero and Leander 1598*. Menston: Scolar Press, 1968.

Marriott, J. A. R. *England Since Waterloo*. London: Methuen, 1913.

Marvell, Andrew. *Poems and Letters*. Edited by H. M. Margoliouth. Revised by Pierre Legouis and E. E. Duncan-Jones. 2 vols. Oxford: Clarendon Press, 1971.

Masson, David. *Wordsworth, Shelley, Keats, and Other Essays*. London: Macmillan, 1875.

Mayall, A. "Leigh Hunt." *Notes and Queries*, 9th ser., 11 January 1902, 34.

Mellor, Anne K. "On Romanticism and Feminism." In *Romanticism and Feminism*, edited by Anne K. Mellor, 3–12. Bloomington and Indianapolis: University of Indiana Press, 1988.

Miller, Barnette. *Leigh Hunt's Relations with Byron, Shelley and Keats*. New York: Columbia University Press, 1910.

Milton, John. *The Complete Poems and Major Prose*. Edited by Merritt Y. Hughes. New York: Odyssey Press, 1957.

Monkhouse, Cosmo. *Life of Leigh Hunt*. London: Walter Scott, 1893.

Moore, Doris Langley. "Byron, Leigh Hunt, and the Shelleys: New Light on Certain Old Scandals." *Keats–Shelley Memorial Bulletin* 10 (1959): 20–29.

Moore, Thomas. *The Complete Poetical Works of Thomas Moore*. London: Longmans, Green, Reader and Dyer, 1869.

Morgan, Edwin. "Reply." *Notes and Queries* 1104 (1961): 436.

Murray, Peter, and Linda Murray. *A Dictionary of Art and Artists*. Harmondsworth: Penguin, 1959.

Norman, Sylva. "Leigh Hunt, Moore and Byron." *Times Literary Supplement*, 2 January 1953, 16.

O'Leary, Patrick. "John Scott and Leigh Hunt." *Keats-Shelley Journal* 33 (1984): 51.

Ovid. *Heroides and Amores*. Translated by Grant Showerman. London: William Heinemann, 1914.

Paton, W. R., trans. *The Greek Anthology*. 5 vols. London: William Heinemann, 1914–16.

Peacock, W., ed. *English Verse*. 5 vols. London: Oxford University Press, 1952.

Pereira, Ernest. "Keats and Leigh Hunt: A Note on *Floridize*." *Notes and Queries* 32 (1985): 341–43.

———. "Sonnet Contests and Verse Compliments in the Keats-Hunt Circle." *Unisa English Studies* 1 (1987): 13–23.

Philostratus. *The Life of Apollonius of Tyana, The Epistles of Apollonius and The Treatise of Eusebius*. Translated by F. C. Conybeare. London: William Heinemann, 1912.

Pomfret, John. *Poems upon Several Occasions*. 10th ed. London: Ed. Cook, 1736.

Poovey, Mary. *The Proper Lady and the Woman Writer: Ideology as Style in the Works of Mary Wollstonecraft, Mary Shelley and Jane Austen*. Chicago: University of Chicago Press, 1984.

Pope, Alexander. *The Poems: A One-Volume Edition of the Twickenham Text with Selected Annotations*. Edited by John Butt. London: Methuen, 1963.

Pope, Willard B. "Leigh Hunt & His Companions." *Keats-Shelley Journal* 8 (1959): 89–91.

Posner, Donald. *Antoine Watteau*. London: Weidenfeld and Nicolson, 1984.

Quinn, Mary A. "Leigh Hunt's Presentation of Shelley's *Alastor* Volume." *Keats-Shelley Journal* 35 (1986): 17–20.

Radcliffe, Ann. *The Mysteries of Udolpho*. Edited and introduced by Bonamy Dobrée with Explanatory Notes by Frederick Garber. New York: Oxford University Press, 1966.

Reese, M. M., ed. *Elizabethan Verse Romances*. London: Routledge and Kegan Paul, 1968.

Reiman, Donald H. "Leigh Hunt in Literary History: A Response." In *The Life & Times of Leigh Hunt: Papers Delivered at a Symposium at the University of Iowa, April 13, 1984, Commemorating the 200th Anniversary of Leigh Hunt's Birth*, edited by Robert A. McCown. Iowa City: Friends of the University of Iowa Libraries, 1985.

Richardson, Alan. "Romanticism and the Colonization of the Feminine." In *Romanticism and Feminism*, edited by Anne K. Mellor, 13–25. Bloomington and Indianapolis: Indiana University Press, 1988.

Richardson, Joanna. "Friend of Genius." *The Listener*, 17 September 1959, 426.

Ristine, Frank. "Leigh Hunt's Horace." *Modern Language Notes* 66 (1951): 540–43.

Roberts, Michael. "Leigh Hunt's Place in the Reform Movement, 1808–1810." *Review of English Studies* 11 (1935): 58–65.

Robinson, Charles E. "Leigh Hunt's Dramatic Success: *A Legend of Florence*." In *The Life & Times of Leigh Hunt: Papers Delivered at a Symposium at the University of Iowa, April 13, 1984, Commemorating the 200th Anniversary of Leigh Hunt's Birth*, edited by Robert A. McCown. Iowa City: Friends of the University of Iowa Libraries, 1985.

———. "Shelley to the Editor of the *Morning Chronicle*: A Second New Letter of 5 April 1821." *Keats-Shelley Memorial Bulletin* 32 (1981): 55–58.

———. "The Shelleys to Leigh Hunt: A New Letter of 5 April 1821." *Keats-Shelley Memorial Bulletin* 31 (1980): 52–56.

Roe, Nicholas. "Leigh Hunt and Wordsworth's *Poems*." *The Wordsworth Circle* 12 (1981): 89–91.

Ross, Marlon B. *The Contours of Masculine Desire: Romanticism and the Rise of Women's Poetry*. New York: Oxford University Press, 1989.

———. "Romantic Quest and Conquest: Troping Masculine Power in the Crisis of Poetic Identity." In *Romanticism and Feminism*, edited by Anne K. Mellor, 26–51. Bloomington and Indianapolis: Indiana University Press, 1988.

Ruskin, Ariane. *Seventeenth- and Eighteenth-Century Art*. New York: McGraw-Hill, 1969.

Russell, Richard. "The Portraiture of Leigh Hunt." *Keats-Shelley Memorial Bulletin*, 1959, 7–9.

Sampson, George. *The Concise Cambridge History of English Literature*. Cambridge: Cambridge University Press, 1949.

Sanders, Margaret. "Literary Hampstead." *The Listener*, 7 August 1958, 190.

Schiller, Friedrich. *Essays Aesthetical & Philosophical Including the Dissertation on the "Connexion between the Animal and the Spiritual in Man."* London: George Bell & Sons, 1900.

———. *The Poems and Ballads*. Translated by Sir Edward Bulwer-Lytton. London: Frederick Warne, 1887.

Scoggins, James. *Imagination and Fancy: Complementary Modes in the Poetry of Wordsworth*. Lincoln: University of Nebraska Press, 1966.

Sewter, A. C. *Baroque and Rococo*. New York: Harcourt Brace Jovanovich, 1972.

Shakespeare, William. *Hamlet*. Edited by Harold Jenkins. London: Methuen, 1982.

———. *King Henry VIII*. Edited by R. A. Foakes. London: Methuen, 1957.

———. *King Lear*. Edited by Kenneth Muir. London: Methuen, 1963.

———. *Macbeth*. Edited by Kenneth Muir. London: Methuen, 1964.

———. *Measure for Measure*. Edited by J. W. Lever. London: Methuen, 1967.

———. *The Merchant of Venice*. Edited by John Russell Brown. London: Methuen, 1964.

———. *A Midsummer Night's Dream*. Edited by Harold F. Brooks. London: Methuen, 1979.

———. *The Sonnets*. Edited by John Dover Wilson. Cambridge: Cambridge University Press, 1969.

Shelley, Percy Bysshe. *The Complete Poetical Works of Shelley, Including Materials Never Before Printed in Any Edition of the Poems*. Edited by Thomas Hutchinson. Oxford: Clarendon Press, 1904.

———. *Selected Poems*. Edited by Timothy Webb. London: J. M. Dent, 1977.

Short, Clarice. "The Composition of Hunt's *The Story of Rimini*." *Keats-Shelley Journal* 21 (1972): 207–18.

Smith, Adam. *The Theory of Moral Sentiments*. 2 vols. London: T. Cadell & W. Davies, 1804.

Smith, Barbara Herrnstein. *Poetic Closure: A Study of How Poems End.* Chicago: Chicago University Press, 1968.

Smith, David Q. "Genius and Common Sense: The Romantics and Leigh Hunt." *Books at Iowa* 40 (1984): 41–57.

Soloway, R. A. *Prelates and People: Ecclesiastical Social Thought in England, 1783–1852.* London: Routledge and Kegan Paul, 1969.

Southey, Robert. *Poems.* Edited by Maurice H. Fitzgerald. London: Oxford University Press, 1909.

Stam, David H. "The Doors and Windows of the Library: Leigh Hunt and Special Collections." *The Book Collector* 35 (1986): 67–75.

Sterbini, Cesare. *Il Barbiere di Siviglia.* Libretto to the RCA recording of Rossini's opera. New York, n.d. C 30.212.

Stonyk, Margaret. *Nineteenth-Century Literature.* London: Macmillan, 1983.

Strachan, L. R. M. "'Fry' in Dryden and Leigh Hunt." *Notes and Queries* 11 (1910): 321–22.

Strout, Alan Lang. "Hunt, Hazlitt, and *Maga.*" *ELH* 4 (1937): 151–59.

Suckling, John. *The Non-Dramatic Works.* Edited with introduction and commentary by Thomas Clayton. Oxford: Clarendon Press, 1971.

Swann, Karen. "Harassing the Muse." In *Romanticism and Feminism*, edited by Anne K. Mellor, 81–92. Bloomington and Indianapolis: Indiana Unversity Press, 1988.

Sypher, Wylie. *Four Stages of Renaissance Style: Transformations in Art and Literature, 1400–1700.* New York: Doubleday, 1955.

Tatchell, Molly. "Leigh Hunt Recollected by His Son-in-Law." *Keats-Shelley Memorial Bulletin* 35 (1984): 71–74.

———. "Leigh Hunt's Impecuniosity: A Pension for His Daughter." *Keats-Shelley Memorial Bulletin* 33 (1982): 66–69.

Tave, Stuart M. *The Amiable Humorist: A Study in the Comic Theory and Criticism of the Eighteenth and Early Nineteenth Centuries.* Chicago: University of Chicago Press, 1960.

Tennyson, Alfred. *The Poems of Tennyson.* Edited by Christopher Ricks. London: Longman's, 1969.

Thackeray, William Makepeace. *Vanity Fair: A Novel without a Hero.* Edited and introduced by John Sutherland. London: Oxford University Press, 1983.

Thompson, James R. *Leigh Hunt.* Boston: Twayne, 1977.

———. "'Mild Singing Clothes': The Poetry of Leigh Hunt." *Books at Iowa* 40 (1984): 21–30.

Thorpe, Clarence deWitt. "The Nymphs." *Keats-Shelley Memorial Bulletin* 10 (1959): 33–47.

Thuillier, Jacques, and Albert Châtelet. *French Painting from Le Nain to Fragonard.* Translated by James Emmons. Geneva: Albert Skira, 1964.

Tighe, Mrs. Henry. *Psyche, With Other Poems.* London: Longman, Hurst, Rees, Orme, and Brown, 1816.

Tillyard, E. M. W. *The English Epic and Its Background.* London: Chatto and Windus, 1954.

Trevor, Meriol. *Newman: Light in Winter*. London: Macmillan, 1962.

Trewin, J. C. "Leigh Hunt as a Dramatic Critic." *Keats-Shelley Memorial Bulletin* 10 (1959): 14–19.

Vargo, Lisa. "Unmasking Shelley's *Mask of Anarchy*." *English Studies in Canada* 13 (1987): 49–64.

Wallace, Catherine Miles. *The Design of Biographia Literaria*. London: George Allen & Unwin, 1983.

Waltman, John L. "'And Beauty Draws Us with a Single Hair': Leigh Hunt as Collector." *Keats-Shelley Memorial Bulletin* 31 (1980): 61–67.

Watson, Melvin R. "The *Spectator* Tradition and the Development of the Familiar Essay." *ELH* 13 (1946): 189–215.

Weld, Mary. "Charles Lamb: Friend and Critic." *Charles Lamb Bulletin* 51 (1985): 61–67.

Wells, Robert. *The Winter's Task: Poems*. Manchester: Carcanet, 1977.

Wheeler, Paul Mowbray. "The Great Quarterlies of the Early Nineteenth Century and Leigh Hunt." *South Atlantic Quarterly* 29 (1930): 282–303.

Wilder, Thornton. *Our Town, The Skin of Our Teeth, The Matchmaker*. Harmondsworth: Penguin, 1962.

Williams, Charles. *The Figure of Beatrice: A Study in Dante*. London: Faber, 1943.

Wittkower, Rudolf. *Art and Architecture in Italy, 1600–1750*. Harmondsworth: Penguin, 1973.

Wolfe, Joseph, and Linda Wolfe. "An Earlier Version of 'Abou.'" *Notes and Queries* 105 (1960): 113.

Wollstonecraft, Mary. *A Vindication of the Rights of Woman*. Edited by Carol H. Potson. New York: Norton, 1975.

Woodring, Carl. "The Hunt Trials: Informations and Manoeuvres." *Keats-Shelley Memorial Bulletin* 10 (1959): 10–13.

———. "*Inter Pares*: Leigh Hunt as Personal Essayist." In *The Life & Times of Leigh Hunt: Papers Delivered at the University of Iowa, April 13, 1984, Commemorating the 200th Anniversary of Leigh Hunt's Birth*, edited by Robert A. McCown. Iowa City: Friends of the University of Iowa Libraries, 1985.

Wordsworth, William. *The Poems*. Edited by John O. Hayden. 2 vols. Harmondsworth: Penguin, 1977.

———. *The Prelude: A Parallel Text*. Edited by J. C. Maxwell. Harmondsworth: Penguin, 1971.

———. *The Prose Works of William Wordsworth*. Edited by W. J. B. Owen and Jane Worthington Smyser. 3 vols. Oxford: Clarendon Press, 1974.

Young, Percy M. "Leigh Hunt—Music Critic." *Music and Letters* 25 (1944): 86–94.

Index

Aesthetic Movement, 76, 152
Ainsworth's Magazine, 94
Akenside, Mark: *Hymn to the Naiads,* 230
Alexander, Mrs. C. F.: *Hymns for Little Children,* 138
Alighieri, Dante. *See* Dante
Amulet, The, 116
Anacreon, 211
Anthony, Saint, 213
Ariosto, Ludovico, 85
Arnold, Matthew, 19, 97
Auber, Daniel François Esprit, 59
Auden, W. H., 70
Austen, Jane, 238

Barnes, Thomas, 204
Barnes, William, 175
Baroque, aesthetics of, 27, 40
Beaumont, Francis, and John Fletcher: *The Woman-Hater,* 100, 172
Benedicite (hymn), 211
Bentham, Jeremy, 198–99
Bergson, Henri, 177
Berkeley, George (bishop of Cloyne), 79, 197
Berlioz, Hector: *Symphonie Fantastique,* 218
Bernini, Gianlorenzo, 27, 162
Blackwood's Magazine, 25, 33, 36–37, 78, 125, 148, 180, 191, 215, 237
Blake, William: *London,* 102
Boccaccio, Giovanni, 68
Boileau, Nicholas: *Le Lutrin,* 188
Boucher, Françoise, 22–23, 27–28, 48
Bowles, William Lisle, 206
Bramante, Donato, 84
Brome, Alexander, 42

Brontë, Emily: *Wuthering Heights,* 92
Brooke, Rupert: *Grantchester,* 205–6
Browning, Robert, 105; *My Last Duchess,* 75; *The Pied Piper of Hamelin,* 138
Burke, Edmund, 32, 44
Burney, Fanny, 164
Burns, Robert, 168
Butler, Samuel, 127
Byron, George Gordon, Lord, 12, 28, 33, 35, 73, 96, 119, 138, 159–60, 178, 183, 203, 229, 238

Campbell, Thomas, 44, 159–60
Canaletto, (Giovanni) Antonio, 26
Carew, Thomas, 158
Carlyle, Thomas, 137
Cato: *Disticha de moribus ad filium,* 191
Catullus, 175, 182, 199, 202
Cézanne, Paul, 26
Chapman, George, 99, 102, 171, 224; *Ode to Pan,* 128
Charles II, 40
Chatterton, Thomas, 57
Chaucer, Geoffrey, 40, 59, 70, 188; *The Franklin's Tale,* 87, 169; *The Knight's Tale,* 52, 54; Prologue to *The Canterbury Tales,* 52; *Troilus and Criseyde,* 35
Cicero, 44
Clarke, Charles Cowden, 113
Clarke, Mary Cowden, 90, 113
Coleridge, Samuel Taylor, 10, 17, 19, 66, 159, 238; *Biographia Literaria,* 18; *Dejection: An Ode,* 67; *Kubla Khan,* 29, 79; *The Rime of the Ancient Mariner,* 141; *This Lime-Tree Bower My Prison,* 205

Collins, William, 9, 56, 70, 238; *Ode to Evening,* 166, 204–6, 209, 230; *Song from Shakespeare's Cymbeline,* 84, 91–92

Correggio, Antonio, 186

Cowley, Abraham, 211

Cowper, William, 28, 37, 42, 56, 209, 223; *Table Talk,* 193; *The Task,* 219

Crabbe, George, 10–11, 41, 120, 158; *The Frank Courtship,* 65; *The Library,* 146; *The Patron,* 68; *Tales of the Hall,* 73

Croker, J. W., 26, 33

Dali, Salvador, 216

D'Annunzio, Gabriele, 78

Dante, 9, 46, 50, 61, 80, 87, 118, 222

David, Jacques Louis, 23

Denham, John: *Coopers Hill,* 74

Dibden, Charles, 158

Dickens, Charles, 11, 19, 200, 239; *American Notes,* 177; *Barnaby Rudge,* 175; *The Battle of Life,* 130; *Bleak House,* 12, 96, 122; *A Christmas Carol,* 148; *Little Dorrit,* 122; *Nicholas Nickleby,* 90; *The Old Curiosity Shop,* 195; *The Pickwick Papers,* 147; *Our Mutual Friend,* 117

Diderot, Denis, 23

Dies Irae (hymn), 178

Donizetti, Gaetano: *La Favorite,* 233

Donne, John: *The Canonization,* 91; *Love's Progress,* 156

Dryden, John, 40, 51, 218; *Ceyx and Alcyone,* 56, 95–96; *Theodore and Honoria,* 68

Edgeworth, Maria, 164; *The Absentee,* 34

Edward I, 123

Elgar, Sir Edward, 213

Examiner, The, 36, 93, 139, 153, 173, 175, 183

Faber, Frederick William, 192

Fine Old English Gentleman, The (song), 122

Finita iam sunt proelia (hymn), 86

Firbank, Ronald, 10

Forster, E. M., 110

Forster, John, 117

Fragonard, Jean Honoré, 22

Froude, Hurrell, 93

Futurism, 174

Garth, Sir Samuel, 174

Gautier, Théophile, 185

Gay, John: *The Beggars' Opera,* 127

George IV, 22, 174, 178, 179, 181

Gifford, William, 158, 168–70, 173, 192

Gilbert, W. S., 50; *Iolanthe,* 50; *The Mikado,* 50; *Patience,* 50; *Ruddigore,*147

Godwin, William, 10

Goldsmith, Oliver: *The Deserted Village,* 208; *An Elegy on the Death of a Mad Dog,* 173; *The Traveller,* 187–88

Goethe, Johann Wolfgang, 46, 77, 97; *Ganymed,* 222

Goncourt, Edmond de, 23

Goncourt, Jules de, 23

Gounod, Charles, 46

Gozzoli, Benozzo, 53

Gray, Thomas, 9, 37, 55, 70, 89, 183–84, 187, 189–190, 235, 238; *The Alliance of Education and Government,* 187; *The Bard,* 53, 106, 185, 230; *The Candidate,* 157; *Elegy Written in a Country Churchyard,* 71, 88; *[Lines on Beech Trees],* 151; *A Long Story,* 155; *Lines Spoken by John Dennis,* 147; *Ode on a Distant Prospect of Eton College,* 82, 129; *Ode on the Spring,* 150; *The Progress of Poesy,* 53, 86, 115, 149–50, 188, 216, 231

Guardi, Francesco, 26, 28, 233

Hadfield, John, 72

Hadrian, 221

Halévy, Jacques François (Fromental Elias): *La Juive,* 59

Handel, George Frideric: *Acis and Galatea,* 196

Haydn, Josef, 221

Haydon, Benjamin Robert, 73, 113

Hayley, William, 158

Hazlitt, William, 10, 22, 24, 66, 194, 211; *The Plain Speaker,* 48; *The Spirit of the Age,* 21

Heine, Heinrich, 39

Hemans, Felicia, 35
Henry III, 123
Herbert, George: *The Collar*, 144; *Dialogue*, 132; *Prayer (I)*, 221; *The Pulley*, 103
Herrick, Robert, 9–10; *Oberon's Feast*, 163
Hesiod, 29, 231
Hobbes, Thomas, 143
Homer, 146, 171; *Iliad*, 52
Hood, Thomas, 99
Horace, 25, 85, 143, 147, 172, 182–84, 193–94, 197, 201, 203, 234; *Ars Poetica*, 171; *Epistula ad Augustum*, 186
Hulme, T. E., 19
Hunt, (James Henry) Leigh: fancy, theory of, 18; "feminine" aspects, 33; homosexuality, views on, 62; paintings, critical treatment of, 22; pastiche, use of, 55, 64–65, 85; religious beliefs, 98–99; "rococo" qualities of, 40, 78, 82; satire, mode of, 143. Works: *Abou ben Adhem*, 55, 105, 116; *Abraham and the Fire-Worshipper*, 117; *Alter et Idem*, 229; *Angel in the House*, 229; *Apollo and the Sunbeams*, 216; *Autobiography*, 12, 47, 168; *Bacchus and Ariadne*, 95, 107, 166; *The Ballads of Robin Hood*, 95, 138; *The Bitter Gourd*, 117; *Blue-Stocking Revels*, 35, 43, 164; *Bodryddan*, 220; *The Book of Beginnings*, 171; *Captain Sword and Captain Pen*, 35, 95, 120, 126, 127, 181; *Caractacus*, 114; *A Chemico-Poetical Thought*, 229; *The "Choice,"* 49, 232; *Christmas*, 228; *The Descent of Liberty*, 12, 21, 39; *Doggrel on Double Columns*, 233; *The Dogs*, 178, 238; *A Dream in Heaven*, 229; *A Dream Within a Dream*, 229; *An Excellent Scotch Parody*, 175; *Extract from Another Letter to the Same*, 194, 197; *The Extraordinary Case of the Late Mr. Southey*, 157–58; *A Fancy Concert*, 187; *Fancy's Party*, 231; *The Feast of the Poets*, 153, 165, 168; *The Fish, the Man, and the Spirit*, 209; *The Gentle Armour*, 118, 123; *The Glove and the Lions*, 126; *Godiva*, 126; *Hampstead Sonnets*, 205; *Hero and Leander*, 95, 109–10, 113, 207; *His Departed Love*, 221; *A Human Being in a Crowd*, 172; *A Hymn to Bishop St. Valentine*, 229; *Imagination and Fancy*, 18–19; *The Indicator*, 97, 99, 100, 104, 115, 172, 177; *The Inevitable*, 117; *Iterating Sonnet*, 209; *Jaffàr*, 117; *A Jar of Honey from Mount Hybla*, 237–38; *Juvenilia*, 12, 115, 238; *Killispindie*, 141; *Lawyer's Lament*, 175; *Lord Byron and Some of His Contemporaries*, 90, 119, 143; *Love Letters*, 229; *The Lord Mayor and the Butcher*, 175; *Mahmoud*, 114, 116; *Memory or Want of Memory*, 176; *National Song*, 227; *A New Chaunt*, 176; *An Nursery Song*, 227; *The Nymphs*, 41, 230; *The Nile*, 12, 211; *Paganini*, 218; *The Palfrey*, 95, 118, 121, 153; *The Panther*, 114–15, 117; *Politics and Poetics*, 144, 231; *Power and Gentleness*, 235; Preface to *Foliage*, 28; *The Progress of Painting*, 52, 150; *Ode for the Spring of 1814*, 226; *An Offering of Gratitude*, 229; *On Hearing a Little Musical Box*, 227; *On a Print of One of Them*, 229; *Our Cottage*, 219, 224; *Quiet Evenings*, 204; *Reflections of a Dead Body*, 221; *The Religion of the Heart*, 97, 110, 116–17, 128; *Reverend Magistracy*, 175–76; *Ronald of the Perfect Hand*, 235; *A Rustic Walk and Dinner*, 223; *The Seer*, 115, 157, 172; *The Shew of Faire Seeming*, 57; *A Song for the Young and Wise*, 228; *Songs and Chorus of the Flowers*, 50; *The St. James's Phenomenon*, 173–74; *The Story of Rimini*, 40–41, 46, 50, 51, 96, 102–3, 106, 109, 112, 118–19, 124, 128, 156, 165, 215, 227; *Talari Innamorati*, 169; *The Tapiser's Tale*, 57, 118, 141; *A Thought on Music*, 215, 221; *Thoughts in Bed*, 214, 219, 231; *Thoughts of the Avon*, 235; *Three Visions*, 230; *To Barron Field*, 201; *To Charles Lamb*, 202; *To the Grasshopper*

Hunt, Leigh *(continued):*
  and the Cricket, 210–11; *To the Infant
    Princess,* 230; *To the Lares,* 228; *To the
    Queen,* 229; *To the Right Honourable
    Lord byron,* 183; *To June,* 228; *To
    May,* 228; *To Miss K.,* 209; *To Mrs.
    L. H.,* 209; *To a Spider Running Across
    the Room,* 168; *To Thomas Moore,* 191;
    To William Hazlitt, 196; *The True
    Story of Vertumnus and Pomona,* 113;
    The Trumpets of Doolkarnein, 117;
    Ultra-Crepidarius, 168; *Verses on a
    Full-Flowing Peruke,* 229; *Wallace and
    Fawdon,* 141; *Wit and Humour,* 143,
    146
Isocrates: *Ad demonicum,* 191

Jeffrey, Francis, 41
Jerome, Saint, *180*
Jerusalem, My Happy Home (hymn), 220
Johnson, Dr. Samuel, 58, 87, 197, 216;
    The Vanity of Human Wishes, 115
Jones, William, 76
Jonson, Ben, 153
Juvenal, 58, 170

Keats, John, 9, 12, 25, 28, 34, 38, 40, 42,
    44, 56, 68, 70, 135, 172, 192, 198,
    231, 237; *La Belle Dame Sans Merci,*
    141; *Bright Star,* 77, 105; *Endymion,*
    238; *The Eve of St. Agnes,* 55, 61, 71,
    101, 166; *Hyperion,* 11; *Ode on
    Melancholy,* 87; *Ode to a Nightingale,*
    152, 192, 232; *Ode to Psyche,* 114; *On
    the Sea,* 212; *Sleep and Poetry,* 33, 110,
    150, 152, 188; *Specimen of an
    Induction to a Poem,* 63; *To Charles
    Cowden Clarke,* 171; *To One Who Has
    Been Long in City Pent,* 205
Keble, John, 33, 133
Kemble, John Philip, 154, 197
Kipling, Rudyard, 175

Lamb, Charles, 73
Langland, William: *Piers Plowman,* 138,
    174
Legitimism, 93
Lewes, G. H., 66
Lewis, Matthew: *The Monk,* 172

Liberal, The, 115, 139, 171, 181
Locke, John, 81
Lockhart, John Gibson, 25, 81, 90, 181
Longfellow, Henry Wadsworth, 139;
    Excelsior, 213
Longus, 10
Lorraine, Claude, *29*
Louis XV, 22
Lovelace, Richard, 192, 211
Lucian, 154, 164

Macpherson, James, 57
Malthus, Thomas, 10
Marcello, Benedetto, 187
Marlowe, Christopher, 62, 99–100, 115;
    Tamburlaine, 115
Marvell, Andrew, 166–67, 174, 196;
    Bermudas, 39, 84; *The Garden,* 149–
    50; *Upon Appleton House,* 210
Mason, William, 183
Masson, David, 19, 25
Mayr, Simon, 233
Menotti, Gian-Carlo, 228
Meyerbeer, Giacomo, 59
Mill, John Stuart, 19
Milton, John, 9, 29–30, 40, 50, 146,
    188, 219; *L'Allegro,* 149, 228; *On
    the Morning of Christ's Nativity,*
    226; *Paradise Lost,* 11, 43, 72, 94,
    133
Mitford, Mary, 164, 219
Montefeltro, Giovanni, 74
Montesquieu, Charles, 187
Monteverdi, Claudio, 187
Montgomery, James, 158
Moore, Thomas, 21–22, 33, 160, 166–67,
    214; *Irish Melodies,* 159
Morgan, Edwin, 209
Mozart, Wolfgang Amadeus, 198–99; *Don
    Giovanni,* 162, 176; *Musikalischer
    Spass,* 191
Murray, John, 158
Musaeus, 99, 101–2, 106
Musical Times, 44

Napoleon Bonaparte, 136
Newman, Cardinal John Henry: *The
    Dream of Gerontius,* 221–22
New Monthly Magazine, 22

Nicias, 210
Novello, Vincent, 113
Noyes, Alfred: *The Highwayman*, 138

Ollier, Charles, 30
Ostade, Isak van, 25
Ovid, 96, 108, 110, 205; *Heroides*, 99, 102, 107; *Metamorphoses*, 186
Owen, Wilfred, 135
Oxford Movement, 93

Paganini, Niccolo, 218
Peacock, H. B., 46
Peacock, Thomas Love, 44, 94
Petrarch, 238
Phos hilaron (hymn), 99
Picasso, Pablo, 39
Piero della Francesca, 74
Pindar, 49, 231
Pomfret, John: *The Choice*, 233
Pope, Alexander, 40, 153, 158, 182, 186, 187, 201, 220; *Autumn*, 108; *The Dunciad*, 164, 169; *Eloisa to Abelard*, 68; *Epistle to Dr. Arbuthnot*, 144; *An Essay on Criticism*, 171; *The First Epistle of the Second Book of Horace*, 189; *The Rape of the Lock*, 118, 145–47, 163, 169, 204; *Summer*, 151
Portici, Palace of, 26
Poussin, Nicolas, 40, 43–44, 47–49, 186
Pozzo, Andrea, 162, 186
Prior, Matthew, 172
Puccini, Giacomo, 228
Pushkin, Alexander: *Eugene Onegin*, 90

Quarterly Review, 168

Rabelais, François, 179
Radcliffe, Ann: *The Mysteries of Udolpho*, 67
Ransom, John Crowe, 137
Raphael, 48, 186
Reni, Guido, 23, 186
Retrospective Review, 58
Reynolds, Sir Joshua, 27
Richardson, Samuel: *Clarissa*, 87
Rococo, aesthetics of, 23, 85
Rogers, Samuel, 158

Rossini, Gioacchino, *Guillaume Tell*, 59; *Il Barbiere di Siviglia*, 176
Roubiliac, Louis François, 48
Rousseau, Jean-Jacques, 138

Sanzio, Raffaello. *See* Raphael
Schiller, Friedrich: *Der Handschuh*, 126; *Ode to Joy*, 136
Schönberg, Arnold, 39
Scott, John, 90
Scott, Sir Walter, 39, 53, 55, 57, 124–25, 159, 163
Scribe, Eugène, 59
Shakespeare, William, 19, 39, 188; *Antony and Cleopatra*, 115; *Henry VIII*, 216; *Hamlet*, 74, 132, 191; *Julius Caesar*, 95; *King Lear*, 117, 148, 171; *Macbeth*, 100; *Measure for Measure*, 77, 100; *A Midsummer Night's Dream*, 170, 220; *Romeo and Juliet*, 92; *Sonnet 18*, 158; *Sonnet 73*, 91; *The Tempest*, 11, 85; *Twelfth Night*, 92
Shelley, Percy Bysshe, 10, 12, 28, 38, 89, 99, 101, 117–18, 159–60, 212, 225, 231, 237; *I Arise from Dreams of Thee*, 150; *The Cenci*, 58, 94; *Hellas*, 136, 230; *The Mask of Anarchy*, 40; *Ozymandias*, 187
Shenstone, William, 127
Sheridan, Richard Brinsley, 47, 77; *The Rivals*, 90
Sir Patrick Spens (ballad), 139
Skelton, John, 42, 127, 170
Smart, Christopher, 37
Smith, Adam, 36
Smith, Charlotte, 35
Southey, Robert, 159, 163; *The Battle of Blenheim*, 130, 135
Spencer, William Robert, 158
Spenser, Edmund, 22, 49, 53, 55, 188; *The Faerie Queene*, 152, 196
Stabat Mater (hymn), 92, 186
Suckling, Sir John, 153, 157–59, 168
Sullivan, Arthur, 50
Superman (film), 155
Swift, Jonathan, 176; *A Description of the Morning*, 196; *A Description of a City Shower*, 196
Symphosius, 209

Tasso, Torquato, 146
Tchaikovsky, Peter Ilyich: *Pique Dame,* 57;
    The Sleeping Beauty, 57
Teniers, David, 25
Tennyson, Alfred, Lord, 12, 33, 175;
    Fatima, 150; *In Memoriam,* 106, 206;
    Tears, Idle Tears, 106, 151
Thackeray, William Makepeace: *Vanity
    Fair,* 132
Thomson, James: *Alfred,* 115
Tiepolo, Giovanni Battista, 50
Tighe, Mary, 35, 43
Titian, 27, 110–12

Uhland, Ludwig, 39

Vecelli, Tiziano. *See* Titian
Verdi, Giuseppe, 228
Victoria, Queen, 123, 125, 207, 230
Virgil, 229–30; *Aeneid,* 52, 91, 118, 162

Watteau, (Jean) Antoine, 23–25, 27–30,
    47, 49–50, 77, 192, 233
Watts, Isaac, 138
Wellington, Duke of, 136

Wells, Robert: *The Winter's Task,* 207
Wilde, Oscar, 10, 23, 39
Wilder, Thornton: *Our Town,* 221
Wilson, John (pseud. Christopher North),
    180
Wolcot, John: *A Cut at a Cobbler,* 168
Wollstonecroft, Mary: *A Vindication of the
    Rights of Woman,* 37
Wordsworth, Dorothy, 33
Wordsworth, Mary, 33
Wordsworth, William, 11, 17–20, 30–34,
    40, 43, 49, 160, 164, 206, 214, 224,
    237; *Anecdote for Fathers,* 161;
    Daffodils, 161; *The Excursion,* 161–62;
    Home at Grasmere, 33; *Intimations
    Ode,* 161; *Lyrical Ballads,* 159; *Point
    Rash Judgement,* 200; *The Prelude,* 32–
    33; *Resolution and Independence,* 82;
    Tintern Abbey, 216–17; *We Are Seven,*
    161; *The World Is Too Much With Us,*
    104, 161, 185
Wren, Sir Christopher, 145

Zandonai, Riccardo, 78